Spirits of the Water

Native Art Collected on Expeditions
to Alaska and British Columbia, 1774–1910

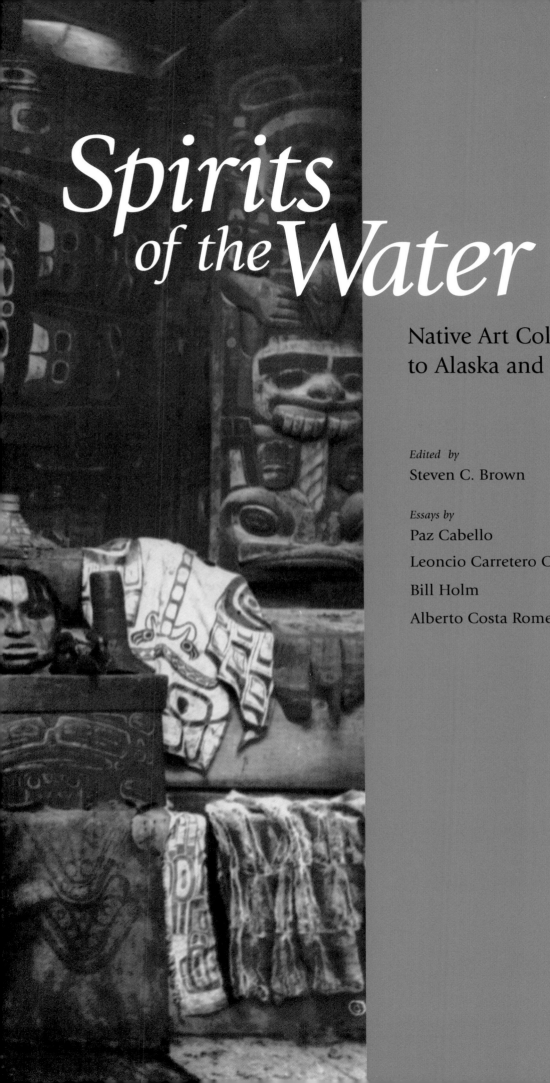

Spirits
of the Water

Native Art Collected on Expeditions
to Alaska and British Columbia, 1774–1910

Edited by
Steven C. Brown

Essays by
Paz Cabello

Leoncio Carretero Collado

Bill Holm

Alberto Costa Romero de Tejada

Exhibition organized by

Fundación "la Caixa"
Barcelona

University of Washington Press
Seattle

Douglas & McIntyre
Vancouver/Toronto

This publication accompanies the exhibition "Spirits of the Water: Native Art Collected on Expeditions to Alaska and British Columbia, 1774–1910," organized by Fundación "la Caixa," Barcelona, and curated by Paz Cabello and Alberto Costa Romero de Tejada.

Texts copyright © 2000 by the authors: Paz Cabello, Leoncio Carretero Collado, Bill Holm, and Alberto Costa Romero de Tejada; and the translators: Ignasi Sardà and Patricia Mathews

Copyright © 2000 Fundación "la Caixa"
Avenue Diagonal, 621
08028 Barcelona

Published simultaneously in the United States of America by the University of Washington Press, PO Box 50096, Seattle, WA 98145-5096 and in Canada by Douglas & McIntyre, 2323 Quebec Street, Suite 201, Vancouver, British Columbia V5T 4S7.

Library of Congress Catalogue Card Number 00-101611
ISBN 0-295-97986-0

Cover: Forehead Mask, *Tsimshian*, mid nineteenth century, north coast of British Columbia (cat. no. 99). © Canadian Museum of Civilization, Hull, Quebec (no. VII-B-17)

A catalogue record for this publication is available from the National Library of Canada.
ISBN 1-55054-712-7

Frontispiece: Interior of Tlingit Whale House in Klukwan, with its Hits.áati (house leader), Shartrich. Photograph by Lloyd Winter and Percy Pond, 1895. Alaska State Library– Historical Collections, Juneau

The paper used in this publication meets the minimum requirements of American National Standard for Information Sciences—Permanence of Paper for Printed Library Materials, ANSI Z39.48–1984.

CONTENTS

LENDERS TO THE EXHIBITION

American Museum of Natural History, New York

Armed Forces Geographic Service.
Cartoteca Histórica y Museo de Aparatos, Madrid

Brooklyn Museum of Art

Canadian Museum of Civilization, Hull, Quebec

Library of the Ministry of Foreign Affairs, Madrid

Musée de l'Homme, Paris

Museo de América, Madrid

Museo Naval, Madrid

André Nasser Collection, New York

Museum für Volkerkunde, Vienna

Peabody Museum of Archaeology and Ethnology,
Harvard University, Cambridge, Massachusetts

Peter the Great Museum of Anthropology
and Ethnology (Kunstkamera) of the
Russian Academy of Sciences, Saint Petersburg

Sheldon Jackson Museum, Sitka, Alaska

The Menil Collection, Houston

University of Cambridge, Museum of
Archaeology & Anthropology, Cambridge

and anonymous lenders

Warrior's Shirt (detail), *Tlingit*,
collected c. 1839–45, southeast
Alaska. Peter the Great Museum
of Anthropology and Ethnology
(Kunstkamera) of the Russian
Academy of Sciences, Saint
Petersburg (see cat. no. 82)

ACKNOWLEDGMENTS

The Fundación "la Caixa" wishes to thank the museums and private collectors who generously lent to the exhibition; their names appear at left. This diverse group of international lenders has enabled the exhibition to bring together for the first time objects collected by early expeditions to the Northwest Coast that now reside in locations around the world. For the English edition of the catalogue, Steven C. Brown generously accepted the task of editing the Spanish text and clarifying translation issues; his assistance has been invaluable.

Many individuals have assisted in preparing this exhibition and both the Spanish and English editions of its publication. They include: María José Albo, Geraldine Aramanda, Julie Bakke, Oliver M. Bakke, Jean Paul Barbier, James H. Barker, Deborah Brauer, Lisa Cain, Louis Campeau, Manuela Cervantes, John Corneil, Susan Davidson, James Donnelly, Galina Dzeniskevich, Diana Fane, Yann Ferrandin, Genevieve Fisher, André Fourquet, Ellen V. Futter, François Gendron, Joe Geurts, José Ignacio González-Aller, Gail and Bertrand Goy, Susan Haskell, Anita Herle, Max Itzikovitz, Rush Janson, Mary Kadish, Peter Kann, Julie Kasper, Belinda Kaye, Martha Labell, Michelle Labelle, Andrea Laforet, Arnold Lehman, Javier Lentini, Daniel Lévine, Basha and Perry Lewis, Diana Loffredo, Laurence Mattet, Alain de Monbrison, Sylvie A. M. Morel, Craig Morris, Kenneth S. Moser, Jeffrey Myers, André Nasser, Ron Nasser, Ángel Paladini, David W. Phillipson, Mawena Quayson, Bettina Raphael, Elizabeth Reynolds, Anna Ricart and Amadeu Cuito, Pierre Robbe, Flora Rodríguez, Robert S. Rubin, Enid Schildkourt, Chuner M. Taksami, Leslie Tapper, George Terasaki, Serge Tornay, Ricardo Tur Serra, Maria Yakimov, Christine Valluet, Gerald W. Van Bossel, Anne Vitart, Rubin Watson, and Paul Winkler.

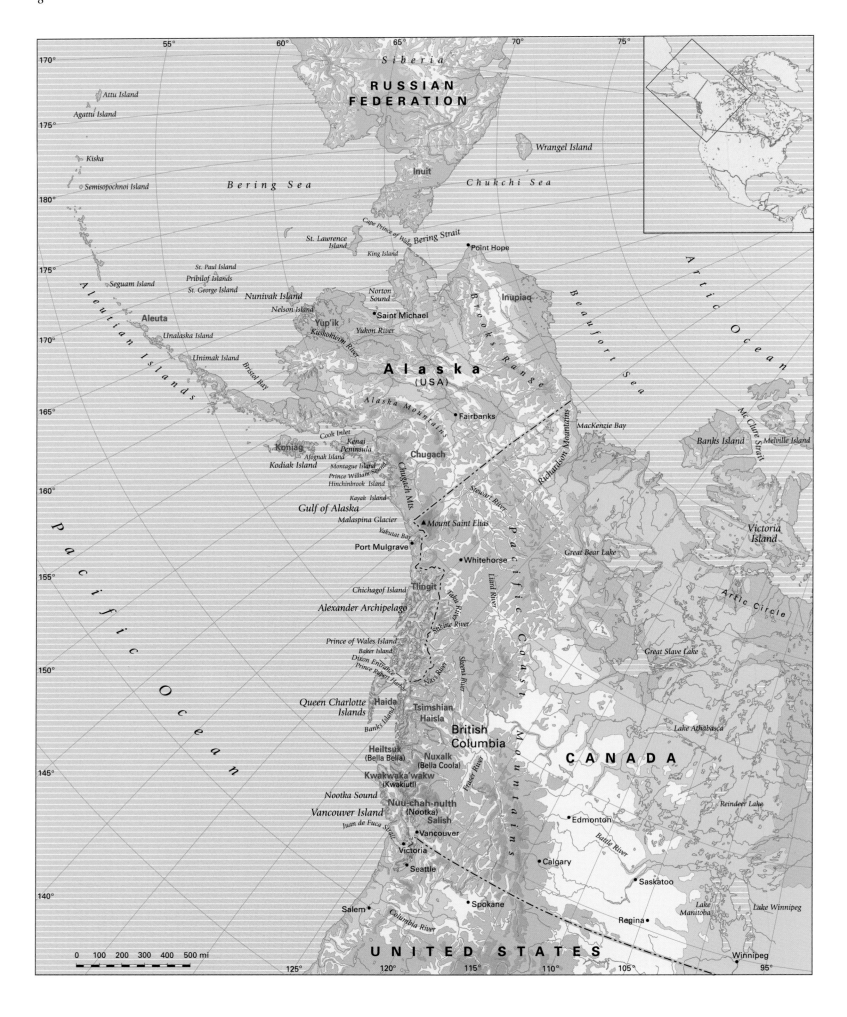

170°
55°
60°
65°
70°
75°

Siberia

RUSSIAN FEDERATION

175°

Wrangel Island

Attu Island

Agattu Island

Inuit

Chukchi Sea

Bering Sea

180°

Kiska

Semisopochnoi Island

Cape Prince of Wales Bering Strait

• Point Hope

Arctic Ocean

175°

St. Lawrence Island

King Island

Aleutian Islands

Seguam Island

St. Paul Island
Pribilof Islands
St. George Island

Nunivak Island

Norton Sound

Inupiaq

Beaufort Sea

170°

Aleuta

Nelson Island

Yup'ik

• Saint Michael

Unalaska Island

Yukon River

Brooks Range

Banks Island
Melville Island

Mc Clure Strait

Unimak Island

Bristol Bay

A l a s k a
(USA)

Alaska Mountains

• Fairbanks

MacKenzie Bay

165°

Cook Inlet

Koniag

Kenai Peninsula

Chugach

Richardson Mountains

Victoria Island

Afognak Island
Kodiak Island

Montague Island
Prince William Sound
Hinchinbrook Island

Stewart River

160°

Kayak Island

Gulf of Alaska

Malaspina Glacier

Chugach Mts.

▲ Mount Saint Elias

Pacific Coast

Great Bear Lake

155°

Yakutat Bay

Port Mulgrave

• Whitehorse

Arctic Circle

Chichagof Island

Tlingit

Taku River

Liard River

Alexander Archipelago

Stikine River

Great Slave Lake

Prince of Wales Island
Baker Island
Dixon Entrance
Prince Rupert Harbor

Nass River

Skeena River

150°

Queen Charlotte Islands

Haida

Tsimshian
Haisla

Lake Athabasca

Banks Island

British Columbia

C A N A D A

Heiltsuk
(Bella Bella)

Nuxalk
(Bella Coola)

145°

Kwakwaka'wakw
(Kwakiutl)

Fraser River

Mountains

Reindeer Lake

Nootka Sound

Nuu-chah-nulth
(Nootka)

• Edmonton

Vancouver Island

Salish

Battle River

Juan de Fuca Strait

• Vancouver

• Victoria

• Calgary

Pacific Ocean

• Seattle

• Saskatoo

Lake Manitoba
Lake Winnipeg

140°

• Spokane

• Regina

• Salem

Columbia River

U N I T E D   S T A T E S

• Winnipeg

0   100   200   300   400   500 mi

125°
120°
115°
110°
105°
95°

PREFACE

At the end of the sixteenth century, when the world map still remained incomplete, legend has it that Juan de Fuca reached the southern coast of Vancouver Island. Almost 150 years later, Vitus Bering's attempt to find the link between the Asian and American continents by exploring the Pacific claimed his life and the lives of many of his Russian crew. Then, in 1774, it was once again the Spanish who set foot on the far Northwest Coast of what is now British Columbia.

Between 1774 and 1795, the Spanish took the lead, exploring and mapping the unknown coasts of present-day Alaska and British Columbia, sending out expeditions led by Juan Pérez, Juan de la Bodega y Quadra, and Alejandro Malaspina. They did not simply produce maps, but also made scientific studies of the geology, flora, and fauna of the new territories, paying special attention to their inhabitants. Subscribers to the Enlightenment's humanistic views, the Spanish explorers scrupulously noted the details of Native life on the Northwest Coast, frequently accompanying their reports with handsome drawings. In addition, they collected numerous masks, rattles, weapons, fishhooks, and utilitarian objects offered by the Native peoples in exchange for European goods. These are now among the oldest works of Northwest Coast art that have been collected and preserved. The surviving objects from these Spanish expeditions are in the Museo de América in Madrid. They are presented in this exhibition together with objects collected on Captain James Cook's British expedition in 1778, by the numerous Russian explorers and scientists in the eighteenth century, and by the North American explorers and anthropologists whose expeditions lasted until the early twentieth century. The aim of this publication is to relate the history of these early expeditions with the discovery of the magnificent art indigenous to the region. The publication also illustrates the drawings and engravings made by Spanish, British, and Russian artists who witnessed and recorded these extraordinary lands and their remarkable inhabitants.

Although little remained widely known about this diversity of Native North American Cultures, many twentieth-century intellectuals and artists were fascinated by the peoples of America's Northwest Coast. In 1925, Marcel Mauss published *Essai sur le don*, drawing the attention of the public to the potlatch ceremonies celebrated by some of the British Columbian tribes. George Bataille saw ceremonies like these as a way of regaining a generous, even orgiastic life of excess, and the youthful movements of the 1960s made the potlatch a central symbol (the Situationists even published a journal entitled *Potlatch*). The visions of artists of this region captivated members of the Surrealist group, some of whom were exiled in America during World War II and while there collected Eskimo masks and Northwest Coast artifacts available through collectors and dealers in New York City.

Alberto Costa Romero de Tejada and Paz Cabello
Curators

Mámałni: Politics, Trade, and Collectionism on the Northwest Coast during the Eighteenth and Nineteenth Centuries

Leoncio Carretero Collado

One and a half centuries after Columbus' arrival in the Americas and despite numerous expeditions that had girdled the planet, a large part of the world, including much of the Americas, Asia, Africa, and Australia as well as the entirety of Antarctica, continued to be a vague, unknown territory for both Western governments and scientists. In Asia and the Americas, which by then had been explored by numerous short or moderately long land and sea expeditions, the partial discoveries were proving more of a drawback than an advantage, further complicating the internal politics of powers such as Spain and Russia while stirring up the international political scene as other European (and later also American) countries began pushing to become international powers themselves. Of course, apart from the imperialist interests of the Eurasian countries, there was no actual need to "discover" new lands, given that every continent on earth, with the exception of Antarctica, had already been occupied for hundreds or sometimes thousands of years by other human beings and other societies, even if they did not mean much to these powerful colonizing countries.

IMPERIAL SPAIN AND RUSSIA

At the beginning of the eighteenth century, Spain and Russia no longer knew where the boundaries of their empires lay and where they could legitimately claim lands as theirs. This uncertainty became a constant source of trouble as other world powers emerged, aspiring to establish their own empires in whatever part of the planet was still unknown or at least not under prior imperial control. Moreover, firmly entrenched commercial interests were requiring new, shorter, and safer maritime routes for everyone. In light of this, an ignorance of their own domains, including geography, climate, resources, and commercial possibilities, not only interfered with Spain's and Russia's planning but threatened the polit-

ical, economic, and military efficiency necessary to guarantee control over their lands.

At that time, Spain, which had never been noted for its organization, was plagued by upheavals in both internal and European politics that were eating up all the capital that arrived from the Americas. Its exploratory fervor was further tempered by the fact that once the Spanish colonists had acquired some land and a steady source of income, they saw no need to discover anything other than the best possible way of life. In contrast, Russian exploration was hampered by the hostile environment it faced east of the Ural Mountains, and no matter how much the government encouraged colonization, only hunters were able to penetrate the new territories in search of animals whose pelts could be sold. Indeed, it was thanks to the hunters and fur traders, traversing one river after another, following them upward as far as they could go, and then returning again to the ocean, that most of the Asian coast of Russia was explored.

Peter the Great nevertheless realized the scientific and political importance of completing the fragmented information about his country's eastern boundaries and putting it into some kind of order. He decided to undertake three major expeditions: to the Arctic, the Pacific, and the North American coasts. Organizing these expeditions involved such a tremendous amount of work that the first of them did not set out until seven years after the ruler's death in 1725. This major exploratory effort concluded with Vitus Bering's second voyage in 1741. The mission of all three expeditions was to map the coast, describe the territories, identify their resources and people, and take possession of all newly discovered lands, establishing Russian sovereignty there.

Bering's final expedition was the first to reach the Alaskan coast of the North American continent and to make contact with the Native Alaskans there. It would set the pattern for all subsequent journeys to that region of the north Pacific. Two weeks after sailing from Petropavlosk in Siberia, the *Saint Peter*, commanded by

fig. 1 Haida men of Masset village in masks and ceremonial dress. Photograph by Edward Dossetter, 1881. British Columbia Archives, Victoria

Bering, and the *Saint Paul*, commanded by Alexsei Tchirikov, were permanently separated in the fog. Bering continued northward along the coast of the Gulf of Alaska, following the Aleutian Islands chain; he eventually died on the island now bearing his name. Tchirikov continued eastward until he glimpsed the Dixon Entrance, then sailed north to the northern tip of Chichagof Island and the Lisianskii Strait. There he sent Captain Dementiev and ten men ashore to explore and take possession of the land, as well as to bring back water. He later sent a second boat to discover what had happened to the first. Nothing more was heard of either boat, and some days later two canoes filled with Tlingit approached the ship in what Tchirikov considered an unfriendly fashion. He was forced to resume his voyage with no lifeboats and missing one-third of his crew. In 1774, Juan Pérez, commanding a Spanish expedition, observed that the Haida from north of the Queen Charlotte Islands were wearing a number of articles that he attributed to Tchirikov's lost crew. A year later, six members of another Spanish expedition would suffer a similar fate at the hands of the Quileute in what is now Washington.

Relations between foreign visitors and the Native peoples remained uneasy. But Bering's and Tchirikov's tragic voyage was only the beginning, and by 1745 fur traders and Kamchatka hunters were moving eastward along the Aleutian Islands chain. Twenty years later, they had reached Prince William Sound. The Native Pacific Yup'ik continued to resist Russian encroachment, and in December 1763 the Aleuts, the Unalaska, and the Unimak destroyed four Russian ships, leaving only a dozen survivors. But Ivan Soloviev and his men struck back in harsh retaliation, and by 1766 the Aleuts and the Pacific Yup'ik had completely lost their autonomy. A wary combativeness persisted, and it was only after the Levashev-Krenitsyn expedition two years later that written and illustrated records of Alaska's Native cultures began to appear.

When the Spanish authorities heard about the Russian expansion and began suspecting that other countries had similar territorial designs, they decided to undertake a series of expeditions of their own. The first was the aforementioned expedition led by Pérez in 1774 and the last was led by Juan Tovar in 1796, after six years of Spanish occupation of Nootka Island had come to an end the year before. These expeditions are described in "Eighteenth-Century Spanish Expeditions, Discoveries, and Collections in the Northwest Coast," in this publication. However, it is worth noting that in 1774, when the Hesquiaht and Mowachaht tribes saw their first European visitors approaching in their floating houses rigged with sails, they thought these starving, sickly, pale, womenless men were creatures from another world, spirits perhaps, in any case disinherited beings who lived in the water and had nowhere else to go. They therefore called them *mámałni*, which continues to be the name they use to designate all non-aboriginal people.

PERMANENT COLONIZATION AND THE FUR TRADE

Meanwhile, the British had their own plans to explore the Northwest Coast and Alaska in order to claim rights of discovery. The British expedition led by James Cook in 1778 so interested all European, Asian, and American powers in the geography, resources, and Native peoples of the Northwest Coast and Alaska that this part of the planet became a center of scientific life and Euro-American politics.

With so many countries interested in North America's northern Pacific coast, the explorers were obliged to go one step further and establish permanent settlements so they could truly control and defend the sovereignty of their territories. Russians and Spaniards, who led the race, chose different alternatives. While the Spaniards eventually opted for costly expeditions and the establishment of military bases controlled from distant Mexico, the Russians quickly realized that settlements in the area would be a success only if they were economically profitable and controlled from close at hand.

To that end, Grigori Shelikhov sailed for Alaska in 1783 with three ships, envisioning settlements that would include colonists, priests, cities, cathedrals, schools, shipyards, and everything else a permanent empire could require. Three years later, he had built forts on Kodiak and Afognak islands and on the Kenai Peninsula, all the while continuing to treat the Native Alaskans as brutally as before. His successor, Aleksandr Baranov, penetrated deeper into Tlingit territory in 1796 when he founded the Yakutat and Sitka settlements, eventually moving his headquarters there. To further encourage and give legal weight to this settlement policy, in 1799 Russia's Emperor Paul I granted Shelikhov's heirs a sort of franchise and monopoly similar to the one held by the Hudson's Bay Company on the other side of the North American continent.

But the Native Alaskans resented the way the Russians treated them, forcing them to work in semi-slavery and against their will. In the Tlingit, the Russian American Company confronted a society more complex than those of the Native peoples governed by the Hudson's Bay Company, a society moreover armed with guns purchased from the British. Conflict was inevitable, and on June 18, 1802, the Sitka settlement was destroyed. It was rebuilt on its current site two years later, but in the following year the Yakutat settlement

fig. 2 John Webber, *Interior of the Mowachaht house in Yuquot village (Friendly Cove), Nootka Sound,* 1778. British Columbia Archives, Victoria

was likewise destroyed, never to be rebuilt. The Russians persisted, however, and their establishment of Novo-Arkhangel'sk (now Sitka) finally forced a radical structural change on the Tlingit peoples of southeastern Alaska: the visitors had come to stay and they continued increasing in numbers and strength.

Further to the south, a different, more explosive growth in the European presence was going on. The furs acquired by Cook's crew to protect themselves from the harsh climate were fetching astronomical prices in Canton, China, a year later. This triggered a fur rush that was as great as or greater than the next century's gold rushes. But to acquire furs meant that expeditions had to be organized and the Pacific Ocean crossed. The first British trader to arrive was James Hanna in 1785, and once again, the impression made upon the Native peoples was not very good: Hanna not only scorched the Mowachaht Chief Maquinna's backside with gunpowder in a joke of questionable taste, but later turned his cannons on the Native village. By the time he returned in 1786, however, seven British trading ships had visited this part of the northern Pacific coast, as well as a French expedition led by Jean François de La Pérouse. American traders John Kendrick, Robert Gray, and Simon Metcalfe followed them in 1788.

As fur traders' expeditions became more numerous, intense, and competitive, they fell into the same pattern: departing from Canton and southeast Asia, they stopped off in Hawaii, and then sailed up the Northwest Coast, stopping to trade at a number of established ports, with Nootka always as their meeting place. The

Native peoples for the most part sought an honest trade (though they were not adverse to a bit of thievery), primarily because they were tremendously interested in all metal tools, arms, and ornaments as well as firearms the British and others offered. This form of maritime trade prevailed until 1843.

Nevertheless, only those traders with a land base had any real power. In 1792, one of the early land explorations saw Alexander MacKenzie of the Northwest Company, the Hudson's Bay Company's rival at the time, follow the Bella Coola River to the sea. Later, in 1805, American explorers Merriwether Lewis and William Clark reached the mouth of the Columbia River, and in the following year, MacKenzie's colleague, Simon Fraser, explored the river that bears his name. These were round-trip expeditions, returning to the East Coast, until 1811 when John Jacob Astor arrived by sea to found the Astoria settlement in the Columbia River estuary. Once again, visitors of another nationality ("Bostonmen," as the Native peoples called them) had come with no intention of ever leaving Chinook territory.

The race tightened between the foreigners as they competed for control of the area's trade and territory. The Russians did not remain passively on the borders of Tlingit territory but moved down as far as northern California, seeking food supplies for their bases in the north. In 1812, they founded Fort Ross, about one hundred kilometers north of San Francisco, which remained in operation until 1841. In addition, at least four other Russian ships were trading up and down the coast.

By the turn of the century, however, fur, particularly

fig. 3 John Webber, *Interior of a Home in Unalaska*, 1778. Peabody Museum of Archaeology and Ethnology, Harvard University, Cambridge, Massachusetts

the most valuable sea otter pelts, had become scarce, and by mid nineteenth century, the fur trade was no longer profitable. The British members of the Hudson's Bay Company, which had merged with the Northwest Company in 1821, thus decided to shift from sea trade to land settlements, turning their trading posts into crop-growing and cattle-raising colonies, extending sovereignty over a different swath of territory. In 1843, a good number of British traders moved to the southern tip of Vancouver Island, where they founded Fort Victoria. The Coast Salish now also had visitors that would not leave. They called the British settlers King George men after King George III, the king of the first British travelers.

The future did not look bright for the Native peoples of the coast. Although the entire period of maritime trade had considerably altered their traditional cultures, and land trade had changed things still more, these changes were more or less voluntary, adaptive behavior over which the Native people had a reasonable amount of control. In contrast, those visitors who were bent on remaining wanted the Native people's land and, by extension, their resources and everything that sustained them as an autonomous culture. The Native people had no place in the new order, which began with gunboat diplomacy and concluded with the prohibition of their languages, religion, and culture. After that, the transformations were drastic and dramatic, taking place at a dizzying speed.

THE COLLECTION OF NATIVE AMERICAN OBJECTS AND RECORDS

People and cultures change, but something always remains to testify to the events that took place at a given moment. Writings, drawings, artifacts, and registers of the most diverse type can provide a contextual picture of what has gone before. Because the Northwest Coast and Alaska aroused such tremendous political, scientific, and economic interest, and because rights of discovery had to be justified in order to claim sovereignty over a given piece of territory, all the explorers and many of the traders, missionaries, and officials left records of their observations. Unfortunately, few of these people had any scientific training: i.e., most of them never learned more than a few words of any Native language, and the interests and personal circumstances of each of them were also significantly different from one another and from the people they wrote about.

Thus, the fur traders left only a few widely dispersed records. Not much could be expected of the fur traders in the way of comprehensive collections of Native Alaskan or Northwest Coast objects either: they were only interested in purchasing pelts and never had sufficient extra space in their boats. The Russian traders, however, proved to be an exception. Ever since Peter I created the Saint Petersburg Kunstkamera as a state museum, all artifacts collected along the north Pacific were kept in the same institution. After the museum

fig. 4 Main street of Alert Bay, a Kwakwa̱ka'wakw (Namgis band) village, c. 1910. British Columbia Archives, Victoria

became an affiliate of the Russian Academy of Sciences in 1724, other types of records were also housed there. After being reorganized in 1831, it was called the Peter the Great Museum of Anthropology and Ethnography. It continues to reside in its original building in Saint Petersburg, housing more than 11,000 artifacts from Native Alaskan cultures, mostly Aleut, Yup'ik, Athapaskan, and Tlingit.

Of all the Russian voyages, the scientific and political expeditions understandably were the ones that made the greatest and most regular contributions to the museum. Although the few survivors of the first of these voyages were fortunate simply to have escaped with their lives, they nevertheless managed to bring back records, such as the naturalist Georg Wilhelm Steller's diary. As the Russians organized a further series of round-the-world expeditions, more material from the American north Pacific ended up in Russian museums. The first of these expeditions took place between 1803 and 1806, led by Iurii Lisianskii and S. Krusenstern, respective commanders of the *Nadezhda* and the *Neva*. The second was headed by Vasilii M. Golovnin in 1817–18. The third was F. Petrovich Lütke's expedition, which lasted from 1817 to 1819. Also deserving of mention are I. Arkhimandritov, who provided the Russians with a great deal of information about the Aleut culture, and I. G. Voznesenskii, who in 1839 was sent to collect artifacts from the Native

cultures and returned with more than one thousand, mostly from the north Pacific coast. Voznesenskii's enthusiasm was equalled by L. A. Zagoskin, a lieutenant in the Russian Navy who brought back important ethnographic material from his Alaskan travels between 1842 and 1844. And we cannot overlook the clergyman E. P. Veniaminov and his Aleut ethnography. After the Alaska territory was sold to the United States in 1867, the Russian collection of local artifacts dwindled, but did not entirely cease, as evidenced by the Tlingit artifacts contributed by Father Georgi Chudnovsky, a missionary on Admiralty Island in 1890. The list of Russian contributors to our knowledge of the ethnography, geography, and natural history of the area far exceeds the limits of these pages.

In contrast, the British collections are scattered in public and private collections all over the world. Particularly worth mentioning is the material collected on the voyages of Cook in 1778 and George Vancouver from 1792 to 1795. While Vancouver's material is all in the British Museum, the survivors of Cook's expedition donated their material to the Leverian Museum, which went out of existence in 1785. Pieces from Cook's collection ended up in the British Museum in London, the University of Cambridge Museum, the Royal Albert Memorial Museum in Exeter, the Museum für Völkerkunde in Vienna, the Museo Nazionale di Antropologia ed Etnologia in Florence, the present-day

fig. 5 Chilkat-style ceremonial robe

National Museum of Ireland in Dublin, the governor of Kamchatka's collection, and the Saint Petersburg Museum of Anthropology and Ethnography. The entire body of work by John Webber, the expedition's artist, went to the Bernisches Historisches Museum in Bern, Switzerland; it is now at the Peabody Museum, Harvard University. British collections are particularly abundant in written and illustrated documents from explorers' numerous trips to the area. They contain invaluable ethnographic descriptions of most of the cultures in the area and even include descriptions of lengthy sojourns by men like John MacKay, who was left in Nootka Sound between 1786 and 1787 to promote trade for James Strange's company, or John R. Jewitt, who was a slave in the same area from 1803 to 1805.

Some French traders in the area, such as Étienne Marchand who was there in 1791, left records, but it was La Pérouse who led the major expedition. Before vanishing at sea, he sent his diaries and drawings from Kamchatka, Yakutat Bay, and Australia to Paris.

Germany neither aspired to territorial claims nor took part in the fur trade, but its mid nineteenth-century explorations made a powerful and decisive contribution to knowledge of the area. The Bremen Geographic Society first sent out Aurel and Arthur Krause on an expedition in 1878–79 to continue Nordeskiöld's work in Alaska. Because European museums in general had few ethnographic objects from the north Pacific, Berlin's Museum für Völkerkunde

then sent Johan Adrian Jacobsen out in 1881–83 to fill that void. His expedition was such a success that he also brought back a group of Nuxalk peoples (formerly known as the Bella Coola). Jacobsen's artifacts, and the Nuxalk who returned with him, proved so fascinating that another German geographer set out immediately on his own expedition to Alaska in 1885. Franz Boas would remain permanently in North America where he became the father of academic anthropology and the leading collector of objects from this area for New York's Museum of Natural History. Since then, Germany has always maintained close and permanent contacts with the Native peoples of the entire north Pacific area and has excellent public and private collections of their art and cultures.

American explorers deserve a special mention here because they began collecting documents and material from the very outset, and the young nation's economic power always far exceeded European expectations. Not only did ocean travelers and land-based fur traders record their activities in the early nineteenth century, but many of them collected objects that ended up in varied hands. Paradoxically, all the efforts the visitors made to put an end to the Native cultures in the late nineteenth century were transformed into an equally passionate interest in collecting their artifacts and records—as soon as their traditional cultures were, or were about to be, nearly eliminated. Thus, the end of the last century saw two complementary fevers. On the one hand, tycoons raced one another to sponsor scientific expeditions to carry out exhaustive studies of the geography, natural history, and ethnography of the vast continent, about which there was still much that was totally unknown. On the other hand, as the museums of the eastern part of the United States saw many Native cultures vanishing daily before their eyes and anticipated that others were also destined to disappear, they embarked on a race to collect the largest possible number of documents, ethnographic records, and artifacts of these cultures.

The competition was particularly intense between the two most powerful museums of the time. Morris K. Jesup, a business magnate and president of New York's Museum of Natural History, sponsored an expedition bearing his name to carry out a complete study of the Asian and American north Pacific. The expedition was to last six years, beginning in 1897 under the direction of Franz Boas, the museum's curator of ethnography. On the Northwest Coast, Boas encountered George Dorsey of Chicago's Field Museum of Natural History, who was heading another, more modest expedition for the same purpose. Their rivalry fueled a competition in the fields of both science and collecting, which drove Boas and his half-Tlingit associate, George Hunt of Fort Rupert, British Columbia, to assemble more than 16,760 artifacts from the Northwest Coast for the New York museum.

Many expeditions of this type were swept up in this competition to collect ethnographic objects and artworks from the Northwest Coast, including efforts by George Heye on behalf of his Museum of the American Indian. What few people could have suspected then is that this would in time create a robust market for the work of renowned Native American artists and that these same extensive museum collections would eventually assist the Northwest Coast peoples most devastated by the entire conquest and colonization process recover their cultural identities. Today, many of the Northwest Coast and Alaskan Native cultures are experiencing a powerful revitalization of their cultural arts, and a subsequent increase in their sense of place and importance in the overall fabric of life in this part of the world.

BIBLIOGRAPHY

Damas, David, and William C. Sturtevant, eds.
1984   *Handbook of North American Indians*, vol. 5, *Artic*. Washington, DC: Smithsonian Institution.

Fisher, Robin A.
1977   *Contact and Conflict: Indian-European Relations in British Columbia, 1774–1890*. Vancouver: University of British Columbia Press.

Fitzhugh, William W., and Aron Crowell, eds.
1988   *Crossroads of Continents: Cultures of Siberia and Alaska*. Washington, DC, and London: Smithsonian Institution Press.

King, Jonathan C. H.
1981   *Artificial Curiosities from the Northwest Coast of America: Native American Artifacts in the British Museum Collected on the Third Voyage of Captain James Cook and Acquired Through Sir Joseph Banks*. London: British Museum Publications.

Suttles, Wayne P., and William C. Sturtevant, eds.
1990   *Handbook of North American Indians*, vol. 7, *Northwest Coast*. Washington, DC: Smithsonian Institution.

Walbran, John T.
[1909] 1997   *British Columbia Coast Names, 1592–1906*. Reprint, Seattle: University of Washington Press.

Eighteenth-Century Spanish Expeditions, Discoveries, and Collections in the Northwest Coast

Paz Cabello

THE RUSSIAN ADVANCE AND THE SPANISH SITUATION

Spanish journeys to the north Pacific coast in the eighteenth century marked the European discovery and first explorations of North America's Northwest Coast and Alaska as far as the natural barrier shaped by the Alaska Peninsula and the Aleutian Islands. The Spanish explorers were immediately followed by other seamen competing for control of the recently opened territory. Only the Russians, who had crossed Siberia and reached the Kamchatka Peninsula, continued their advance from the east, entering the American territory of Alaska along the same route from Asia that the Eskimos had begun using several centuries earlier and that American First Peoples had followed thousands of years ago.

The new wave of European explorers, however, did not follow this ancient trail into North America, but moved in the opposite direction, following the route initiated with the discovery of the North American continent, working their way from east to west around South America until they encountered the Russian outpost.

In 1728, Vitus Bering, a Dane who worked for Russia, explored the Bering Sea separating Asia from America. On his second voyage in 1741, he reached the Aleutian Islands, dying on the island that today bears his name. The abundance of fur pelts discovered during these explorations led Russian traders to sponsor expeditions. The Spanish government found out about them through Antonio de Ulloa, an enlightened Spanish naval officer, and later from the ambassadors who were permanently posted to the Court of Saint Petersburg from 1761.[1] Both sources reported that the Russians were sending expeditions to some eastern coasts that turned out to be the westernmost coasts of North America, at that time the only part of the world, other than the Poles, that had not yet been explored. In those days the northwestern part of America was perceived as the end of the world, the furthest point from any European port, so inaccessible that to reach it one had to sail around South America via the infamous Cape Horn. Upon their arrival, explorers and navigators began to search for the fabled Northwest Passage, which geographers assumed united the Pacific and Atlantic oceans somewhere in the north. The only other possible route, crossing the continent by land from east to west, would not be explored until Alexander MacKenzie reached the Pacific via the Bella Coola River (in 1792), and the American expedition led by Lewis and Clark arrived on the coast via the Columbia River in 1805.

At the time of the early Russian expeditions, Spain was firmly entrenched in the heart of the Americas and had begun moving outward into such sparsely inhabited areas as Rio de la Plata and the southern tip of South America. It was also colonizing the vast expanse of land to the north that spread across what is now the states of Florida, Texas, New Mexico, Arizona, and California, territory belonging to the viceroyship of New Spain, whose capital was in Mexico. England's concurrent aggressive pursuit of its efforts to rule the seas and dominate maritime trade in the Atlantic and Pacific led to constant clashes with Spain. In response, Spain introduced in 1726 a policy designed to strengthen its navy and related industries and sciences, first under the direction of José Patiño and later under Zenón de Somodevilla, Marquis of Ensenada. By solidifying its maritime strengths throughout the reigns of Philip V, Ferdinand VI, and Charles III, Spain was able to settle in areas such as Alta California (now the state of California), which was supplied and communicated with Mexico by sea (fig. 7).

It was while the Spaniards were in the process of colonizing Alta California that they heard the Russians had reached what was feared to be the lands just north of them. Spain immediately organized a series of expeditions northward. Although precise individual instructions were given for each of these expeditions, they all involved verifying the presence of the Russians, learning the extent of their expansion, ratifying the Spanish king's rights to the American lands by taking possession of any new territory discovered, exploring and mapping the new

fig. 7 Map showing the route traveled by the Spanish explorers from Mexico to the Northwest Coast

coasts, and making thorough reports. (The expedition leaders and officers were to keep two copies of a journal, one of which was to be sent to the viceroy as soon as they arrived in port.) The leaders were also given strict orders to treat the Native peoples with the utmost delicacy and patience and to avoid any form of confrontation.[2]

The artifacts that were gathered during these expeditions joined other objects in Spain's newly institutionalized collections. In 1753 Ulloa had created a Real Gabinete de Historia Natural [Royal Cabinet of Natural History]. Five years later Pedro Franco Dávila offered his own collection to Ferdinand VI. After negotiations were concluded in 1771, by which time Charles III was on the throne, a new Real Gabinete de Historia Natural was formed, which included the artifacts collected by both Ulloa and Dávila. It was this collection that was subsequently enhanced with new objects from America's Northwest Coast. In the early nineteenth century, the collection was renamed the Museo de Ciencias Naturales, and in 1868 all historical and ethnographic collections were transferred to the Museo Arqueológico Nacional. Finally, in 1941 the Museo de América was created to house the collections from the *Indias*.

THE FIRST EXPEDITION TO THE NORTHWEST COAST: PÉREZ IN 1774

While a team of officers, trained at the naval school in Cádiz, was being organized to sail for Mexico with a group of scientists to start exploring the Northwest Coast, Viceroy Bucareli ordered Juan Pérez, a Majorcan sea pilot, to undertake a reconnaissance voyage. Pérez was already familiar with the northern Pacific coasts and currents, having captained the ships that supplied the Alta California colonies of San Diego, Monterey, and San Francisco. Following copies of maps that had been printed in Saint Petersburg in 1758 and 1773 and the viceroy's precise instructions, he sailed from San Blas on Mexico's Pacific coast on January 25, 1774. Traveling with him aboard the *Santiago* were Esteban Martínez, his second in command, and Father Junípero Serra, who was set ashore in San Diego. In Monterey Pérez picked up two other priests, Father Juan de la Peña and Father Juan Crespí, both of whom kept journals. To avoid the southwestern currents, Pérez sailed the open sea directly north until he reached 53° 58' north latitude (now known as the Dixon Entrance, to the north of the Queen Charlotte Islands). He called the spot Santa Margarita.

There, according to Crespí's journal, one of the sailors traded some of the red ribbons used to tie up documents for "a well-woven grass hat in various colors, with a pyramid-shaped crown about a third of a yard high."[3] Peña also describes in detail the cargo the Native people carried in their canoe: mats, furs, fish, grass [spruce-root] hats, leather caps adorned with feathers and various figures, and, above all, many well-woven blankets with brightly colored designs and fringes, for which the Spaniards traded clothing, knives, and beads.[4] Some sixteen leagues further on, more Native people appeared in various canoes, singing and making music. As Crespí describes it, "a fair" was soon set up and more goods traded, a list of which he includes in his journal.[5] A shortage of water then forced the Spaniards to sail southward to 49° 30' north latitude where they dropped anchor in a place Pérez called San Lorenzo. His second in command, Martínez, called the same place Santa Cruz, and James Cook later would call it Friendly Cove, although it was more generally known as Nootka (in Spanish, *Nutka*) Sound, on the west coast of Vancouver Island. Crespí describes how on August 8, just as they were about to take on water, some fifteen canoes arrived carrying Native women who began trading the skins of otters and other unfamiliar animals, as well as "grass hats painted like the pointed ones from Santa Margarita except that in these the pyramid-shaped crowns were finished off with pear-shaped knobs and some were woven of a

fig. 8   Hats collected in 1774 by Juan Pérez on the first recorded European expedition to the area. Museo de América, Madrid (nos. 13571 and 13567)

The first objects—the blankets, the sash, and the spruce-root hat that were reportedly among the items traded at Dixon Entrance—are not in the Museo de América. Perhaps they did not survive the years and their infestation by insects: as Crespí recounts, some sailors who had bought blankets spent an uncomfortable night "because, having wrapped themselves in them, they had to scratch the bites they got from the little animals these people brought in their clothing."[8] Although it proved impossible to identify the set of wooden sticks listed in the inventory from among the sets that exist in the collection, it was not difficult to locate the plain hat and the bone bird (a little duck) that the Native woman—probably a Haida—wore around her neck (see fig. 8, left, and cat. no. 18). The duck's beak is broken in two places; one of the breaks is ancient, and the other more recent. With the aid of Bill Holm, the classic Nootka hat with the canoe design was identified (see fig. 8, right), differing slightly from three other apparently identical hats that must have been collected several years later (i.e., cat. no. 24). These are the oldest objects from the Northwest Coast collected during Spain's first expedition, now in the Museo de América.[9]

material very similar to rush, with fringes of the same material."[6] Unlike the hats from Santa Margarita, they did not include woven wool or hair. The Native peoples were interested in trading their goods for red ribbons and shells, such as abalone from the beaches of Monterey. Bad weather and scurvy caused the Spaniards to hug the coast on their return voyage, mapping it as they went.

In the archives of the Museo de Ciencias Naturales and the Museo Arqueológico Nacional is a copy of a document sent from Mexico, dated December 27, 1774, and titled *Inventario de las piezas cambalacheadas con los indios descubiertos a la altura de 55 grados y 19 minutos por los individuos de la fragata* Santiago *destinada a explorar la costa septentrional de California que se remitió a S.M. por el Virrey de Nueva España* [*Inventory of the items traded with the Indians discovered at latitude 55° 19' by the individuals aboard the frigate* Santiago *charged with exploring the northern coast of California, which was sent to His Majesty by the Viceroy of New Spain*]. The items are:

one blanket that appears to be made of coconut fiber [yellow cedar bark]; another of the same, made with greater care and embroidered on one side in white and black, with squares of otter fur in a checkerboard design on both sides; a cummerbund or sash apparently of wool and well-woven, with the ends embroidered in black; a leather cap, which appears to be of deerskin with a sort of black sealskin visor adorned with two rows of what seem to be fish teeth on the edge; a very carefully woven hat apparently of fine ipecac fiber [or red cedar bark]; another of the same in a Chinese style, much more exquisite in its weave and because it has a pattern of canoes made with ipecac dyed black; a seamless oblong bag also of ipecac, with twenty of the finely carved wooden sticks the natives use, and inside it a sort of bone bird with its upper beak broken, which was retrieved from an Indian woman who wore it around her neck with a string of little teeth that appeared to be those of a baby alligator [probably sea otter.][7]

THE SECOND EXPEDITION TO THE NORTHWEST COAST: HEZETA AND BODEGA IN 1775

After Pérez returned, preparations immediately got under way for a second expedition to include the Cádiz officers and scientists. Two ships sailed from San Blas in March 1775: the frigate *Santiago*, commanded by Bruno de Hezeta, chief of the expedition, and carrying as navigators Pérez and Martínez, who had been on the earlier voyage, and the schooner *Sonora*, under the command of Juan Francisco de la Bodega y Quadra, with Antonio Mourelle as second in command. The ships sailed north, ceremoniously taking possession of Vancouver Island in July. A few days later, bad weather and an ailing crew forced the *Santiago* to embark on its return trip, during which Pérez died of fever. Despite its precarious condition, the *Sonora* continued northward.

Like the previous year's expedition, the *Sonora* reached 55° north latitude and continued up the Alaskan coast until it came in sight of Mount Saint Elias, reaching 59° north latitude in August. An outbreak of scurvy forced the ship to return, although its exploration of the coast continued, stopping at the islands of the Alexander Archipelago (southeast Alaska), where the crew recuperated to some extent, then sailing down to Floridablanca Island (now known as the Queen Charlotte Islands), and from there to Vancouver Island. Bodega and Mourelle entered the details in their journals, describing their contacts with the Native peoples

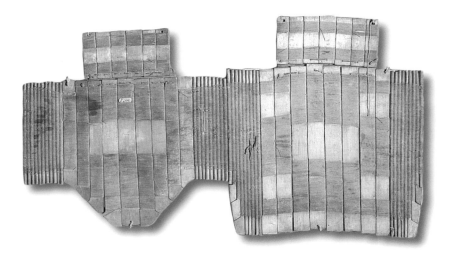

figs. 9a, b, & c Three of the four sets of armor collected by the Spanish explorers. Museo de América, Madrid (nos. 13934, 13883, and 13822)

and listing several trading sessions, some near Mount Saint Elias.[10] They reached San Blas at the end of November. Mourelle's journal was later published in London and used by James Cook on his third and final voyage in 1778, when he explored the Alaskan coast and disembarked at Nootka Sound on Vancouver Island. No evidence of objects collected on the 1775 expedition appears in the Museo de América.

BODEGA'S EXPEDITION IN 1779 AND ACQUISITION OF A BATTLE DRESS

Preparations for another expedition got under way in May 1776, but sailing was delayed as new ships had to be built. In February 1779, the sloops *Princesa* and *Favorita* set sail with orders to reach 70° north latitude. The *Princesa* was commanded by Ignacio de Arteaga, chief of the expedition, with Fernando de Quirós as second in command. The *Favorita* was under the command of Bodega with Mourelle once again serving as his second in command. At the beginning of May, they reached Bucareli Bay between what are today Guemez and Baker islands in the Prince of Wales Cape. They spent two months there, mapping and describing the area. At the beginning of July, they continued their journey north as far as the *Santiago* had reached on its previous voyage. They came to Carmen Island (now Kayak Island) and followed the coast as far as a port they called Santiago on Magdalena Island (now Hinchinbrook Island). They then sailed around Quirós Island (now Montague Island), exploring what is today known as Prince William Sound. All of this area was Pacific Yup'ik (Eskimo) country. In August they reached Regla Island, which may have been what is now Chugach Island near the Kenai Peninsula, although they apparently saw no Native people there. Scurvy finally forced them to turn back. When they put into port at the end of November, Spain and England were at war.

Although they reported only sporadic contact with the Pacific Yup'ik, the crews were in daily touch with the Alaskan peoples who came to trade with them during the two months they were in Bucareli Bay (either Tlingits or Kaigani Haidas). Mourelle reports bartering with the Native peoples of the Bucareli area on several occasions and carefully describes the objects acquired, among them "helmets that represent the head of some very ferocious animal" and "whistles that they played like flutes." He goes on to note, "And of all of this, the Captains took what they considered special, leaving the rest to be bargained for by our people."[11]

Letters exist written by Bodega, when he arrived in Mexico, to the viceroy. In one, he explains that the trifles collected during the expedition have been delivered to Commissioner Francisco Hijosa.[12] Records also show

fig. 10   Together with a stone club and a set of armor, this helmet and visor were most likely part of the battle dress collected by Juan de la Bodega y Quadra in 1779. Museo de América, Madrid (nos. 13913 and 13908) (see cat. nos. 8 and 9)

fig. 11   Tomás Suría, *Port Mulgrave (Yakutat) Tlingit Wearing Wood-Slat Armor, a Visor, and a Helmet*, 1791. Yale University Library, New Haven

that a chest filled with Native artifacts was sent to the Spanish court, arriving at El Ferrol aboard the frigate *El Aguila*. A document dated July 18, 1780, which is preserved in the Archivo General de Indias with a copy in the archives of the Museo Arqueológico Nacional, states that Joseph Ivargoyen, cashier for the tobacco factory in Guadalajara, sent the viceroy a collection (destined for the Real Gabinete de Historia Natural) consisting of "two stone figures, which are believed to have been Indian idols, [and] some articles used by the Indians that were recently discovered in Northwest California. They consist of a cape, a breastplate, a backplate, two arrows, a stone hatchet, and a bag containing some little sticks with which these Indians play."[13]

Various examples conserved in the Museo de América could have come from the Bodega expedition. They include two complete suits of armor, one entirely covered with paintings and the other only partly decorated (see figs. 9a, b, and cat. no. 20); three helmets, two of which have visors that covered the neck and face up to the eyes (see fig. 10 and cat. nos. 6, 7, 8, 9, and 10); a beautiful club (hatchet) with a green stone blade (cat. no. 17); and various sets of little sticks (used in a gambling game). According to Bodega's journal:

The Indians, whose martial temperament no doubt led them to invent defensive weapons, go to war wearing breastplates and back plates made of narrow slats woven together with many threads, making them flexible enough to be wrapped around their bodies, leaving their arms free; around their necks they wear a wide strip of thick wood in the shape of a gorget, which covers them nearly to their eyes, and on their heads they wear a helmet that usually depicts a fearsome animal. From the waist down, they wear a wooden apron, and on their backs a handsome leather cape that covers them to their ankles . . . The offensive weapons they generally use are hatchets of flintstone and another green stone, so hard that they cut any wood, although there is not a single tooth on their blades.[14]

A drawing from a later expedition led by Alejandro Malaspina portrays an Indian from Port Mulgrave (Yakutat Bay, where the explorers collected numerous objects) in battle dress, and one of the three helmets preserved in the Museo de América is similar to the one in the drawing (fig. 11). The other two helmets portray animals as described by Bodega and others. Of the two visors or gorgets in the collection, one matches a helmet in the shape of a "fearsome animal" while the other might match either of the remaining two helmets.

Because the stone club, the helmet adorned with a fearsome animal, and its matching visor are all decorated with inset shells, it seems likely that these objects formed a set and are the articles sent to Spain by Bodega, along with a suit of armor. The armor is probably the example that is decorated all over, its construction from flat boards differentiating it from the others preserved in the Museo de América, all of which are made of cylindrical boards and likely date from the Malaspina expedition (the armor with all-over painted decoration is most likely of Pacific Yup'ik origin and would most likely have been acquired in Prince William Sound). It is still unknown whether the painted visor goes with the helmet decorated with an image of a bird or with the one apparently collected in Yakutat (Port Mulgrave).

THE FOURTH EXPEDITION TO ESKIMO AND RUSSIAN LANDS: LÓPEZ AND MARTÍNEZ IN 1788

The United States made its Declaration of Independence in 1776 and went to war against England. Spain, still pressed by England's policy of expansion by sea and anxious to recover enclaves like Minorca and Gibraltar, entered the war in 1779, fighting on the side of the former colonies. The skilled officers who had been stationed in San Blas for the Northwest Coast expeditions soon left for other parts. As the war drew to a close, however, new reports of Russian settlements in the Aleutian Islands and Prince William Sound led the Spaniards to organize further voyages. In March 1788, the frigate *Princesa* and the packet-boat *San Carlos* set sail. They were commanded by Gonzalo López de Haro and Martínez, Pérez's second in command who had taken part in the earlier expeditions and continued after Pérez's death sailing from Mexico to supply the Alta California colonies.

They went directly to what is now Montague Island in Prince William Sound, where they traded with the Pacific Yup'ik. From there, they went up Cook Inlet, locating a Russian settlement and other anchoring grounds and factories. They passed Kodiak and Unimak islands, visited Unalaska in the Aleutian Islands, and traded with the Aleuts, Pacific Yup'ik, and Russians. They returned in September with the news that the Russians planned to settle in Nootka the following year. Although various Pacific Yup'ik objects in the Museo de América might have been collected on this voyage, no documents have been located to prove that this was the case.

THE FIFTH EXPEDITION, THE NOOTKA CRISIS, AND A NEW COLLECTION: MARTÍNEZ IN 1789

The Russian plan to settle in Nootka, much further south than they usually ventured, was an attempt to stop the British from taking over the fur trade the Russians had dominated up until 1786. When the Spaniards learned about this, however, they saw it as a territorial encroachment and immediately organized a new expedition. Martínez set sail in February 1789 with orders to establish a permanent settlement in Nootka Sound, doing everything possible to gain the Native peoples' goodwill while treating both the Russians and British civilly, all in order to foster Spain's commercial interests. On May 5, the expedition reached Nootka (Yuquot village), on a small island very close to the larger Vancouver Island, where it met two ships, one sailing under the United States flag and the other under the flag of Portugal. The Spaniards renewed their friendly relations with Chief Maquinna (or Macuina, in Spanish), the tribal leader at Nootka, and began building a fort and barracks, digging trenches, and preparing six batteries of guns to defend the settlement.

During a luncheon in Madrid in 1997, I asked the current Nootka chief, Mike Maquinna (a descendent of the eighteenth century's Chief Maquinna), how the Native peoples were able to distinguish the Spaniards from the other Europeans. Though he clearly believed that relations with the Spaniards had always been good, he nevertheless drew himself to his full height and quickly replied with certainty that his tribe's traditional lore relates how the Spaniards set up batteries of cannons on the tip of the island and opened fire. (In 1992 I saw only a single Native dwelling on Yuquot beach. By the end of the nineteenth century, European trade had gone elsewhere. The Nuu-chah-nulth [Nootka] people now live at the end of the deep inlet that forms the upper reaches of Nootka Sound, where they are connected to the road system of Vancouver Island.)

The subsequent Nootka crisis entailed a clash, not with the Russians, but with a succession of British ships. We know from Mike Maquinna that Martínez opened fire. After a slight skirmish with a British ship belonging to the South Seas Company, Martínez invoked Spain's authority, but permitted the ship to leave. The packet-boat *Argonaut* arrived on July 2. It was also owned by the South Seas Company and commanded by "Jaime Colnet" (James Colnett), who had instructions from his company in Macao to settle in Nootka as a scout. When Colnett refused to recognize Spain's authority, Martínez took him prisoner, sending him and his ship back to San Blas in Mexico. Somewhat later, Thomas Hudson, captain of the *Princess Royal*, an-

fig. 12 One of the Hawaiian feathered headdresses and cloaks that Estaban Martínez seized from the British in Nootka in 1789 and later sent to the Royal Cabinet in Madrid. Museo de América, Madrid (nos. 13562 and 13021)

which was in the government's general archive and burned during the Spanish Civil War) records a "memorandum of the shipment made by 'Estevan Josef Martínez'" and contains a note explaining that "by order of the King, these objects from the Northern Coast of California were transferred in four crates, together with the pelts of various animals, to the Real Gabinete de Historia Natural on March 21, 1790."[16]

Why did Martínez send feather capes, caps, and other objects from the Sandwich Islands (see fig. 12), together with the furs and garments worn by the Nuu-chah-nulth? It is easy to deduce the reason: all the ships belonging to the South Seas Company that arrived in Nootka had come from Macao and stopped off in the Sandwich Islands (now Hawaii). According to the anonymous Franciscan friar who wrote the *Relación de los hechos acaecidos en Nutka en 1788* [*Report of the Events that Took Place in Nootka in 1788*], "among Captain Colnett's crew was an Indian from those Islands (Sandwich), a young man of some twenty years, who followed the other sailors onto our ships."[17] This Hawaiian remained in the Franciscan school in Mexico until Colnett was set free, then went with him to England. It was with his help that Father Lorenzo Socies put together a Sandwich Islands glossary, which he attached to a report sent to Spain, along with another of the Nootkan language included as an appendix. The magnificent collection sent by Martínez is preserved in the Museo de América. Later in 1876, museum curator Juan Sala would write an article incorrectly attributing the collection to the Malaspina expedition.[18]

The Nuu-chah-nulth garment sent back with the collection was probably a military garment (the Nuu-chah-nulth usually went naked). None of the capes or skirts they used, which are depicted in other drawings, has been preserved. However, Martínez had been on the 1779 expedition during which Bodega acquired the battle dress he sent back to Spain. It therefore seems likely that Martínez sent one of the plain suits of armor now in the Museo de América or else the one that is partially decorated, as well as the bird-shaped helmet similar to the one worn by a Nuu-chah-nulth in the drawing of Maquinna dancing for Bodega's expedition in 1792 (see fig. 6 and cat. nos. 10 and 28).

SIXTH EXPEDITION TO THE NORTHWEST COAST: ELIZA IN 1790

At the time of the Nootka crisis in 1789, both Spain's new Viceroy Revillagigedo and Bodega arrived in Mexico aboard the same ship from Spain. With them was a new group of officers trained in Cádiz and destined to consolidate Spain's presence in the Department of San Blas, whose port was Spain's

other ship belonging to the South Seas Company, met the same fate. This eventually launched Spain into another war with England, bringing the first series of Spanish expeditions to the Northwest Coast to an end. Negotiations began that led to the beginning of a second stage, which was to mark the highest point of Spain's presence in the area.

Documents in the Museo de Ciencias Naturales authenticate objects in the collection of the Museo de América that coincide with these events. On March 4, 1790, the king's minister Antonio Valdés sent the Real Gabinete de Historia Natural four crates containing the pelts of animals from the north coast of California along with some curiosities and ornaments from both the Northwest Coast and the Sandwich Islands. The crates had been shipped from Nootka on July 9, 1789, and contained "some curiosities woven by the Indians of Meza or Sandwich Island"; two blankets made of "red and yellow feathers and used by King Tayana of Owihee Island"; two feather capes for women, two "chokers" for women, and a feather fan; a "carpet" of feathers in red, yellow, and black stripes; three feather hats "fashioned like helmets"; five coins that had been given out by Captain Kendrick, commander of a sloop from Boston on a voyage commissioned by the American Congress; another coin that Cook had given to Native people, as well as another bearing a likeness of King George III; three small dead birds whose feathers are used in the aforementioned woven goods; and, lastly, a garment such as those used by the Natives of Puerto San Lorenzo in Nootka.[15] A copy of a document in the Museo Arqueológico Nacional (the original of

fig. 13 Fernando Brambila,
*View of the Settlement and Port
of Nootka.* Museo de
América, Madrid (no. 2271)

connection to the north Pacific. From San Blas, they would supply the settlements in the two Californias (Baja California, now a part of Mexico, and Alta California, now in the United States), sustain the new colony at Nootka, resume the explorations interrupted by the war, and settle the Nootka conflict.

The viceroy sent out a sizable expedition under the command of Francisco de Eliza. The expedition consisted of the frigate *Concepción*, the packet-boat *San Carlos*, and the sloop *Princesa*. They set sail in February 1790 and after delivering supplies to the presidios (military posts) in Alta California, continued northward, arriving in Nootka Sound in March. Eliza set up his headquarters there and sent Commander Salvador Fidalgo and the *San Carlos* to continue their explorations further north. Like the expedition that had preceded him along the Alaskan coast, Fidalgo and his men reached what is now Hinchinbrook Island, explored Prince William Sound, and visited the Russian settlements in Cook Inlet, filling in their maps and knowledge of the geography and trading with the Russians until bad weather forced them to return. Meanwhile, Eliza's first lieutenant, Manuel Quimper, reconnoitered Juan de Fuca Strait and the entire complex coastline near what are currently the island and city named after Vancouver. There are no records of any objects sent back to Spain.

THE MALASPINA EXPEDITION IN THE NORTHWEST COAST

Malaspina proposed and subsequently commanded a scientific expedition that plied the Pacific for almost five years, from July 1789 to September 1793. The expedition consisted of the corvettes *Descubierta* and *Atrevida*, respectively commanded by Malaspina and José Bustamante. They had a crew of highly trained officers and carried with them naturalists such as Luis Née, Tadeo Hanke, and Antonio Pineda and artists such as Fernando Brambila, Tomás Suría, and Ravenet. The expedition, outfitted with scientific and technical equipment, followed the same research model as Cook's and Jean François de La Pérouse's expeditions. But the Malaspina expedition also conducted astronomical studies and made hydrographic and coastal maps that would eventually lead to a reorganization of maritime traffic in the Pacific, which was increasingly attracting Russian, British, and French ships. The expedition's objectives were to study the political situation in the *Indias*, the trade potential, the potential capacity of the Spanish colonists to attack and to defend themselves, the suitability of their ports, shipbuilding and the resources to encourage it, the use of natural resources, and their particular systems of government. The geographic and scientific findings were made public while the description of the viceroyship's political and defense systems remained confidential.

In June 1791, *Descubierta* and *Atrevida* sailed northward, exploring the waters where Fidalgo had already been and reconnoitering the coast in search of the fabled Northwest Passage. They dropped anchor in Port Mulgrave (Yakutat Bay), where the "Tejunes," or Tlingit, lived. They explored Prince William Sound and the adjacent islands, and then sailed back down to Nootka, returning in October with one ship destined for Acapulco and the other for San Blas. Several different journals were kept and drawings made, and these were eventually brought together and preserved in the Museo de América and the Museo Naval (a few of them ended up in the Ministry of Foreign Affairs and others at Yale University). Thanks to these drawings, we have not only journal descriptions but also visual depictions of the area and its people (see fig. 13 and cat. nos. 30, 31, 33, 34, and 35), including incomparable portraits of some of their chiefs, particularly Tetaku and the Nootka chief, Maquinna (see fig. 14 and cat. nos. 29 and 32). It is a collection of great historical, ethnographic, and in many cases, artistic interest. Although it is not limited to the Northwest Coast, a great deal of the material concentrates on this area, given that the land and its people were hitherto unknown.

Reports from Port Mulgrave describe a woman's labret, which was sent back to Spain, as well as "utensils, arms and manufactures for the Royal Cabinet in Madrid."[19] Other journals also report sending to Madrid all manner of fishing and household utensils such as "various dolls, some spoons and wooden boxes, the little sticks they play with, tightly woven baskets for the kitchen, and some stone axes and hammers that are well counterbalanced."[20] The expedition also acquired "a bow, its arrow, a dagger, and a sort of wooden battle dress," fabrics, and a blanket.[21] One distinctive acquisition was a casket, carved and decorated with inlaid shells, which they bartered for and sent back to Spain. Inside was another casket that contained the burned bones taken from the grave of a local chief. The expedition artists made drawings of both the grave and the casket. The Museo Naval's archives confirm these shipments: On December 20, 1791, a shipment of animals, herbs, drawings, and manuscripts was sent from Mexico; a second shipment included a crate belonging to the naturalist Pineda that contained a "collection of all manner of utensils from Port Mulgrave," while other crates contained various stuffed animals and still another held "a small coffin with bows and arrows from the ports visited."[22]

Other than the shipping documents preserved in the Museo Naval, no records exist of these objects having entered the Real Gabinete de Historia Natural. This was by no means unusual: only when the members of an expedition returned to Spain did they begin to organize

the material they had sent back. The situation was complicated by the fact that Malaspina fell out of favor immediately upon his return and was imprisoned, then exiled to his Italian birthplace. The Age of Enlightenment and the reign of Charles III had come to an end. It was the time of Charles IV's weak reign, the Godoy government, and its attempts to ensure that the ideas of the French Revolution did not take root in Spain. Enlightened individuals, among them some of the most brilliant Spanish naturalists of the time, were accused of being "Frenchified." Malaspina's name was eradicated from the writings of the day as well as from later publications. The expedition's journals were never finished and would remain unpublished for another century.

Despite the lack of records, some objects from the Malaspina expedition might have made it into the Royal Cabinet. The Museo de América collections, however, only partly coincide with the shipping and journal descriptions: a variety of goods, among them a battle dress, some little sticks, various spoons, a few bowls, and fishing gear, can be documented, but none of the more significant pieces are there. These would have been easy to identify because they were exhaustively described (the labret and the boxes) or because drawings were made (the casket). So it would appear that at most only part of the material collected by Malaspina

fig. 14 Tomás Suría, *Maquinna, Leading Chief,* 1791. Museo Naval, Madrid (folder 1-27, no. 2936) (see cat. no. 29)

was delivered to the Real Gabinete de Historia Natural: utensils, among which was a doll, and one or two pieces of armor along with the helmet mentioned in the discussion of Bodega's expedition in 1779, all of which matched the drawings made in the journal by Suría, the expedition's artist (see fig. 11 and cat. nos. 27 and 29).[23]

THE EXPEDITION OF THE SCHOONERS SUTIL AND MEXICANA AND THE CAAMAÑO EXPEDITION IN 1792

Having lost all hope of finding the fabled Northwest Passage that supposedly connected the Pacific and Atlantic oceans, Viceroy Revillagigedo of New Spain sent two expeditions to further explore the Juan de Fuca Strait and the coastlines near what is now Vancouver Island, at the extreme west of which lay the Nootka settlement. For the first of these expeditions, the schooners Sutil and Mexicana were fitted out and commanded by men who had been with the Malaspina expedition: Dionisio Alcalá Galiano and Cayetano Valdés.[24]

The schooners left Acapulco in March 1792 and reached Nootka Sound in May. Bodega, leader of the second 1792 expedition, whose principal mission was peace negotiations with England (see below), was already there commanding the fort. The schooners also met up with the Aránzazu, captained by Jacinto Caamaño and part of Bodega's group. Galiano and Valdés made observations involving astronomy and physics while cultivating cordial relations with Chief Maquinna's community. Their journals make special mention of Maquinna's character and leadership qualities in their description of the expedition's fairly strained political relations with Europeans from other ships and its more complex relations with the other neighboring Native people. The schooners then explored the Juan de Fuca Strait, where they met Fidalgo and the Princesa, also part of the Bodega expedition, and the British delegates en route to meet Bodega in Nootka Sound.

In addition to observing the territory and making maps, the members of the Sutil and Mexicana expedition developed special relations with Tetaku, a chief who was particularly feared in the area. They also initiated contact with other communities, all very different from one another, noting the differences and describing some of the customs. The best descriptions focused on the settlement at Nootka, details of which were mostly acquired from the naturalist José Mariano Mociño. They also traded with the Native people, acquiring both fish and objects, among them a blanket, bows, arrows, flint-edged wooden sabers, and canoe paddles. North of Nootka Sound, they encountered Nootkan-speaking peoples whose chief, according to the report published in 1802, wore "a hat very similar to the one we had seen a year earlier on the chief in Port Mulgrave . . . [He] held his hat in great esteem, having acquired it from his enemies in a battle. We purchased it . . ."[25] On another occasion, the report laments the fact that the expedition was unable to buy more utensils and arms from other Native peoples, which indicates that this expedition put together a collection of artifacts, although there is no record of it ever being sent to Spain or entering the Real Gabinete de Historia Natural.

Meanwhile Caamaño, charged with exploring Bucareli Bay and the adjacent islands in what is today known as Dixon Entrance and the Queen Charlotte Islands, sailed from San Blas in March aboard the Aránzazu, arriving at Nootka Sound in May. He then began his explorations of the area, including Calamity Island (now Banks Island) and various contacts with the Native peoples (this was Haida country). His journal is one of the few that makes a single brief mention of the bad smell the Native people left on the ship (due to their use of seal and whale fat). Although this must have been common, it is scarcely mentioned by the extremely decorous sailors and naturalists, who were influenced by Enlightenment ideas about the noble savage and under constant orders to treat the Native people politely. Aware of their role in history as the first Europeans to describe these unknown peoples, they avoided making indelicate comments (journals from the Malaspina expedition also make one mention of the bad smell of the objects being sent back to Spain).[26] Caamaño exchanged gifts and established a stable and cordial relationship with Chief Jammisit's community, who were apparently Haida (also possibly a Heiltsuk name, perhaps Hamsid), located somewhere around 53° 24' north latitude on the rugged coastline.

DIPLOMATIC NEGOTIATIONS AND NATURAL HISTORY IN NOOTKA: THE BODEGA EXPEDITION IN 1792

The Nootka crisis, which brought Spain and England back to war, had interfered with the foreign policy of Spain's Secretary of State, Count Floridablanca, who hoped to avoid any type of conflict and instead create a widespread diplomatic network that would keep the peace. Spain's war against England in support of United States independence had caused the country serious damage and paralyzed its American trade. Floridablanca therefore quickly negotiated a peace with England, which was finalized when the Spaniards gave up their claim to Nootka Sound.

Bodega's 1792 expedition was part of these negotiations. As commander of the Department of San Blas, Bodega was to meet with a British delegate at Nootka to discuss boundaries and other points of conflict. Before embarking on his voyage, Bodega met with the British captains Colnett, Hudson, and Temple, who had been taken prisoner during the Nootka crisis, conferred with the departing and incoming viceroys, and carefully prepared his expedition. The 1792 expedition then sailed from San Blas in February. A large expedition, it consisted of the frigates *Santa Gertrudis, Aránzazu,* and *Princesa,* and the schooner *Activa.*

In addition to negotiating a peace, the expedition was to continue both building the Nootka settlement and exploring the area for the purpose of making maps. After relieving Eliza, commander of the *Concepción,* who was working in Nootka Sound when the expedition arrived, Bodega finished fortifying the harbor, constructed some buildings, and even planted a vegetable garden. He also ordered Caamaño to sail the *Aránzazu* into northern waters and sent Fidalgo and the *Princesa* to explore the shores of the Juan de Fuca Strait and other points as far as the Russian settlements and the Sandwich Islands. (Although both ships were part of the Bodega expedition, technical reasons forced them to embark on their journeys at different times.)

The Bodega expedition also accommodated portions of a lengthy botanical expedition to New Spain that was taking place under the leadership of the naturalist Martín Sessé. This scientific study had been long in the planning. The viceroy had probably spoken to Bodega during their trip together from Spain to Mexico in 1789 and on subsequent occasions about Bodega's plans for a scientific expedition (Bodega had drafted a proposal similar to the one Malaspina proposed and carried out). Now he took advantage of Bodega's journey and sent part of the Mexican expedition to Nootka including Echevarría, the expedition's artist, the naturalist Mociño, and José Maldonado, a surgeon with a knowledge of botany and natural history. Maldonado accompanied Caamaño on his solitary explorations, while Mociño spent five months in Nootka, producing a series of illustrations of local flora and fauna that are now preserved in the Ministry of Foreign Affairs along with other documents and ethnographic drawings from the expedition. Mociño also wrote the first study of Nootka, with detailed descriptions of the Native customs. In order to do this, he first learned their language, concluding his study with a glossary that was published under the title *Noticias de Nutka* in 1913, then republished that same year.

Among the Museo de América collections are a series of objects that appear to have come from Nootka. Although customarily attributed to the Malaspina expedition (during his brief sojourn in Nootka Sound, Malaspina produced some magnificent drawings), there is no indication that he collected or sent back any artifacts from there. Moreover, an inventory taken by

fig. 15 Nuu-chah-nulth (Nootkan) mask. Museo de América, Madrid (no. 13917) (see cat. no. 14)

Florencio Janer of the Museo de Ciencias Naturales between 1858 and 1860 includes within the sparse information available some unusual notations about the origin of several objects from the Northwest Coast.[27] One of the masks clearly from the Northwest Coast (cat. no. 13) was said to be a theater mask made by Peruvian Indians and collected by Hipólito Ruíz and José Pavón, who had led a botanical expedition to Peru at the end of the eighteenth century. The same was said of some hats that, thirty years later, appeared in the catalogue of an 1893 exhibition of American history in Madrid as having been collected by the Malaspina expedition (i.e., from the Northwest Coast). An 1871 file from the Museo Arqueológico Nacional, where the collections were then stored, also notes that Janer sold a "Peruvian Indian theatre mask" brought to Spain by an expedition that took place during the reign of Charles III;[28] the same piece was then published the following year with the notation that it had been collected by Ruíz and Pavón in Peru when it is obviously a Nootkan mask (fig. 15 and cat. no. 14).

A double check of the Janer inventory produced a collection of labels that were clearly the wrappings or references for the objects he had inventoried. Many of them were indeed from the Ruíz and Pavón expedition and had been turned over to the Museo de Ciencias Naturales following the death of Pavón in 1840. The objects probably came in crates with which Janer had never worked. He simply listed them all in his inventory (which he began in 1858 after the historical-ethnographic collections had fallen into a state of abandon) as belonging to the Ruíz and Pavón collection, unaware that it was impossible for some of the objects to be Peruvian. As it happens, when Mociño returned to Spain from the Northwest Coast, he made a written request to be permitted to store his crates of scientific materials in the office of the botanists Ruíz and Pavón.[29] Shortly afterward, Mociño was accused of being "Frenchified" and left the country. He returned to Spain, but not Madrid, only shortly before his death. I concluded that Mociño had left the crates containing his collections in Ruíz and Pavón's offices and died before he had a chance to retrieve them. The crates then remained in the office untouched until Pavón died in 1840, when they were sent with his scientific belongings to the Jardín Botánico and the Real Gabinete de Historia Natural where Janer must have opened them and assumed that they were all of the same provenance.

A comparison of the Malaspina expedition's handsome portraits of Maquinna wearing his chief's hat with its bulbous top and designs of whale-hunting canoes with the hats in the natural history collections led to the conclusion that the same expedition that made the drawings instead must have also collected the hats. However, the collector instead must have been Mociño, who spent five months in Nootka (in contrast to Malaspina, who was there only a few days the previous year), worked as a naturalist on a scientific expedition, learned the language, and had drawings made that show the Native people in these same hats (although the drawings are not as good as those of the Malaspina expedition). Indeed, Mociño was particularly interested in these hats, and his description of Nootkan clothing goes into particular detail about them:

> I noticed that in order to protect themselves from the sun, some of them wore caps or visors of beaver or badger skin. But the most common are two types of hats, woven on special forms. Although the hats appear to be made of flexible reed mace, they are really thin sheets taken from the ribs of feathers to form a white field that sets off the designs that decorate them, which always depict the instrument they use to hunt whales. These hats are a more or less high conical shape atop which the leading people place another small cone that ends in a point. The commoners' hats are more roughly woven and have no designs. They are both fastened with bonnet strings or some other kind of tie.[30]

It was probably also Mociño who collected the two masks, one extremely large, that are listed as being from Peru, although they are clearly Nootkan, and that

are very similar to the faces carved on the interior house posts shown in the drawings of the interior of Maquinna's home made by artists with the Cook, Malaspina, and Bodega expeditions (figs. 2, 3, and 6 and cat. no. 28). It seems likely that some of the material from the Northwest Coast that is now in the Museo de América, such as the utensils mentioned in the discussion of the Malaspina collection, was also collected by the 1792 Bodega expedition, whose diplomatic mandate has completely overshadowed its scientific purposes.

This is understandable, given the elaborate nature of those negotiations. Bodega had been in the area for months before Captain George Vancouver arrived, and although the two men reached no agreement, they got along so well that they each baptized the island where they met, according to their journals, with both their names: Quadra and Vancouver Island. Bodega meanwhile was in constant negotiation with the numerous ships that dropped anchor in Nootka during his sojourn there, then with Vancouver and the British, and finally with the Native peoples, particularly their Chief Maquinna, Bodega's principal diplomatic target. The chief's descendants, Ambrose Maquinna and his son Mike Maquinna, still recount stories of the solid friendship between Bodega and their ancestor. Bodega and the other captains who anchored in the port, including Vancouver himself, have all left descriptions of the exceptionally polite and cordial relations that were the order of the day.

A drawing from the Bodega expedition and the journals of both captains depict a particular event: the welcoming dance Maquinna performed on two occasions. The first was in honor of Bodega and is described in his journal. The second was in honor of Vancouver and is mentioned by Bodega but described in more detail by Vancouver himself. The drawing shows the interior of Maquinna's house (with only one carved house post instead of the two that appear in the drawings done by John Webber of Cook's expedition). Maquinna's daughter occupies the place of honor; Maquinna himself is dancing, his brother and servants are singing, and the artist is standing in a corner. In the background, near the chief's daughter, are the Europeans. The man in the top hat is probably Mociño; the man who is enthusiastically welcoming his neighbor with broad, almost hostlike gestures, must be Bodega; and the object of his attention must be Vancouver, the long-faced captain who is standing politely with his hat in his hands. In his journal, Bodega recounts how Maquinna "gave me a dance, dancing alone to the sound of the song sung by his relatives and servants, beating the ground with lance points and rifles to provide the music's bass line, which was, however, difficult to understand. At the end of every brief dance, he had his brother Qua-tla-zape present me with a rich otter pelt, shouting out his expressions of goodwill."[31] Somewhat further on, Bodega writes, "Captain Vancouver was desirous of seeing Maquinna's settlement and getting to know his daughter Es-to-coti-tle-mog. We arrived in time to eat with him and his daughter, and enjoy the strange dances with which they presented us."[32] According to Vancouver's diary, "After the meal, Maquinna gave us a demonstration of his nation's war maneuvers. Twelve soldiers armed with rifles and other military equipment appeared and stationed themselves in good order at the entrance to the house . . . but all was done with rough and crude manners. Many of their movements represented attack and defense . . . They performed a masked dance that was so extravagant it made us laugh: Maquinna, who played a leading role, was a great success."[33]

THE SPANISH WITHDRAWAL

Spain ultimately withdrew from Nootka Sound, which was later depopulated and nearly forgotten, at least by Europeans. Spain also abandoned its pretensions of controlling the coasts north of the Californias. The French invasion and other political events further diminished Spain's influence, which vanished entirely when the former viceroyships achieved their independence. Mexico's subsequent loss to the United States of the vast area of land that stretches from the Atlantic to the Pacific (including the states of Texas, New Mexico, Arizona, and California) brought an end to officially Hispanic California and other more northern settlements. Still, twenty years of Spanish explorations and discoveries, of charting some extremely rugged and complex coastlines, punctuated with rivers, inlets, islands, and keys, produced maps that are still preserved today. They were also years of close contact with a range of Native peoples, whose societies were at their height and whose thousand-year-old traditions were irreplaceably recorded in the explorers' journals, drawings, and collections.

NOTES

1. Bernabeu Albert "Introduction" in Bodega 1990: 12.

2. Each expedition had its own instructions, depending on the results of the previous expeditions. In their journals, the members of the expedition make reference to the instructions they received, especially in the beginnings, which summarize the objectives of the trip. Bodega begins the journal of the expedition to Nootka in 1792 by summarizing the instructions received and describing the orders from members of other expeditions in response to the instructions in question (Bodega 1990: 159–62). Peña, on the other hand, begins to explain the instructions in the title of his journal (Peña 1774), like Mourelle in the account of his trip of 1779 (Landín 1978: 220ff.). They also refer to the instructions throughout their journals to justify their behavior, as in the ceremonies described by Mourelle on June 11, 1775 (Landín 1978: 182). This was mainly to justify the compliant or passive attitude displayed before certain hostile Native actions, like the inactivity in the face of the death of his seamen, described by Bodega, when raided in 1775 at the present Point Grenville, Washington (Bodega 1990: 83–87). The commentary of Mourelle when he could not recover stolen utensils explains that failure ". . . the softness with which I was ordered to treat the Indians whenever possible made it necessary for me to tolerate the defect and bear his impudence" (Landín 1978: 240). Moreover, the editors of the expedition journals, in their introductions and notes, indicate the correlative sources of these journals, like the correspondence and instructions given to Bodega for his expedition to Nootka in 1792, in the Archivo General de Indias; Sevilla, the Archivo General de la Nación, Mexico City; and the Archivo Histórico Nacional, Madrid (Bernabeu Albert "Introduction" in Bodega 1990: 62), and also in the Museo Naval (Palau 1998b: p. 220). The bibliography of this article contains a large number of the principal journals of the expeditions described herein. Some, like *Nutka 1792* (Palau 1998b), include valuable catalogues and documented appendices containing the expeditions' instructions.

3. Crespí 1774: 51v.

4. Peña 1774: 10.

5. Crespí 1774: 54v–56.

6. Crespí 1774: 69–69v.

7. A manuscript from Mexico dated December 27, 1774, in the archive of the Real Gabinete de Historia Natural (now Museo de Ciencias Naturales); a copy from 1875 is in the Museo Arqueológico Nacional.

8. Crespí 1774: 58.

9. It should be noted here that a good part of the collection from the Northwest Coast was once believed to have been brought back by Malaspina from his 1789–93 expedition. Smaller, less representative, and generally less important pieces were not even publicized, classified, or attributed. In the 1980s, when I was attempting to identify the exact origin of these pieces, I searched a number of archives and compared the records with the objects. This enabled me to discover something new: that parts of the collection had been brought back from voyages other than the Malaspina expedition. This opened a whole new line of research into those preliminary voyages, during which explorers mapped the territory and collected geographical and anthropological information, as well as objects that testified to their travels and encounters, and sent this material to Real Gabinete de Historia Natural. This development is discussed at length in Cabello 1989: 110–31. See also Cabello 1989b, 1992, and 1992b.

10. Bodega 1990: 55–110; Landín 1978, which contains the diary of Mourelle.

11. Landín 1978: 254. Earlier on (252–53) Landín carefully describes the armor worn and the rest of the armaments.

12. See the letter from Bodega to Mayorga dated November 28,

1779, in the Archivo General de la Nación, Mexico City, Historia, 63, fols. 252–58 (Bernabeu Albert "Introduction" in Bodega 1990: 38). Regarding the shipment of a chest with Indian objects, see the letter from Mayorga to Gálvez, Mexico City, December 27, 1779, in the Archivo General de Indias, Sevilla, Estado, 20 (28) (Bernabeu Albert, "Introduction"in Bodega 1990: 39).

13. A manuscript copy from 1880, of an original dated 1780 from the Archivo General de Indias, Sevilla, is in the archive of the Museo Arqueológico Nacional.

14. Bodega 1990: 137.

15. See the letter from Joseph Clavijo, director of the Real Gabinete de Historia Natural, to Count Floridablanca, dated March 27, 1790, in the archive of the Real Gabinete de Historia Natural, now Museo de Ciencias Naturales. A copy from 1875 is also in the archive of the Museo Arqueológico Nacional.

16. See the copy from 1880 of a document dated March 21, 1790, in the Archivo General Central (now Archivo General de la Administración del Estado), copied from the archive of the Museo Arqueológico Nacional. During the Spanish Civil War, the Estado section of the archive of the administration was burned and their documents were lost. The existing copies in the Museo Arqueológico Nacional were authenticated when they were made and represent an important collection, mainly because the originals no longer exist.

17. Relación 1788: 57.

18. Sala 1876. A reminder that the American objects soon went from the Real Gabinete de Historia Natural to the Museo Arqueológico Nacional, then to the Museo de América, when it was established.

19. Novo 1885: 168.

20. Novo 1885: 348.

21. Novo 1885: 161, 346; Tova 1988: 364.

22. For the shipment from Acapulco, see MS 583: 87v and MS 427: 184, and for the shipment from Pineda, see MS 583: 98–99, located in the archive of the Museo Naval.

23. By the end of the last century, with the publication of Malaspina's journals, all attractive or aesthetically valuable objects from the Northwest Coast and Alaska held by Spain had been attributed to the Malaspina expedition. Based on supposition rather than documented facts, this attribution lives on. However, recently discovered historical documents testify that at least some of these objects were collected by other explorers on expeditions hitherto known only to specialists. It is only now that they are beginning to attract the interest they deserve.

24. Their journal, the only chronicle of the expedition to be published, came out in 1802 as an anonymous report, with a long introduction that described Spanish voyages to northern California since the fifteenth century, using excerpts from various shipping logs. Somehow this trip, although independent, relates to the expedition of Malaspina, as does the trip of Bodega in 1792.

25. Relación 1802: 93.

26. Relación 1802: CXXIX-CXXX.

27. Janer 1860.

28. The record of the sale of 1871 is located in the archive of the Museo Arqueológico Nacional, published by Janer in 1872.

29. Jaramillo in Ruiz 1952: XXXVII; Arias 1968: 287–88.

30. Mociño 1913: 13.

31. Bodega 1990: 177.

32. Bodega 1990: 191.

33. Vancouver 1799: 449.

BIBLIOGRAPHY

Alcina, José, and Mercedes Palau
1988 *El ojo del totem: Arte y cultura de los indios del Noroeste de América*. Madrid: Comisión Nacional Quinto Centenario.

Arias Divito, Juan Carlos
1968 *Las expediciones científicas españolas durante el siglo XVIII: Expedición botánica des Nueva España*. Madrid: Ediciones de Cultura Hispánica.

Bernabeu Albert, Salvador
1995 *Trillar los mares: La expedición descubridora de Bruno de Hezeta al Noroeste de América 1775)*. Madrid: Fundación Banco Bilbao-Vizcaya, Consejo Superior de Investigaciones Científicas. (Contains the journals of Hezeta.)

Bodega y Quadra, Juan Francisco de la
1990 *El descubrimiento del fín del mundo (1775-1792)*. Introduction, notes, and edited by Salvador Bernabeu Albert. Madrid: Alianza. (Contains the journals of the Northwest Coast expeditions.)

Cabello Carro, Paz
1983 "Coleccionismo americano y expediciones científicas del siglo XVIII en la Museología española." *Archivio per l'Antropología e la Etnología*: 113.

1984 "Expediciones científicas, museología y coleccionismo americanista en la España del XVIII." In *Actas del II Congreso de la Sociedad Española de Historia de las Ciencias*, vol. 3. Zaragoza.

1986 "Amerikanische Sammlungen des 18 Jarrhunderts." In *Gold und Macht: Spanien in der Neuen Welt*. Vienna: Kremayr und Scheriau.

1989 *Coleccionismo americano indígena en la España del siglo XVIII*. Madrid: Ediciones de Cultura Hispánica.

1989b "Materiales etnográficos de la costa noroeste recogidos en el siglo XVIII por viajeros españoles." In *Culturas de la Costa Noroeste de América*. Edited by José Luis Peset. Madrid: Turner.

1992 "The Ethnographic Collections: A Special Legacy of the Spanish Presence on the Northwest Coast, 1774–1792." In *Spain and the North Pacific Coast: Essays in Recognition of the Bicentennial of the Malaspina Expedition, 1791–1792*. Edited by Robin Inglis. Vancouver : Vancouver Maritime Museum Society.

1992b "Ancient Spanish Collections from North America." *European Review of Native American Studies: 6(2)*.

Calatayud Arinero, María de los Ángeles
1984 *Catálogo de las expediciones y viajes científicos españoles a América y Filipinas (siglos XVIII y XIX)*. Madrid: Consejo Superior de Investigaciones Científicas, Museo de Ciencias Naturales.

Crespí, Fr. Juan
1774 "Diario que yo Fr. Juan Crespí missionero del app. Colegio de Propaganda Fide de S. Fernando de México, formo del viage de la Fragata de su Mag. nombrada *Santiago*, alias la *Nueva Galicia*, mandada por su Capitán y Alférez de Fragata D. Juan Pérez . . ." In *Papeles Varios de Interés Americano de la Colección Borbón-Lorenzana*, vol. 65: 1–82. Toledo: Biblioteca Pública.

Diez Torre, Alejandro, *et al.*, eds.
1990 *La ciencia española en Ultramar: Actas de las I Jornadas sobe "España y las expediciones científicas en Emérica y Filipinas*. Madrid: Doce Calles.

Feder, Norman
1972 "The Malaspina Collection." *American Indian Art Magazine* 2:3.

Fuster Ruiz, Francisco
1998 *El final del descubrimiento de América. California, Canadá y Alaska (1765–1822)*. Murcia: Universidad de Murcia.

Gunther, Erna
1975 *Indian Life of the Northwest Coast of North America, as Seen by the Early Explorers and Fur Traders during the Last Decades of the Eighteenth Century*. Chicago: University of Chicago Press.

Inglis, Robin, ed.
1992 *Spain and the North Pacific Coast: Essays in Recognition of the Bicentennial of the Malaspina Expedition, 1791–1792*. Vancouver: Vancouver Maritime Museum Society.

Janer, Florencio
1860 *Historia, descripción y catálogo de las colecciones hisórico-etnográficas, curiosidades diversas y antigüedades conservadas en el Museo de Ciencias Naturales de Madrid*. Manuscript. Madrid: Museo de América.
1872 "Máscara teatral de los indios del Perú." In *Museo Español de Antigüedades*, vol. 1. Madrid: T. Fortanet.

Landín Carrasco, Amancio
1978 *Mourelle de la Rua, explorador del Pacífico*. Madrid: Ediciones de Cultura Hispánica. (Contains the journals of Mourelle.)

Longinos, José
1994 *Diario de las expediciones a las Californias*. Introduction, notes, and edited by Salvador Bernabeu Albert. Madrid: Doce Calles.

Lozoya, Xavier
1984 *Plantas y luces en México. La Real Expedición Científica a Nueva España (1787–1803)*. Barcelona: Ediciones del Serbal.

Malaspina, Alejandro
1977 *The Malaspina Expedition: "In the Pursuit of Knowledge."* Santa Fe: Museum of New Mexico.

Martínez Shaw, Carlos, ed.
1988 *El Pacífico español de Magallanes a Malaspina*. Madrid: Ministerio de Asuntos Exteriores.

Mociño Suárez de Figueroa, José Mariano
1913 *Noticias de Nutka: Diccionario de la lengua de los Nutkeses, y descripcion del Volcán de Tuxtla*. Prologue by Alberto M. Carreño. Mexico City: Sociedad Mexicana de Geografía y Estadística.

Novo y Colson, Pedro de, ed.
1885 *Viaje político científico alrededor del mundo por las corbetas. Descubierta y Atrevida al mando de los capitanes de navío D. Alejandro Malaspina y D. José de Bustamante y Guerra desde 1789 a 1794*. Madrid.

Palau Baquero, Mercedes, and Antonio Orozco Acuaviva, eds.
1994 *Malaspina '92. I jornadas internacionales. Madrid, Cádiz, La Coruña. 17 a 25 e septiembre de 1992*. Cádiz: Real Academia Hispanoamericana.

Palau, Mercedes, Marisa Calés, and Araceli Sánchez, eds.
1774 *Nootka: regreso de una historia olvidada*. Madrid: Ministerio de Asuntos Exteriores.

Palau, Mercedes, Freeman Tovell, Pamela Sprätz, and Robin Inglis, eds.
1998b *Nutka 1792. Viaje a la costa noroeste de la América septentrional por don Juan Francisco de la Bodega y Quadra, capitán de navío*. Madrid: Ministerio de Asuntos Exteriores.

Peña, Fr. Juan de la
1774 *Diario del viaje que, que por mandado del R. Pe. Fr. Junípero Serra Predr. Appco., y Presidte. de estas Misiones de Monte-Rey, del cargo de nuestro Stô Colegio de propagande Fide de Sn. Fernando de la Ciudad de Mexico, hago desde este puerto de Monte-Rey sito en la costa de la California Setentrional, hago desde este puerto de Monte-Rey sito en la costa de la California Setentrionales, 30. minutos de Latitud al Norte, en la Fragata de S. M. nombrada Santiago, alias la Nueva Galicia, mandada por Dn. Juan Pérez . . . Capitán y Comandante de esta expedición, qe. por orden de del Excmo. Sr. Dn. Frey Anto. Ma. Bucareli, y Orsua, ha de hacer en dha. Fragata, a fin de reconocer la costa desde dho. Puerto de Monte-Rey hasta la altura de 60. grados de Latitud Norte, comenzando el día 6 de junio de 1774, en que me embarqué en compañía del R. P. Fr. Juan Crespi, predicador Apostólico de dho. Colegio, y Ministro de la Mission de Sn. Carlos de Monte-Rey, vulgo, del Carmelo. Estado, 43*. Sevilla: Archivo General de Indias.

Peset, José Luis, ed.
1988 *Las culturas de la costa noroeste de América*. Madrid: Turner.

Relación
1972 *. . . de la entrada de San Lorenzo de Nutka, formada por individuos de la Expedición que de orden de S.M. el Sr. D. Carlos Tercero salió el año de 1788 del Puerto de San Blas en la Fragata llamada Princesa*. Manuscript 2866: 1–57. Madrid: Biblioteca de Palacio.
1802 *. . . para reconocer el Estrecho de Fuca, con una introducción en que se dá noticia de las expediciones executadas anteriormente por los españoles en busca del paso del noroeste de la América*. Madrid: En la imprenta real.

Ruiz, Hipólito
1952 *Relación histórica del viaje, que hizo a ls reynos del Peru y Chile el botánico D. Hipólito Ruiz en el año 1777 hasta el de 1788, en cuya época regresó a Madrid*. Edited by Jaime Jaramillo Arango. Madrid.

Rüstow, A. von
1939 "Die objecte der Malaspina-Expeditan in Archaologistchen Museum zu Madrid." In *Vassler-Archiv*, vol. 2. Berlin.

Sala, Juan
1876 "Cascos y mantos guerreros procedentes de las islas Sandwich conservados in la Sección Etnográfica del Museo Arqueológico Nacional." In *Museo Español de Antiguedades*, vol. 7. Madrid: T. Fortanet.

Tova Arredondo, Antonio
1988 *62 meses a Bordo. Diario de D. Antonio Tova Arredondo, 2° Comandante de la "Atrevida" 1784–1794*. Edited by Lorenzo Sanfeliú Ortiz. Madrid: Editorial Naval.

Vancouver, George
1799 *Voyage de découvertes, a l'Ocean pacifiquedu Nord et aoutour du monde*, vol 1. Paris: Imprimerie de la Republique, année VIII.

Reason and Dreams:
Eskimos and Northwest Native Americans in Art and Legend

Alberto Costa Romero de Tejada

THE POWER OF THE IMAGE

There is in New York, a magic place where the dreams of childhood hold a rendezvous, where century-old tree trunks sing and speak, where indefinable objects watch out for the visitor, with the anxious stare of human faces, where animals of superhuman gentleness join their little paws like hands in prayer for the privilege of building the palace of the beaver for the chosen one, of guiding him to the realm of the seals, or of teaching him, with a mystic kiss, the language of the frog or the kingfisher...[1]

—*Claude Lévi-Strauss, 1943*

This magic place is the Alaska and British Columbia room of the American Museum of Natural History. Lévi-Strauss adds, "Surely it will not be long before we see the collections from this part of the world moved from ethnographic to fine arts museums to take their just place amidst the antiquities of Egypt or Persia and the works of medieval Europe."[2] These objects, immobile but filled with life, call out from their display cases to seduce and invite the viewer to explore the mystery contained in the closed universe of their forms.

Lévi-Strauss began his vocation as an ethnologist exploring the Paris *marché aux puces*, or flea market. In *Tristes Tropiques* (1955), he confesses, "from my earliest childhood, it had been my hobby to collect exotic curios."[3] Elsewhere Lévi-Strauss writes about his trips to villages in the French countryside and his visits to the antiquarians there, always in an attempt to slake his thirst for intriguing objects. In 1941, after carrying out fieldwork in Brazil, he left France for the United States. André Breton sailed on the same ship and they became close friends. No doubt Lévi-Strauss' interest in what Breton called "art sauvage" was a bond between them.

In those days, New York was the refuge of European artists fleeing from World War II: Marcel Duchamp, Yves Tanguy, André Masson, Robert Lebel, Georges Duthuit, Max Ernst, and Breton all gathered there. Lévi-Strauss felt comfortable in the climate of intellectual exaltation that prevailed in the group. He became especially close to Ernst, whose work showed an affin-ity with the structuralist methodology the anthropologist later made famous. The construction of the artist's collages was reminiscent of the way Lévi-Strauss explored the myths of different peoples, searching for their meaning: they were cut in pieces, glued down, and rearranged as often as necessary until they took on an apparently coherent form.

The Surrealists were looking for a new, more truthful style of art, as well as a new approach to life. They called on anthropology and psychoanalysis to aid them in their search. In *The Golden Bough* (1890), James George Frazer recounted a multitude of myths from all over the world and showed how primitive man believed that dreams revealed higher truths. Sigmund Freud found symbols that enabled him to interpret dreams and to search for the secret of neuroses in the unconscious; in *Totem and Taboo* (1913), he linked the psychology of primitive people with the neuroses of contemporary individuals, as though they were a survival from ancient times. In the 1920s, the Surrealists adopted Freud's principles, considering primitive art to be an expression of the essential truths hidden in myths, the unconscious, and dreams—in other words, a higher form of art. The artist is always a magician, and if his work is to be authentic, it should be intuitive and oneiric, not the result of a rational process.

One day, probably early in 1942, Ernst entered the Third Avenue gallery in New York of Julius Carlebach, a German-born antiquarian. Carlebach recognized him instantly. "I'm going to show you something extraordinary,"

fig. 16 Blankets stacked for distribution during a potlatch, end of the nineteenth century. Department of Library Services, American Museum of Natural History, New York (neg. 22861)

fetishes covered with nails that came from the Congo. One explanation may be that the Africans were expert at handling form, which is why the Cubists were so fascinated with their art, while the Surrealists were interested more in the color and the mobility found, for example, in the masks of New Guinea. Furthermore, representation of the human body, while a central feature of African art, was rarely found on America's Northwest Coast. African objects in general seem to be more rooted in stable, religious principles. In contrast, despite the high quality of the best Tlingit and Haida work, Northwest Coast art seems somehow more fluid, closer to the magmatic process by which myths are made. (Although the Surrealists had a greater aesthetic affinity with the art of the Northwest Coast tribes, Breton nevertheless had a few samples of African art that he kept until his death.)

Elisabeth Cowling explains that when Breton and Paul Eluard, the most active collectors among the Surrealists, prowled the Paris antique shops in the 1920s, objects from America were very rare and Eskimo masks almost nonexistent.[5] This became clear when financial difficulties forced both men to sell their collections in 1931: the majority of their collections were works from the South Pacific—the Eskimos were represented solely by a few ivories whose quality was at best discreet. Difficulties in directly acquiring such works of art forced the Surrealists to search for information about the ethnic groups that most interested them in books and museums. Books about the rich American collections of Northwest Coast and Eskimo art could usually be found in the French bookstores; the New York museums in particular housed thousands of objects that had been brought back from expeditions organized at the end of the nineteenth century, when Native American homes still preserved many ancient artifacts and ceremonies still played an important role in their cultures. The Surrealists also devoured the Annual Reports published by the Smithsonian Institution's Bureau of Ethnology, among them Edward William Nelson's classic article on the Eskimos of the Yukon and Kuskokwim river basins in Alaska. Some European museums had collections as well: the marvelous objects collected by Alphonse Pinart in the 1870s are now in Boulogne-sur-Mer and the British Museum, and several German museums also house important collections, particularly Berlin's Museum für Völkerkunde, which financed Johan Adrian Jacobsen's expedition to the Northwest Coast and Alaska in the early 1880s.

Despite such a shortage on the market, Charles Ratton, an antiquarian friend of the Surrealists and one of the people who did much to publicize "primitive" art at this time, organized in the early 1930s the first European exhibition of Eskimo and Northwest Coast art in

fig. 17   André Breton in his Paris studio. On the wall are some of the Northwest Coast objects he collected, including the Yup'ik mask acquired by the merchant A. H. Twichell at the end of the nineteenth century. Photograph by Sabine Weiss, May 1960

he said, leading Ernst into the back room where the walls were covered with marvelous masks from America's Northwest Coast and, what impressed Ernst even more, Eskimo masks that appeared to have only just emerged from a dream.[4]

In 1929 the Surrealists had published a world map whose relative scale was based on the intensity of their interests (fig. 18). Thus, Alaska and the Arctic, home of the Eskimo people, and the South Pacific, home of the Melanesian and Polynesian peoples, occupied most of the earth. The most important part of North America was the Queen Charlotte Islands, where the Haida live. Russia also loomed very large because the Surrealists were sympathetic to the Communist cause. Their lack of interest in African art, however, is striking; one would think they would have been intrigued by huge

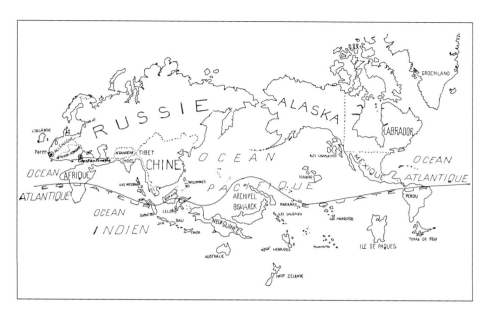

fig. 18   The Surrealist map of the world, first published in the French periodical *Variétés*, June 1929

his gallery.[6] Because New York's Heye Foundation was experiencing financial difficulties due to the Great Depression, Ratton was able to purchase a considerable number of objects from the foundation's owner and founder, George Heye (Heye was much more interested in art from Mexico and Peru, which he considered to be of higher quality than the Native American art of his own country). Man Ray was the only member of the Surrealist group who could actually afford to buy anything from the gallery, and even he purchased the least expensive Eskimo mask. The rest of the exhibition attracted only eighty visitors. Ratton eventually sold more of the pieces, but in 1936 he still had enough to include them in an exhibition of Surrealist objects, where Breton was at last able to purchase an Eskimo mask.

Given this scarcity and the Surrealist interest, it is not surprising that when Carlebach led him into the back room of his little shop on Third Avenue, Ernst felt that he had been transported to the magical center of the world. Most Surrealists were not exactly adventurers, and the only ones who actually traveled to the Northwest Coast were Kurt Seligmann and Wolfgang Paalen. Seligmann later published an article on Tsimshian totemism in *Minotaure*. After traveling to the Northwest Coast, Paalen went to Mexico where he spent many years. A great connoisseur, the artist put together a valuable collection of Native American art, although he also made room for objects from the South Pacific.

Ernst apparently kept his discovery of Carlebach's shop a secret from his friends, which demonstrates how they vied with one another to acquire such objects. Still, Breton came across the shop on one of his wanderings, and soon everyone knew about it. Carlebach eventually introduced Breton, Lebel, Matta, and the other Surrealists, including Lévi-Strauss, to Heye, from whom they purchased whatever masks they could

afford. Heyes' prices were very reasonable: around fifty dollars each.[7] The artists put together a notebook of their own drawings of some of these masks and sculptures, which is now a valuable document in itself.

Upon their return to Europe after the war, the Surrealists displayed the Eskimo and Northwest Coast art in their homes, alongside the *kachinas* of the Pueblo Indians and sculptures from Melanesia. Photographs of Breton's home prove that he was a passionate collector (fig. 17).[8] Lévi-Strauss also put together a notable collection, which he later sold in 1951. (A few years earlier, when serving as a cultural attaché at the French Embassy in the United States, he had tried to purchase a number of high-quality pieces of Native American art for France, but the French authorities were not interested.)

As is so often the case, artists were the first to discover the hidden values of these objects. Today, many art lovers share the Surrealists' delight as they contemplate the works of the Eskimos and the Northwest Coast tribes. One source of this fascination is how the decoration plays with objects just as it plays with myths. Lévi-Strauss discusses this when writing about a Native American mask: ". . . why the quasi-demonic style resembling nothing else in the neighboring cultures, or even in the culture that gave it birth?"[9] To the Native American's way of thinking, he concludes, the decoration creates the face:

> Decoration is conceived for the face, but the face itself exists only through decoration. In the final analysis, the duality is that of the actor and his role, and the concept of *mask* gives us the key . . . Their function is to offer a series of intermediate forms which insure the transition from symbol to meaning, from magical to normal, from supernatural to social . . . [I]t is the actor himself who becomes all these things . . .[10]

We are indeed in the "kingdom of characters." Similarly theatrical, a box in which ceremonial ornaments are kept is transformed into an eagle, with the figure of the bird split into two halves; when open, the halves adapt to their surface, as decoration and function become integral parts of one another.

Eskimo art appeals to the romantic imagination. Inhabitants of the earth's most inhospitable lands, the Arctic tundra stretching down to the somewhat milder zones of the northern forests, Eskimos are admirable as much for their ability to survive as for their lust for life. This spirit is manifested in the Yup'ik masks—cult objects for the Surrealists, who maintained a passionate, intuitive relationship with them. The Surrealists did not know what the masks were: they simply saw the creatures imagined by them and by the Eskimos. Interpreting their language, they believed that the objects would tell the story of their world.

Yup'ik masks are used in the men's ceremonial

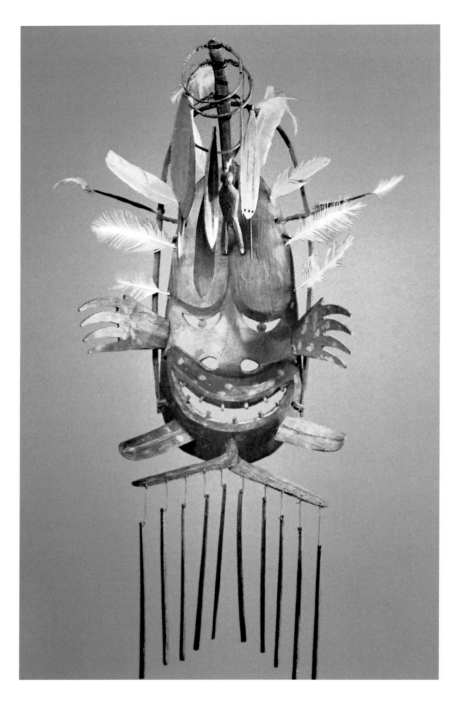

a face, which is often distorted—maybe a circle with a hole in the center. This is a *tunghak*, or evil spirit, which must be propitiated. The forms are a fascinating combination of abstraction and naturalism, and because the artists had tremendous freedom when making these masks, they are far more varied than objects usually found in the world of "art sauvage." But the style is recognizable: they all have seal faces, as though thousands of years of interdependence had grafted the genealogical trees of humans and animals.

Feathers, harpoons, hands and legs, and fish tails decorate the edges of the masks, generating no sensation of weight but rather restoring equilibrium to any possible imbalances in the composition. They capture the symmetry of nature. During the dance, and even in museum display cases, this "lightness" of the masks reveals one of the defining characteristics of Yup'ik Eskimo art: the objects are (or are perceived as) flat. They are also dynamic: feathers and the surrounding features, including the use of colors—white, red, black, and a light blue—invite the viewer to see them in movement. A motionless mask, in a sense, is a dead mask. Sometimes a long spiral emerges from the front of a mask, indicating the spirit of bubbling air underwater (fig. 19). Masks like that should be seen in the dim light of oil lamps, in wooden houses where the air is almost too thick to breathe, moving like ghosts to the shaman's orders while outside there is only the black northern silence. The masks imitate the movement of the planets; they travel the sky, mimicking constellations in space. They illustrate the music of a Joan Miró painting.

The first Eskimo ivories reached American collections at the beginning of the century, but they were considered of too recent origin to arouse much interest. The reason they looked new was because they had been perfectly preserved in the frozen earth, and it wasn't until the 1926 excavations sponsored by the Ottawa Museum on Cape Prince of Wales and the Diomede Islands that Diamond Jenness proved their true antiquity. They belong to what the archaeologist called the "ancient culture of the Bering Sea." Jenness was followed by Henry Collins of the Smithsonian Institution who in 1929 established the chronology that is still used today. Since then, thousands of ivory objects have been found, establishing a reasonable chronicle of the evolution of Eskimo art.

Although some of these small sculptures from as early as 200 B.C. seem to have been carved with iron points that probably came from Asia, they give the impression of being a paleolithic art, similar to Europe's Aurignacian period. In historic times Eskimos are known to have amused themselves by carving walrus tusks, portraying their neighbors or the fauna around

fig. 19   Yup'ik mask depicting *Negaqfaq*, "the spirit who likes cold and stormy weather," from the Napaskiak village on the lower Kuskokwim River, southwest Alaska, collected by A. H. Twitchell in the early 1900s. The Metropolitan Museum of Art, New York, Michael C. Rockefeller Collection, Nelson A. Rockefeller gift, 1961 (1978.417.76 [9/3393])

houses to propitiate the animals to be hunted, during shaman healings, and in funeral rites. As the element depicted in the masks are dreamed or seen by the shaman when he is in a trance, they do not really exist, and the masks are usually destroyed after use. This is one of the reasons why there are so few of them. Many of them represent a human face with an animal figure, such as a seal, surrounding it on one side. The face is the *inua*, a spirit like the human spirit, that is possessed by all creatures. Because nature is seen as uniform, the mask is the complete animal, its spirit and body. Others, simpler in structure, present a sketchy portrayal of

fig. 20   Female torso, ivory, Okvik culture, 250 B.C.–A.D. 100, Bering Strait. Private collection, Paris

fig. 21   Female head, ivory, Okvik culture, 250 B.C.–A.D. 100, Punuk Island, Bering Strait. Private collection

fig. 22   Ivory head depicting a person who was either congenitally deformed or suffered an accident, Ancient Bering Sea culture I-II, 250 B.C.–A.D. 100. Private collection, Barcelona

them, but it is doubtful that they did this in prehistoric times. The pieces dating from the earliest periods, especially the Okvik culture (200 B.C.–A.D. 100), have a formal sobriety and stylistic unity that preclude improvisation (figs. 20 and 21). Using a strictly geometric pattern, these early Eskimo artists achieved an absolute faithfulness to their human type and an inner concentration reminiscent of certain Asian art. The sculptures were undoubtedly ceremonial objects destined for shamanic practices, depicting figures of ancestors, guardian spirits, or people absent from the family during long periods of time. Some of the heads appear to have been deliberately separated from the bodies, perhaps to indicate death or distance. What is evident is that the Eskimos had strong emotional bonds with these little figures. Finely carved snow goggles, finger protectors, harpoon heads, and counterweights also reveal their makers' decorative skills. By A.D. 1000, with the expansion of the Thule culture, the sculptures had lost their geometric rigidity and taken on more organic features, representing the body and the qualities that give it life. Some of these enchanting figures carry a baby on their backs, and others show humor and resignation to accidents and illnesses, among them deformed heads (fig. 22). Their economy of means gives the results all the more merit.

Although the various tribes are culturally different, the broad, flat faces and straight black hair of the Alaskan Eskimos and the Northwest Coast Native peoples reveal their shared Asiatic origins. But the latter inhabited societies where some were poor and others were rich. The rich fought wars while the poor clashed in duels of improvised songs. Perhaps it was this social organization that conditioned their vision and portrayal of the world. The Tlingit, Haida, and other Northwest Coast tribes were painstaking and pragmatic, splitting open the animal represented when the object, such as a box, requires it. They reproduced details in a standardized but effective way—the Ingres or David of the so-called "primitive" people. They seldom depicted the human body, and when they did, the results are disappointing. Paradoxically, their masks are splendid, perhaps because they were placing their illustrative talents at the service of the animals around them. When they managed to integrate the disperse elements of the representative animal, their works are unsurpassed, and the Northwest Coast tribes are considered the best sculptors of the traditional Native American nations. Yet their analysis of forms always leads to the "exterior." In contrast, the Eskimos interpret, their powerful glance avoiding the superfluous as it abstracts. Yup'ik masks, despite their heavy ornamentation, capture the essence. The ancient ivories also explore the spirit of the human and animal, the shared spirit found beneath different skins. The resulting image in both cases is an "interior" one.

THE POWER OF THE WORD

> Novelists' intuitions and presentiments are sometimes as useful as academic sciences in breaking the spell of reality.[11]
>
> —*Gabriel García Márquez*

Nothing exists if it does not have a name—if it cannot be described or recounted. The word, whether spoken or written, whether expressions of love, orders, the prose of Cervantes, or the poetry of a chosen few, arouses feelings. In every corner of the earth, people have told stories, inventing the origin of the world, constructing myths and heroic gestures. Some tales are true, which is why the chronicles of travelers to unfamiliar lands are part of the great tradition of adventure stories. Bernal Diaz, James Cook and Louis-Antoine de Bougainville, Sir Richard Burton, Knud Johan Victor Rasmussen, all recorded their journeys, and millions of people have been thrilled by their feats, which epitomize the exploring spirit and the insatiable curiosity of human beings.

Although less well known, certain anthropological works can arouse the same feelings. The indigenous people of the Trobriand Islands described by Bronislaw Malinowski in *The Argonauts of the Western Pacific* (1922) are as alive and exotic as the Polynesians of Herman Melville and Robert Louis Stevenson. The imagination effortlessly changes Malinowski's subjects from scientific objects to literary characters. Malinowski's "novel" is continued in the diaries he kept while in the field. In them, he clearly describes his doubts, his feelings of loneliness and emptiness, his hatred of the "blacks." Like Gustave Flaubert, he expresses the artist's torment when caught in the creative process, and it is revealing that Malinowski decided to become an anthropologist after being seduced by Frazer's *The Golden Bough*, the same book that, years later, was to inspire the Surrealists. Indeed, anthropologists, explorers, and novelists all share an aesthetic vision of nature. Humans inhabit the world as artists inhabit a studio. The human observer is the creator who alters the landscape and constructs a parallel reality of objects and thoughts. These, in turn, must be observed by others in order to be valued and included in the annotated catalogue that includes all works, material and intellectual, produced by the world's different cultures.

Accounts by Native Americans have brought an inexhaustible supply of adventure and delight to many readers. The Northwest Coast, virtually unknown to Europeans until the eighteenth century, is a world of forests and fog-shrouded islands, of fjords and deep glacial valleys, peopled by tribes who perform strange ceremonies of mock cannibalism and who produce masks and totem poles of legendary beauty. The Native inhabitants of Nootka Sound on Vancouver Island appeared as follows to Cook, who had reached them on his third trip around the world:

> The persons of the natives are, in general, under the common stature; but not slender in proportion, being commonly pretty full or plump, though not muscular . . . The visage of most of them is round and full . . . The forehead rather low; the eyes small, black, and rather languishing than sparkling . . . Their colour we could never positively determine, as their bodies were incrusted with paint and dirt . . . The women are nearly of the same size, colour, and form, with the men; from whom it is not easy to distinguish them, as they possess no natural delicacies sufficient to render their persons agreeable . . . The ears of many of them are perforated in the lobe . . . In these holes they hang bits of bone; quills fixed upon a leathern thong; small shells; bunches of woollen tassels; or pieces of thin copper, which our beads could never supplant. The *septum* of the nose, in many, is also perforated . . . One canoe was remarkable for a singular head, which had a bird's eye and bill, of an enormous size, painted on it; and a person who was in it, who seemed to be a Chief, was no less remarkable for his uncommon appearance; having many feathers hanging from his head, and being painted in an extraordinary manner. He held in his hand a carved bird of wood, as large as a pigeon, with which he rattled . . .[12]

He also writes:

> But the most extraordinary of all the articles, which they brought to the ships for sale, were human skulls, and hands not yet quite stripped of the flesh, which they made our people plainly understand they had eaten . . . We had but too much reason to suspect, from this circumstance, that the horrid practice of feeding on their enemies is . . . prevalent here . . . Though there be but too much reason . . . to infer that they treat their enemies with a degree of brutal cruelty, this circumstance rather marks a general agreement of character with that of almost every tribe of uncivilized man, in every age, and in every part of the globe . . . They seem to be a docile, courteous, good-natured people . . .[13]

Cook was obviously not a disinterested observer. Conscious of his reputation, knowing that he would be read by a public anxious for details about the new lands, he measured the effect of his words and spelled it out: the Native Americans were cannibals. Considered a truthful chronicler, he certified with the precision of a notary in a style that is cold and concise, but his intention was still that of a novelist. Can we really believe that the Nootkan people carried human remains out to Cook's boats in order to sell them?

Let us return to his diary once more:

fig. 23   Tlingit Battle Helmet with a Bear Image. Peter the Great Museum of Anthropology and Ethnology (Kunstkamera) of the Russian Academy of Sciences, Saint Petersburg (no. 5795-10) (see cat. no. 71)

These consist of an endless variety of carved wooden masks or vizors, applied on the face, or to the upper part of the head or forehead. Some of these resemble human faces, furnished with hair, beards, and eyebrows; others, the heads of birds . . . and many, the heads of land and sea-animals, such as wolves, deer, and porpoises . . . Their furniture consists chiefly of a great number of chests and boxes of all sizes, which are generally piled upon each other, close to the sides or ends of the house; and contain their spare garments, skins, masks, and other things which they set a value upon . . . in the houses, many of them are decorated with images. These are nothing more than the trunks of very large trees, four or five feet high, set up singly, or by pairs, at the upper end of the apartment, with the front carved into a human face, the arms and hands cut out upon the sides, and variously painted; so that the whole is a truly monstrous figure.[14]

According to Cook, these are pagans, cannibals, who adorn themselves with feathers, pierce their ears and noses to insert extraneous elements, and use masks. Cook, the most experienced captain of his time, a man with considerable knowledge of human nature, in fact wrote admiringly of what he saw. But while describing the material culture and life style of a people living in the eighteenth century, their physical appearance, and the territory they inhabited, including the flora and fauna, perhaps he could not resist a certain touch of fable. It is anthropology as it has always been: facts must live up to expectations. Things are the way they

are imagined, not the way they are actually seen. Still, it is also the voice of history: the testimony certifies to Cook's presence, and the literary chronicle transmits the image of the times lived. Is a "faithful" picture really necessary?

Scientists began studying the cultures of America's Northwest Coast at the end of the last century, probably too late to get an undistorted view. The Native population had shrunk dramatically since the time of the first contacts, and their culture was undergoing an irreversible change. Still, the best known activities of these tribes remained their winter ceremonies and the potlatch. Masks, totem poles, decorated bowls, beautiful ivories . . . none of these artifacts can be understood except in terms of this ceremonial world. And this ceremonial world, the foundation of their entire culture, can only be understood if it is truly imagined. What follows in this section is a very condensed and free description, taken from various sources, of two of these ceremonies held in the mid nineteenth century when the Northwest Coast culture was still relatively intact and flourishing.[15]

Winter was the season when the powerful Kwakwaka'wakw secret societies performed their rites. The most awaited rite, the one that aroused the most dramatic response among the people, was the cannibal initiation ceremony. For them as for us, the cannibal was the stranger, the transgressor, an apparent alien.

Mysterious and attractive, as evanescent as F. W. Murnau's Nosferatu, he hides in the shadow of all humans.

It is night on a Vancouver beach. Inside a large Kwakwaka'wakw wooden house, lit with a central firepit, the eyes of the bear-man study the men congregated there (see fig. 23). Next to him are the animal-men from other secret societies, who, like him, are moving to the hypnotic rhythm of the drums. The odor of burning fish oil permeates the air. The spectators, seated on benches that line the walls, are silent and motionless, and their faces reflect expectation and excitement. "How can we hide from the bear who moves around the entire world? . . ." They avoid his teeth and the claws that rip their garments made of bark. Like the cannibal himself, the bear-man knows that he is strong. He has had a vision after a time of fasting and withdrawal. The burning embers he holds in his hands make him suffer, but he must not show his pain: he is a member of an important religious society, and any show of weakness means expulsion and shame. If, in his trance, he should make too many mistakes, he will be killed on the spot. The bear-man spins around, claws the earth, and leaps up and down, frothing at the mouth, possessed by his asocial spirit. The sound of the drums fills the entire space in the large building, reverberating against the wooden pillars: the people's ears vibrate with the force of its sound. They shout, then abruptly cease moving. As the ceiling planks are moved aside to create an opening, the cannibal drops to the floor of the fire-lighted house. He begins a crouching dance that conveys his state of trance, but suddenly, agitated by the reemergence of the cannibal spirit, he vanishes through a hidden door. The members of all the secret societies pursue him along the beach, capture him, and return to the house in which the winter ceremonies are performed. Once again the cannibal escapes and is caught, and yet a third time as well. Finally, resigned to enter the village, he follows a female relative who carries the dead body of a slave in her bare arms, dancing backwards and staring into the eyes of the cannibal, who cannot resist her call. Entering the building where he is to meet his destiny, he dances entranced, but in rhythm with the drummers and singers, who sing the cannibal songs especially composed for him. He loses control and lunges, and if he succeeds in capturing victims, he bites small strips of flesh from their arms. Then the cannibal becomes socially dead. His irrational condition persists, however, and to overcome him and calm his terrible passion, four "doctors" begin rites of exorcism. The ability to control the cannibal comes directly from supernatural beings. First they use fire, next water; then they pass a burning torch over him, so that the pain will pacify him. When the cannibal spirit is appeased by the ritualists, he begins to dance upright. He wears cedar bark regalia in place of his first costume of hemlock branches, and he dances with the customary movements that indicate his taming is proceeding. He was dead, insane, and has been revived. Society has recovered one of its own who was lost in madness and irrationality. The world has been restored. The power of the "doctors," the shamans, has been proven once again; the community is safe in their hands.

The rhetoric of the theatrical representation is directly linked to the quality of the works of art used in it and their capacity to convince. An otter mask that is not the animal, that does not move like it, nor emit the same sounds, is rejected. Thus, both the mask and the dancer are essential. But the mask, as a work of art, takes on its meaning from the use made of it. In the case of portrait masks, which represent members of the group valued so highly they remain forever among their people, only a master dancer can retrieve the ancestor's life and merge it into the mask. As with all objects of traditional Native peoples, use is the finishing touch to a work of art: it anoints it with the breath of life and confers on it the patina of art. Only when it has expressed its meaning, has it existed. Today it is fashionable to try to identify the sculptors and artists and to use these names to privilege certain ethnic groups. But these researchers do not realize that in most cases these spirits they attempt to pin down have no names.

The indigenous societies of the Northwest Coast were separated into definite classes: nobles, common folk, and slaves. The nobles were the chiefs of the great houses—possessors of fishing waters, hunting grounds, large harvests, abundant oil, smoked fish, copper, canoes, and Chilkat blankets. But every bit as important as their accumulated wealth were their exclusive titles, recorded in heraldic devices. Animals and sea monsters from whom they were descended were depicted on their huge totem poles and canoes; songs, places of honor in a ceremony, and the use of a celebrated mask reinforced the titles. The emphasis on property and the bonds forged among individuals who shared a chief's wealth led to relations of loyalty and dependence, which were contingent on the chief's ability to maintain his prestige.

How was this done? Not through a display of wisdom or strength, not through bravery in war, and not through shamanic powers, but through the ability to ritually humiliate other chiefs in the course of a ceremony unique in the annals of ethnography: the potlatch. The word, *pach'itl*, which originated in the Nootkan language, is musical and poetic. It refers to the lavish feasts used by the host chief to distribute gifts to his guests who serve as witnesses to the social contracts that were enacted in the potlatch: a marriage, the trans-

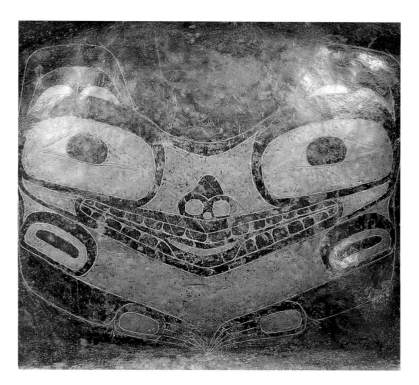

fig. 24   Haida "Copper"
(detail) Brooklyn Museum
of Art (no. 16.749.1)
(see cat. no. 151)

with many other canoes that have come from very far away, they converge on the host beach where a crowd awaits them. The painted paddles slice the water, while on land the drums reverberate. The bear-man looks to his left and admires the assurance of the eagle-man; he looks to his right and smiles at the otter-man's problems. They disembark, and standing on his back legs in the sand, the bear-man begins a clawing, roaring dance while the eagle-man swoops among the crowd. After a while, they all move toward the large potlatch building. Inside, a huge fire throws the shadows of animals and monster-beings on the walls. Behind the fire is a tiered platform where important guests are seated while everyone else takes their assigned places closer to the wall. Young men usher the visiting nobles to seats designated by the chief, and the bear-man hears their mumbling of approval when they see that their places have been appropriately assigned to show their host's respect for them.

When everything is in order, the host appears and welcomes his guests, treating them as great friends and allies, who yet are privileged to be in his presence. "I am the great chief who stands tall among people. I look from one side to the other, and I feel proud. You are welcome to my home." Afterward, with the help of his hereditary speaker, he begins an incantation of all his noble titles. He shows his crests and enumerates the potlatches that entitle him and his ancestors to boast such honors. Meanwhile, the guests listen appreciatively, peering at the curtain that hides the material goods that will be distributed later: they know that some time in the future they must repay in kind to the chief, in order to maintain their responsibility to the traditional community.

At a sign from the master of ceremonies, the animal-men of the clans take their places around the bonfire and perform their customary rituals. Wrapped in his fur garment, the bear-man dances with them, then clambers onto the platform and moves curiously toward the curtain, but he doesn't dare look behind it. Just then a procession of young slaves appears bearing heavy bowls overflowing with food and fish oil. These are set out for the guests, who look at the offered food with interest, although the bowls themselves are more important. Some have been specially made for the occasion, while others are old family heirlooms. They all have names—Wolf, Seal, Otter, Deer—and have been painstakingly carved in cedar, for the largest bowls, or alder wood, for the smaller food or oil dishes, by the best artists of the village.

During the meal, quantities of fish oil are thrown onto the fire through the mouth of a sculpture carved in human form known as "the regurgitator." The flames lick the roof beams, and the nobles seated closest to the

fer of ceremonial names to a new generation. The guests were then obliged to reciprocate with equal or greater gifts at subsequent potlatches for which they were hosts. Relatively modest potlatches were held so a noble could demonstrate his wealth on festive occasions, such as the building of a new home or the birth of a child. But when a particularly wealthy chief held a potlatch to transmit his noble titles to a descendent, the amounts distributed (even today) could reach staggering proportions. The grandiloquence of the great chiefs expressed an exaggerated pride: "I will go out and break Mount Katstais into bits and use them as stones for my bonfire."[16] During the nineteenth century, some of these ceremonies saw as many as three thousand blankets given away (fig. 16) and numerous gallons of fish oil gathered together and burned in the central fireplace of the ceremonial house, sometimes setting the roof on fire. Giving away and even destroying one's possessions, and sacrificing or emancipating slaves, became more common as fur trading made the Northwest Coast tribes increasingly wealthy. This increase in available goods coincided with a drop in the Native population, large numbers of whom succumbed to diseases brought by the colonists, and the demise of traditional leaders unleashed a public contest among survivors hopeful of attaining the names and social positions of the ranking nobility even if their connection by family lineage to the position was tenuous.

The potlatch begins as the guests arrive. The bear-man, guardian of the cannibal, dances in the prow of a large canoe carrying the members of his clan. Together

fig. 25   Tlingit box panel.
Private collection, New York
(see cat. no. 167 a)

fire stoically endure the heat. Even if the roof collapses, they will attempt to remain impassive. Numerous slaves begin to heap piles of leather, fur, and wool blankets at the guests' feet. To the most high ranking among them, particularly those who are descended from people of the northern tribes, go the highly valued Chilkat blankets. The host strolls among the noble guests, and at one point he orders a large canoe to be broken up on the beach and the pieces thrown into the fire. The destruction climaxes when he orders the greatest treasure, a painted "copper," to be destroyed and a slave sacrificed (see fig. 24). The bear-man with the others looks away, hearing only the sound of the falling ax as the order is carried out.

Afterwards, the bear-man once again stands majestically in the prow of his fifty-foot canoe. The canoe is loaded with sealskins filled with fish oil, beautifully painted boxes (fig. 25) of salmon and dried herring, piles of blankets, and half a dozen painted "coppers." On the beach, the host's people beat hollowed log-drums with their time-keeping sticks, and the departing clans keep time on the gunwales of the canoe with their paddles painted with emblematic designs. When the canoes set off, one can almost hear a song of mourning from both those who remain behind and those who are returning to their homes, often several long days distant. The bear-man dances and dances, and when the houses of the village are lost to his sight, he settles down to sleep on the stacks of blankets piled in the bottom of his canoe.

Is there any explanation for this unusual ceremony? Some anthropologists maintain that potlatches are ceremonies for redistributing wealth, providing groups in difficulties with food and other goods that they must later repay. But in *Patterns of Culture* (1934), Ruth

Benedict offers a highly original interpretation. Her book is both a scientific book and a seductive literary adventure, written by a woman who was as much a poet as an anthropologist. Romantic by nature and influenced by psychoanalysis, she believed that cultures, like individuals, have character, and she divided them according to Friedrich Nietzsche's typology in *The Birth of Tragedy* (1872): either Apollonian or Dionysian. In Apollonian cultures, people view life serenely; they are cooperative, rational, and nonviolent. In a Dionysian culture, the tone is antagonistic, dominated by competition and focused on ceaseless activity that is intuitive rather that rational. According to Benedict, among Native American tribes, New Mexico's Pueblos are an example of an Apollonian society while the Northwest Coast societies are Dionysian, as evidenced by their winter ceremonies and potlatch.[17]

In reality, only art exists—that is to say, human beings and their creative capacity. This includes amazing sensations, unforgettable images and sounds, smells that cling to the skin of the actors and the audience. The Northwest Coast winter ceremonies and potlatches are staged rites, like Aztec sacrifices and the Inquisition's autos-da-fé, Mardi Gras and bullfights, even the rioting crowds burning cars and violently destroying property on city streets. These rites are sometimes theatrical, almost always to some degree uncontrolled. The metaphor extends to war as a gigantic performance for which lethal equipment of great beauty is produced. War can be seen as a radical potlatch in which one destroys in order to rebuild and attempts to humiliate the enemy. Cannibals eat human flesh to acquire the virtues of the dead, but what better nourishment than one's own substance? Nature in the end rebels against culture.

NOTES

1. Lévi-Strauss 1982: 11.

2. Lévi-Strauss 1982: 11.

3. Lévi-Strauss 1997: 49.

4. Cowling 1978: 493.

5. Cowling 1978: 48 6, 487.

6. Cowling 1978: 488.

7. Cowling 1978: 493.

8. *André Breton* 1991: 76 (illus.).

9. Lévi-Strauss 1982: 18.

10. Lévi-Strauss 1967: 237.

11. García Márquez 1999.

12. Cook 1774: 266–67, 301, 303, 305.

13. Cook 1774: 271, 309.

14. Cook 1774: 306–7, 316, 317.

15. Benedict [1948] 1955 and Bancroft-Hunt 1979.

16. Benedict [1948] 1955: 191.

17. Benedict [1948] 1955: chapter 4.

BIBLIOGRAPHY

André Breton: La beauté convulsive.
1991   Paris: Musée National d'Art Moderne, Centre Georges Pompidou.

Bancroft-Hunt, Norman
1979   *People of the Totem: The Indians of Pacific Northwest.* London: Orbis Publishing.

Benedict, Ruth
[1948] 1955   *Patterns of Culture.* Reprint, New York: New American Library.

Boas, Franz
[1927] 1955   *Primitive Art.* Reprint, New York: Dover.

Cohen-Solal, A.
1999   "Claude Lévi-Strauss au États-Unis." *Critique:* 620–21.

Cook, James
1774 *A Voyage to the Pacific Ocean. Undertaken, by the Command of His Majesty, for Making Discoveries in the Northern Hemisphere. To Determine the Position and Extent of the West Side of North America; its Distance from Asia; and the Practicability of a Northern Passage to Europe,* vol. 2. London: Lords Commissioners of the Admiralty.

Corbin, George Allen
1988   *Native Arts of North America, Africa and the South Pacific.* New York: Harper and Row.

Cowling, Elisabeth
1978   "The Eskimos, the American Indians and the Surrealists." *Art History* 1: 484–500.

Fiedel, Stuart J.
1992   *Prehistory of the Americas.* Cambridge and New York: Cambridge University Press.

Fienup-Riordan, Ann
1996   *The Living Tradition of Yup'ik Masks: Agayaliyararput = Our Way of Making Prayer.* Translations by Marie Meade. Seattle: University of Washington Press.

García Márquez, Gabriel
1999   In *El Pais.*

Geertz, Clifford
1988   *Words and Lives: The Anthropologist as Author.* Stanford: Stanford University Press.

Lévi-Strauss, Claude
1967   *Structural Anthropology.* Translated by Claire Jacobson and Brooke Grunfest Schoepf. Garden City, NY: Doubleday.

1982   *The Way of the Masks.* Translated by Sylvia Modelski. Seattle and London: University of Washington Press.

1997   *Tristes Tropiques.* Translated by John and Doreen Weightman. New York: The Modern Library.

Maurer, Evan
1987   "Dada and Surrealism." In *"Primitivism" in 20th Century Art: Affinity of the Tribal and the Modern,* vol. 2, pp. 535–93. Edited by William Rubin. New York: The Museum of Modern Art.

Wardwell, Allen
1986   *Ancient Eskimo Ivories of the Bering Strait.* New York: Hudson Hills Press.

Function of Art in Northwest Coast Indian Culture

Bill Holm

Although the Native cultures of the Northwest Coast of North America have often been characterized as homogeneous, there are in fact many distinct traditions of art, social organizations, and ceremonial complexes along this 2,400-kilometer stretch of coast from Oregon to Yakutat Bay in Alaska. Of course, the varied Native groups did share many cultural concepts. The climate and natural resources available all along the coast were similar,[1] and although travel by land was impossible or very difficult over much of the area, the sea and interconnected waterways enabled contact, trade, marriage, and war between tribes. The formidable mountain barrier stretching close to the shore over much of the length of the coast hindered contact with Native peoples of the interior, resulting in relative isolation from those cultures.

But in spite of the general similarity of topography, climate, and food resources, there are regional variations that influenced Native response to the environment. The climate is more severe in the north and the land more rugged, a condition that likely influenced many aspects of culture including social organization and the functions of art. The radical differences between the Tlingit and Coast Salish in the amount of applied art each produced and its function in society may in part be due to the need for a graphically reinforced hierarchy to coordinate resource utilization in the north compared to the relatively more resource-abundant south.[2] Another formidable obstacle to uniformity of art and culture was the great diversity of languages along the coast, with at least a dozen linguistic families and over forty distinct languages identified.[3] The major areas of difference in culture, in fact, coincide roughly with linguistic borders. The southern province is dominated by Salishan speakers, the central coastal province is largely Wakashan, and the northern province is the home of the Haida (fig. 27), Tsimshian, Tlingit, and some northern Wakashan-speaking people.[4] Within these three provinces, art traditions vary from tribe to tribe and even among individuals. In the past, these differences went largely unrecognized or were misunderstood by writers and scholars, but scholarship in recent years has increased awareness of such stylistic variations.[5] And just as art styles differed from one another, the uses to which art was put, or at least the emphasis on art's function, was somewhat different in each of these linguistic provinces.

Before we consider these differences, perhaps the notion of "art" itself should be addressed. In popular thought today, art is often regarded as nonfunctional or something that does not serve any concrete purpose, but is merely enjoyable to look at or designed to stir one's emotions. (Of course, that is in itself a function.) Yet the idea that art has no real function is a relatively recent one in Western thought. The archaic and still the primary dictionary meaning of the English word is "skill."[6] Art once served religion, where it provided spiritual instruction or manifested the supernatural, and nobility, where it glorified lineage and manifested political power. In fact, these were the functions of art in traditional Northwest Coast societies. It has been popular in recent years to describe Native American languages as "having no word for art," implying that art in those societies was not frivolous and decorative, but was truly functional. One could take that idea to mean that Native American art had no aesthetic component, or at least that aesthetics were of subordinate value. The ideas of "skill," "craftsmanship," and "beauty" are all capable of expression in Northwest Coast (indeed in all Native American) languages, and there is, just as there is in English, a "word for art." Clearly, the sophisticated canons of design followed for centuries by the northern artists and the visceral power of art expression evident throughout the Northwest Coast could not have developed without an appreciation of the aesthetic component. Nor would renowned artists as far removed from one another in time and distance as the early nineteenth-century Tlingit master Kajis'du.axtc and the twentieth-century Kwakwaka'wakw artist Willie Seaweed have been commissioned by chiefs from distant villages to produce the masks and poles representing their treasured heritages.

fig. 26 Tlingit shaman posing for the photographer as if working on the cure of an ailing man. The shaman wears a painted robe, a small forehead mask, and carved bone amulets. His right hand holds a rattle depicting the black oyster catcher. Photograph by Edward de Groff, 1889. Special Collections Division, University of Washington Libraries, Seattle

fig. 27 The Haida village
of Xaina on the Queen
Charlotte Islands (Haida
Gwaii) in British Columbia.
Photograph by Richard
Maynard, 1884. Peabody
Museum of Archaeology
and Ethnology, Harvard
University, Cambridge,
Massachusetts

THE SOUTHERN PROVINCE

All the varied cultures of the Northwest Coast produced art that was purely, or at least primarily, decorative. Basketry was such an art, a skill that reached a very high plane everywhere on the coast, but had the greatest emphasis and elaboration at the northern and southern extremes. Basketry incorporated a certain amount of symbolism, but although most makers applied names to design elements, these names were more descriptive than meaningful. In the southern province, among the Chinook of the lower Columbia and the many Salish-speaking peoples of the Puget Sound/Georgia Strait basin, basketry once made up the largest part of the area's graphic arts. The baskets themselves were functional containers for gathering and storing foods, including roots, berries, fish, and shellfish, for preparing foods by stone-boiling, for storing and transporting household goods and clothing, and as cradles. None of these uses required beauty

to function in a perfectly adequate fashion. Yet the fact that these baskets (even undecorated examples, with their perfection of form and construction) are beautiful attests to a cultural appreciation of that quality.

By far the greatest motivation for art in the south, however, was religion. The widespread Native American concept of a guardian or assisting spirit was the prevalent religious credo, and the majority of graphic art (other than basketry) and ceremonial activity revolved around that concept. Some of the painted and sculptured representations were cryptic, the meaning known fully only to the possessor of the specific power, like the painted imagery on the zoomorphic panels used by Puget Sound shamans in the Spirit Canoe soul recovery ceremony.[7] Others were more overt, often more naturalistic sculptural representations of the owner of the power holding the image of his spirit helper. Yet even these preserve an element of mystery, by leaving the details of the power source unstated.

Further north, in the southern Vancouver Island and Georgia Strait area, the graphic art was more elaborate, but the primary impetus was still the representation (still often cryptic) of a source of supernatural power. Monumental art in the form of house posts and grave monuments often depicted encounters with power sources or formed representations of the supernatural beings themselves. A very sophisticated system of two-dimensional design, related distantly to the well-known northern "formline art," developed in this area. It was applied as detail to masks and sculptural monuments, to weapons and tools, and to ritual objects such as the power-imbued rattles made of folded bighorn sheep horn. Wooden whorls, or flywheels, pierced by the long spindles used for producing yarn from mountain goat wool, were often similarly decorated. Although spindle whorls and other implements used by women in their weaving and mat-making, such as mat creasers and needles, wool beaters, and looms, were primarily functional, the applied imagery seems surely to have been religious in content. It may relate to the wealth- (and hence, prestige-) producing products of women's work and perhaps also to the wool itself, important in purification rituals.[8] The meanings of the designs are mysterious partly because of lost knowledge, but also because such knowledge is inherently private.

Although present, masks were relatively little used in the southern province. The best known Salish masks represent the *Sxwayxwey*, a being that appeared to an ancestor, which is depicted by masked and costumed dancers in life-crisis rites. The *Sxwayxwey* dancers function as ritual purifiers of those central to the ceremony (fig. 28). The motivation is both religious and social, purifying in the spiritual sense and increasing prestige in the secular sense.[9]

fig. 28   Cowichan *Sxwayxwey* dancers in Esquimalt, British Columbia. Photograph by Bill Holm, 1956

THE CENTRAL PROVINCE

The narrow, mountain-bound west coast of Vancouver Island and the adjacent shore of Washington State's Olympic Peninsula were home to Wakashan-speaking fishers and sea hunters whose culture and art traditions were interrelated and are identifiable. On Vancouver Island those related groups were historically and generically known as "Nootka," an erroneous term that has since been replaced by a Native reference, "Nuu-chah-nulth" ("All along the mountains").[10] Along with their linguistically related neighbors to the east and north—the Kwakwaka'wakw (Kwakiutl), the Oweekeno, the Heiltsuk (Bella Bella), and the Salishan-speaking Nuxalk (Bella Coola)—they make up the central coastal province, an area extending northwest to the center of the British Columbia coast. Although art traditions vary considerably within the area, concepts and functions are shared sufficiently to warrant describing them together.

Although there certainly were purely aesthetic and religious components to the arts of this central province, the main motivation, in historical times at least, was social—the graphic representation of hereditary privilege. This took two main forms. One, which seems to have had a religious origin related in some way to the religious art and observances of the more southern groups, was the representation in graphic dramatic performances of the supernatural beings encountered by an ancestor and the dances and masks acquired from those beings.[11] The other was the display of crests, emblems also acquired through supernatural encounters by an ancestor, on sculptured house posts and totem poles, on headdresses and dancing robes, and in paintings on house fronts and canoes (fig. 29). The public display of the crests and of the ceremonial arts reinforced the nobility of the privilege owners.

In the dance performances, masks, robes, rattles, painted screens, and other decorated objects portray either the supernatural beings encountered by the ancestor or the powers bestowed by those beings. The artists who produced these objects had considerable leeway in which to use their imagination and creativity. Masks and other objects could be made to suddenly change shape or otherwise alter their form to dramatically illustrate the mythical sources of the privileges being portrayed.

fig. 29   Painted front of a Kwakwaka'wakw dwelling in Alert Bay from the 1870s. The painting depicts a thunderbird and whale. Photograph by Richard Maynard. Peabody Museum of Archaeology and Ethnology, Harvard University, Cambridge, Massachusetts (neg. 2676)

fig. 30 Kwakwa̱ka̱'wakw
Huxwhukw dancer.
Photograph by Bill Holm at
Alert Bay, 1960s

Artists of the Nuu-chah-nulth, Kwakwa̱ka̱'wakw, Heiltsuk, and Nuxalk were noted for their imaginative abilities to create these transformations. In the shadow-rimmed, fire-lit expanse of the great houses in which the dances were performed, the effect was magical (fig. 30). Although the performances were carefully planned and rehearsed, and the effect of supernatural power simulated, the underlying religious motivation is apparent in the frequent references to the supernatural in songs and speech and in the use of shamanic paraphernalia such as rattles and cedar bark regalia. Nevertheless, the principal motivation for the ceremonies in the historic period was, and is still, secular—the display of prestigious privileges owned by noble families. The same can be said of the crest objects—headdresses, robes, feast dishes, carved poles, and painted house fronts, for example—that were also acquired by ancestors from supernatural encounters.

THE NORTHERN PROVINCE

It was the artists of the northern province who produced the works that have come to be commonly characterized as "Northwest Coast art." Massive totem poles, great canoes, and especially the enigmatic "eye-filled" formline art, so familiar from painted boxes and Chilkat dancing robes (see fig. 5), are all typical of northern Northwest Coast art. The idea that the northern styles are the "true art" of the Northwest Coast has been so pervasive that the more southerly work has often been seen as inferior and derivative. Fortunately this attitude is changing, and the southern arts are more and more recognized for their creative and dynamic character.

The very sophisticated system of two-dimensional design, closely adhered to for centuries by artists throughout the northern province, most clearly binds the art of those tribes in stylistic unity.[12] This system, characterized by the use of conventionalized design elements, called formlines, to render more or less abstracted images of animals, gave artists a kind of grammar and vocabulary that allowed them great freedom of expression while simultaneously maintaining a formal unity of design throughout the region. The formline system began developing over a thousand years ago, and by the time of first European contact in the late eighteenth century, it had been fully developed and in use for perhaps several centuries. The painting on square storage boxes that are probably the most common decorated objects collected from the northern coast illustrates the amazing uniformity, and at the same time the individual uniqueness, of the formline art of all the northern artists.[13] Subtle changes in style over time and from tribe to tribe are recognizable, but the very close adherence to the system throughout the north is striking.

Images rendered in formlines are often so abstracted as to make identification difficult or impossible. But the images are still representational, usually depicting the creatures and natural phenomena that are regarded as crests. Like the figures carved on house posts and totem poles, they come from stories that recount the adventures of ancestors who acquired the use of the image as a prestigious emblem. The display of crests on poles, clan hats, staffs, robes, and other regalia makes a statement about the nobility of the family, and the right to use a crest image was, and is, of great social value and jealously guarded (see fig. 31). Attitudes about crest ownership are similar to those of European nobility, perhaps even more intense.

Some masks made and used by the northern tribes are also crest-related. A good example is the Grizzly Bear mask and dress of the Nanya.ayí clan of the Stikine Tlingit.[14] This mask was made of the skin of a bear that, according to tradition, accompanied the people up a mountain to escape a great flood. It became the source of the Grizzly Bear crest of the clan and was subsequently worn in dramatizations of the originating myth.[15]

Other masks were seen as repositories of supernatural power. This is the case of masks used by Tlingit shamans (shamanic art is prominent in the northern province, especially among the Tlingit). Masks carved to represent animal, bird, and human spirits that were controlled by a shaman, and whose power gave him the ability to cure illness, predict the future, or counteract the power of sorcerers, are among the most dramatic examples of Northwest Coast art. Other shamanic objects—rattles, amulets, robes, and headdresses, for example—are equally evocative and powerful. Haida and Tsimshian shamans used similar wonderful objects in

fig. 31   The body of Tlingit Chief Shakes lying in state surrounded by symbols of the Nanya.ayí clan, including the bear costume and mask to the right. Photograph by Davidson in Wrangell, Alaska, 1878. Burke Museum of Natural History and Culture, Seattle

their practice. Their images are enigmatic, typical of shamanic objects, with meanings known clearly only to the individual shamans who owned them. In this respect they are similar to the paraphernalia of southern shamans and characteristic of Northwest Coast religious material in general.

The Tsimshian used masks in dramatic portrayals of inherited spirits called *Naxnox*. These performances resembled some of the masked dramas of the central coastal tribes. Many masks were used, portraying a great range of spirits, including strange or foreign people, animals, and aberrant personalities. Striking illusions, again similar to those created in central coastal ceremonies, were part of *Naxnox* performances. Like those other ceremonies, the *Naxnox* portrayal of spirit power was more truly social than religious in motivation and content.

Everyday tools and implements of the northern province were often elaborated with designs that, in many cases, can be seen as religious in nature, much like the weaving tools of the southern coast. The best known of these implements are the two-piece halibut hooks once used primarily by Tlingit fishermen. The lower shank of the hook was invariably carved in the form of a mystic bird, fish, man, or combination of creatures. When in use, the carved arm faced the ocean bottom, so the power of the spirit figure could lure the

deep-swimming fish to take the bait. Clubs used by fishermen and sea mammal hunters to kill their catch were also often carved with animal images, most commonly the sea lion and killer whale. These sea hunters were probably chosen because of their abilities to capture prey, and hence to imbue the club with their powers.

A similar motivation may lie behind the use of fierce animal and spirit images on sculptured war helmets, combining visual intimidation and the idea of supernatural power against the enemy. Weapons, particularly daggers, were often embellished with carved pommels showing fearsome animals. Some helmets and daggers came to be regarded as clan treasures with the status of crests. When the use of wooden helmets in war ceased with the increased adoption of guns, some ancient helmets, treasured as heirlooms, were validated by potlatch and acquired that use. The Kaguanton Shark Helmet is a good example.[16]

Clan emblems were often carved on bowls and ladles, some of which also achieved clan treasure status. Such vessels were used only on ceremonial occasions, handled ritually and accompanied by formal speeches. Like other clan objects, their appearance emphasized the high rank of the owner and honored the guests. On the other hand, many oil dishes were made in the form of hair seals, arched as if resting on a rock, apparently because the seal is a major source of edible oil.

SUMMARY

The arts of the Northwest Coast have a variety of functions. The purely aesthetic function is present everywhere, and the work of the most skilled and imaginative makers is highly regarded, appreciated, and sought. The religious component is also found the length of the coast, but dominates art production in the southern, primarily Salish-language, area; much of the graphic art there functions as an active part of religious ritual or refers directly to supernatural power.

Although the idea of spiritual power expressed in art is present in the central coastal groups, primarily Wakashan speakers, it is subordinated to the social importance of the display of inherited privilege. For that reason, art's function here can be regarded as primarily social, the expression of family status. An undercurrent of spiritual power is present, especially in the "Winter Ceremonies," but it is overshadowed by the social function.

The art of the northern tribes also combines both spiritual and secular components, but in a somewhat different way. Most of the images expressed in art are derived from supernatural events, but they function primarily as manifestations of noble rank. One exception is in shamanic art, which follows the same aesthetic canons as crest art but refers directly to individual spirit power as a means to curing and prophesying (fig. 26). Another exception is in the evocation of hunting and fishing power through decorated hooks and clubs.

The functions of art in Northwest Coast societies are really not so different from those in Western art traditions. Art has both an aesthetic component and a "practical" component, with the emphasis shifting from one to the other in response to the purpose to which it is put. It can bring joy, stir emotions, glorify the past, honor the present, foster pride, evoke spiritual power, and promote knowledge. Art functioned and continues to function in all these ways on the Northwest Coast.

NOTES

1. Suttles 1989: 16.

2. Goodacre 1972: 25–39.

3. Thompson and Kinkade, 1987: 30–51.

4. Holm 1965.

5. Brown 1987, 1994; Holm 1981, 1983; and Wright 1983, 1992.

6. Many English dictionaries list the aesthetic or imaginative meaning of art far down the list of definitions. The *Oxford English Dictionary* (compact ed., 1971), for example, lists "skill" first and the aesthetic meaning tenth!

7. Miller 1988; Waterman 1930; and Wingert [1949]1976.

8. Suttles 1987: 130.

9. Suttles 1982.

10. Arima 1983: v.

11. Holm 1990b, and Jonaitis 1991.

12. Holm 1965.

13. Holm 1997.

14. Holm 1987: cat. no. 79.

15. Swanton 1909: 231.

16. Shotridge 1929: 329–34.

BIBLIOGRAPHY

Arima, Eugene
1983 *The West Coast People: The Nootka of Vancouver Island and Cape Flattery*. Special Publication, no 6. Victoria: British Columbia Provincial Museum.

Brown, Steven
1987 "From Taquan to Klukwan." In *Faces, Voices, and Dreams: A Celebration of the Centennial of the Sheldon Jackson Museum, Sitka, Alaska, 1888–1988*, pp. 157–74. Sitka: Alaska State Museum.

1994 "In the Shadow of the Wrangell Master: Photo Documentation of the Work of Two Nineteenth Century Tlingit Artists." *American Indian Art Magazine* 19(4):74–85, 104.

Goodacre, Richard
1972 "Habitational and Cultural Variation Between The Tlingit and the Coast Salish of the Northwest Coast." In *Journal of Student Papers in Anthropology*, pp. 25–39. Victoria: University of Victoria.

Holm, Bill
1965 *Northwest Coast Indian Art: An Analysis of Form*. Seattle: University of Washington Press.

1981 "Will the Real Charles Edensaw Please Stand Up?: The Problem of Attribution in Northwest Coast Indian Art." In *The World is as Sharp as a Knife: An Anthology in Honour of Wilson Duff*. Edited by D. N. Abbott, pp. 175–200. Victoria: British Columbia Provincial Museum.

1983 *Smoky-Top: The Art and Times of Willie Seaweed*. Thomas Burke Memorial Washington State Museum, Monographs, 3. Seattle: University of Washington Press.

1987 *Spirit and Ancestor: A Century of Northwest Coast Indian Art at the Burke Museum*. Thomas Burke Memorial Washington State Museum, Monographs, 4. Seattle: University of Washington Press.

1990 "Art." In *Handbook of North American Indians*, vol. 7, *Northwest Coast*, pp. 602–32. Washington, DC: Smithsonian Institution.

1990b "Kwakiutl: Winter Ceremonies." In *Handbook of North American Indians*, vol. 7, *Northwest Coast*, pp. 378–86. Washington, DC: Smithsonian Institution.

1997 "Variations on a Theme: Northern Northwest Coast Painted Boxes." *American Indian Art Magazine* 22(2): 52–61.

Jonaitis, Aldona
1991 *Chiefly Feasts: The Enduring Kwakiutl Potlatch*. Seattle and New York: University of Washington Press and American Museum of Natural History.

Miller, Jay
1988 *Shamanic Odyssey: The Lushootseed Salish Journey to the Land of the Dead*. Ballena Press Anthropological Papers no. 32. Menlo Park: Ballena Press.

Shotridge, Louis
1929 The Kaguanton Shark Helmet. *University of Pennsylvania Museum Journal* 20(3–4): 339–43.

Suttles, Wayne
1982 "The Halkomelem Sxwayxwey." *American Indian Art Magazine* 8(1): 56–65.

1987 "Productivity and Its Constraints: A Coast Salish Case." In *Coast Salish Essays*, pp. 100–33. Seattle: University of Washington Press.

1989 "Environment." In *Handbook of North American Indians*, vol. 7, *Northwest Coast*, pp. 16–29. Washington, DC: Smithsonian Institution.

Swanton, John
1909 *Tlingit Myths and Texts*. Bureau of American Ethnology Bulletin, 39. Washington, DC: U.S. Government Printing Office.

Thompson, Laurence, and M. Dale Kinkade
1987 "Languages." In *Handbook of North American Indians*, vol. 7, *Northwest Coast*, pp. 30–51. Washington, DC: Smithsonian Institution.

Waterman, Thomas T.
1930 "The Paraphernalia of the Duwamish Spirit Canoe Ceremony." *Museum of the American Indian, Heye Foundation. Indian Notes* 7(3): 295–312.

Wingert, Paul
[1949] 1976 *American Indian Sculpture: A Study of the Northwest Coast*. Reprint, New York: Hacker Art Books.

Wright, Robin
1983 "Anonymous Attributions: A Tribute To a Mid-19th Century Haida Argillite Pipe Carver, the Master of the Long Fingers." In *The Box of Daylight: Northwest Coast Indian Art*, pp. 139–42. Seattle: Seattle Art Museum.

1992 "Kadashan's Staff: The Work of a Mid-Nineteenth Century Haida Argillite Carver in Another Medium." *American Indian Art Magazine* 17(4): 48–55.

Spanish Expeditions
1774–1792

page 55
José Cardero, *Grave of the Former Ankau of Port Mulgrave Who Died in a Raid* (detail), 1791. Museo Naval, Madrid (MS 1726–67, cat. 2924) (see cat. no. 34)

1
Head
Chugach (Pacific Yup'ik)
Collected c. 1775–92, Prince William Sound, Alaska

Wood with traces of paint
7 1/2 x 3 1/2 in.
Museo de América, Madrid
(no. 13900)

The schematic features of this portrayal of a human face are carved in relief and highlighted with what are now only traces of red and black paint. The back of the head is flat. It is believed that this wooden head was attached to a body of soft material and used in shamanic magic ceremonies in which "puppets" enacted a variety of situations.

2
Mask
Chugach (Pacific Yup'ik)
Collected c. 1775–92, Prince William Sound, Alaska

Wood with human hair
8⅝ x 6⅛ in.
Museo de América, Madrid
(no. 13899)

This mask represents a human face. The bridge of the large nose is pierced, indicating that the mask may have once had a nose ornament. The eyebrows, mustache, and beard are realistically indicated by human hair inlays, and the small hole beneath the lower lip was probably for a labret, or lip plug. These masks were produced in accordance with shamanic visions. Made either by the shaman himself or by a tribesman working under his direction, these masks, like rattles, were essential features of the shaman's rituals.

3
Human Figure
Chugach (Pacific Yup'ik)
Collected c. 1775–92, Prince William
Sound, Alaska

Stone with leather, metal, animal fiber,
and traces of paint and resin
8⅝ x 4 in.
Museo de América, Madrid (no. 16382)

This appears to be a female figure,
dressed in a leather tunic with metal
rolled tube ornamentations. The head
and trunk are a single piece. There are
traces of resin in the pupils of the eyes
and inside the nose, and red paint appears on the head and neck. Religious
practices in the area since ancient
times have included ceremonies in
which such figures were used, although
generally they were made larger.

4
Hunting Hat
Chugach (Pacific Yup'ik)
Collected c. 1775–92, Prince William
Sound, Alaska

Painted wood with seal whiskers
8⅝ x 6⅛ in.
Museo de América, Madrid (no. 13915)

Particularly worth noting in this realistic depiction of a seal's head are the
inset seal whiskers and the painted
spots, which accurately resemble the
coloring of the animal's fur. A hunting hat such as this was worn in the
kayak by a hunter who most likely
carried a throwing board (*atlatl*) and
hunting dart, or spear. Pacific Yup'ik,
Alutiiq/Sutpiaq, Aleut, and some
western Yup'ik hunters wore related
wooden hunting hats of varying
forms, each distinguished by the
individual cultures and village areas.

5
Human Bust
Chugach (Pacific Yup'ik)
Collected c. 1775–92, Prince William
Sound, Alaska

Wood with leather
11¼ x 7⅝ in.
Museo de América, Madrid (no. 13898)

This flat bust apparently represents a
woman. It is very simple, the features
only roughly indicated and the round
face contrasting with the rectangular
torso. Little is known about the use
and purpose of these figures, although
indications are that they were related
to shamanic practices.

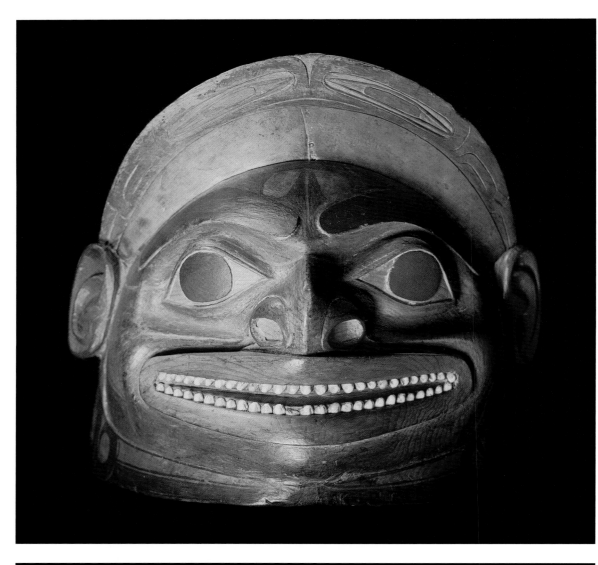

6
Helmet
Tlingit
Collected 1791, southeast Alaska

Painted wood with opercula, copper, and leather
11 1/2 x 10 5/8 in.
Museo de América, Madrid (no. 13909)

This helmet in the shape of a human head has very realistic ears and a sort of diadem made of copper, which was a sign of wealth, equivalent to the gold of other cultures. This appears to be the helmet worn by the Indian dressed in armor pictured in a drawing by Tomás Suría, one of the illustrators who accompanied the Alejandro Malaspina expedition. This would indicate that the helmet was collected by the Malaspina expedition when it was in Yakutat Bay in June 1791. Although the illustrator was evidently fascinated by the helmet, which he enlarged in the drawing, he did not manage to capture its exact shape, but only an approximation (see fig. 11).

7
Helmet Visor
Tlingit
Collected 1791, southeast Alaska

Painted wood with leather
8 1/2 x 10 in.
Museo de América, Madrid (no. 13912)

This visor might have been made with the above helmet (cat. no. 6), although it can be matched with cat. no. 10 as well. The drawing made by Tomás Suría (fig. 11) shows a visor without decoration. It was intended to protect the warrior's neck and the lower face, which were left uncovered by the helmet. Sometimes the Tlingit organized raids against other tribes to take possession of such assets as otter skins, slaves, and ceremonial regalia. The Tlingit would arrive in canoes, disembark, and begin their raids, which eventually ended in a pact requiring the Tlingit to pay compensation for the damages they had caused. The amount of compensation varied depending on the victims' rank.

8
Helmet
Tlingit
Collected 1779, southeast Alaska

Painted wood with opercula and
human hair
8¹/₈ x 14 in.
Museo de América, Madrid (no. 13913)

This helmet, together with a matching
face protector or visor (cat. no. 9), is
part of the battle dress that according
to the records was collected in 1779
by Juan de la Bodega y Quadra and
sent to Madrid a year later (see also
cat. no. 20). Bodega himself described
the Tlingit weapons in detail and
added that the Native peoples used
"helmets that usually depict a fearsome animal." The sculptured figure
embodied in this helmet appears to
represent a wolf. The wolf was one of
the most admired, feared, and respected
animals, due to its strength and ferocity,
and was the highly respected emblem
of certain Tlingit clans.

9
Helmet Visor
Tlingit
Collected 1779, southeast Alaska

Wood with opercula
5¹/₂ x 10³/₄ in.
Museo de América, Madrid
(no. 13908)

Used to protect the lower part of the
face and neck, this visor appears to
match the Bodega helmet (cat. no. 8).
According to the description in Juan
de la Bodega y Quadra's diary, when
both were worn, only the warrior's
eyes were left unprotected. Bodega
collected the battle headdress in 1779
and sent it back to Spain, together
with a stone club (probably cat. no. 17).
The Tlingit warrior would wear armor
of thick sea lion hide or interlaced
wooden slats, with the helmet and
visor to protect his head and neck.
Wars sometimes began when large
canoes commanded by the clan chief
or his nephew made a surprise night
raid. During these raids, authority was
usually shared with a high-ranking,
elderly tribeswoman.

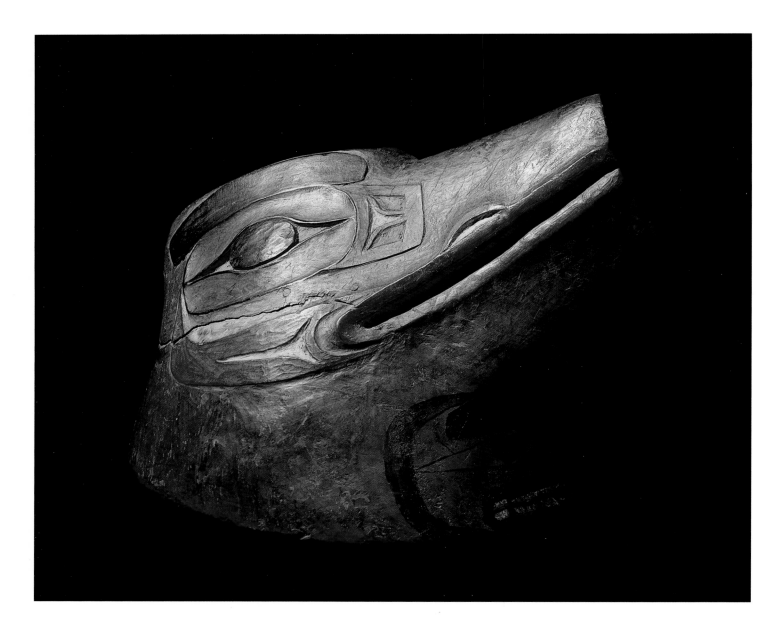

10
Helmet
Tlingit
Collected c. 1775–92, southeast Alaska

Painted spruce with leather
12⅝ x 11⅞ in.
Museo de América, Madrid
(no. 13911)

Helmets like this were a basic part of Tlingit battle dress, along with visors, body armor, and leg guards. This startling attire turned battles with the Tlingit into a fantastic struggle between opposing warriors transformed into supernatural beings such as sea lions, bears, wolves, and other animals. Generally speaking, wars were battles waged between rival clans and not between individuals or nations. Stylistic features of this helmet suggest that it was perhaps a century or more old when it was collected by the Spanish explorers. The wood also clearly shows its origin as a gnarly burl of spruce, selected for its strength and durability to hold up in hand-to-hand battle.

11
Forehead Mask
Tlingit
Collected c. 1775–92, southeast Alaska

Painted wood with opercula, copper, and silver
7³⁄₈ x 7 in.
Museo de América, Madrid (no. 13902)

Below the bird's beak on this head-dress frontlet are broad formlines that represent stylized wing feathers. Two claws grasp onto a large mouth, which displays small opercula, representing the teeth. The ears and claws are copper, while the pupils of the eyes are made of iron. Both metals were a sign of wealth. This portrayal most likely represents an anthropomorphic thunderbird holding onto the mouth of a whale. The thunderbird and whale were frequently combined in carved and painted representations across the entire Northwest Coast culture area. The fine detail and the accomplished woodwork and metalwork in this early frontlet demonstrate the level of artistic development present on the Northwest Coast at the time of the first Euro-American explorers in the late eighteenth century.

12
Forehead Mask
Tlingit
Collected c. 1775–92, southeast Alaska

Painted wood with leather
6¹⁄₄ x 6 in.
Museo de América, Madrid (no. 13905)

The sculpted face of this mask is typical of small Tlingit shaman's masks or maskettes, though the surrounding two-dimensional designs of black formline U-shapes are not a commonly seen feature. Shamans employed such masks to represent the unseen spirits that were their helpers in the healing arts. The labret indicates that this mask represents a female spirit. Shaman's masks were handed down from one practitioner to the next, passing through generations. Some masks collected in the historic period were already several generations old at the time they were acquired, which could easily be the case with this mask.

13
Large Mask
Nuu-chah-nulth (Nootka)
Collected 1792, west coast of
Vancouver Island, British Columbia

Painted wood
27 1/2 x 19 5/8 in.
Museo de América, Madrid (no. 13919)

This large mask of a human face is
made from a single piece of wood,
though it once had another piece attached at the tip of the nose. When
the Spaniards first reached this part
of the world, they did not describe in
their journals the totem poles that are
now emblematic of this area because
they did not exist. Instead, large
masks were displayed in the homes
of distinguished members of the

community, alluding to the lineage of
the inhabitants. This mask, or a very
similar one, can be seen in the drawing of the interior of Chief Maquinna's
dwelling (cat. no. 28). It was collected
in 1792 by José Mariano Mociño, a
naturalist who was a member of the
Juan de la Bodega y Quadro expedition and who appears in the drawing.

14
Mask
Nuu-chah-nulth (Nootka)
Collected 1792, west coast of
Vancouver Island, British Columbia

Painted red cedar
13 x 8¹/₂ in.
Museo de América, Madrid (no. 13917)

This mask depicting a human face with a headdress in the shape of an animal has a twofold design: the face and the emblematic headdress of the figure above. The features are very pronounced, and the mouth is round in the style of other early Nootkan masks, as can be seen in the drawings from the Juan de la Bodega y Quadra and James Cook expeditions showing the interior of Chief Maquinna's home (cat. no. 28). This mask was collected by the naturalist José Mariano Mociño on the Juan de la Bodega y Quadra expedition in 1792.

15
Rattle
Tlingit
Collected c. 1775–92, southeast Alaska

Wood
12¾ x 3⅞ in.
Museo de América, Madrid (no. 13907)

This rattle is made of two pieces, one
of which is carved with the image of
a bird with a slightly curved beak.
On its back is a high-relief carving
of a human figure in a reclining pos-
ture, reminiscent of the raven rattles
common in the nineteenth century.
The head of this bird most resembles
that of the tufted puffin, a seabird with
a beak that features crescent-shaped

slits across its width, much like the
forms carved here. The other half of
the rattle is decorated with a very thick
formline design of a bird's face that
has a small three-dimensional beak
protruding from its center. The very
early style of the two-dimensional
work on this rattle, along with the simplicity of the sculptural forms, suggests
that it was possibly made in the early
part of the eighteenth century, long before it was collected by the Spanish.

16
Rattle
Nuu-chah-nulth (Nootka)
Collected 1792, west coast of
Vancouver Island, British Columbia

Painted wood
6⅛ x 18⅛ in.
Museo de América, Madrid (no. 13897)

Carved in the shape of a bird, with
four human faces depicted on the side,
this rattle was used in shamanic ceremonial rites. The musical instruments
of the Northwest Coast are essentially
percussion instruments. Rattles, which
come in a variety of shapes, are the
most common. These instruments
were used in all ceremonies to propitiate the spirits. This rattle was probably
collected at Nootka Sound by the naturalist José Mariano Mociño, who was
part of the 1792 expedition led by
Juan de la Bodega y Quadra. It is similar to other rattles collected by James
Cook in this same place in 1778 (see
cat. nos. 40 and 41).

17
Ceremonial Club
Tlingit
Collected c. 1775–92, southeast Alaska

Wood with stone, leather, fiber, quills, human hair, opercula, and copper
6$^{1}/_{2}$ x 4$^{1}/_{2}$ in.
Museo de América, Madrid (no. 13916)

This hatchet was probably collected in 1792 by Juan de la Bodega y Quadra at the same time he collected the battle dress (cat. no. 20). It may have been part of a set with the helmet and visor (cat. nos. 8 and 9) also acquired at that time. The materials and crafts-manship are indicative of wealth and status. A green stone blade is attached to the handle by a strip of leather. The handle is carved in the shape of an animal (possibly a wolf or a bear) with shell teeth, and the eyes have copper irises. The shaft of the handle is covered with quills woven in a basketweave pattern. Such a woven quill covering is not commonly seen in Tlingit or other Northwest Coast work, though the sculpture of the head is classically Tlingit in style.

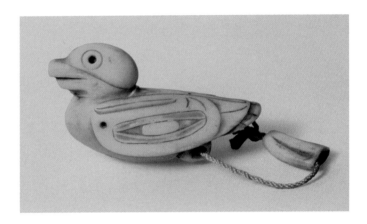

18
Amulet
Haida
Collected 1774, Queen Charlotte Islands, off the north coast of British Columbia

Whale ivory
1³/4 x 2³/4 in.
Museo de América, Madrid
(no. 13042)

Carved from a whale's tooth, this small amulet is currently the oldest documented object of the historic period that is decorated with the northern Northwest Coast conventions of two-dimensional design. The wings are embellished with a formline face that contains an elongated eye socket. The bird was given to Juan Pérez in 1774 by "an Indian woman who wore it around her neck with a string of little teeth that appeared to be those of a baby alligator [probably sea otter teeth]," according to the bill of goods still preserved in the Museo de Ciencias Naturales. The upper part of the beak was already broken at the time Pérez acquired the figure. Its delicate workmanship and great beauty make it an exceptional artifact from the first journey of European exploration in the area.

19
Halibut Hook
Tlingit
Collected c. 1775–92, southeast Alaska

Wood with spruce root and bone
13³/4 x 12¹/4 in.
Museo de América, Madrid
(no. 2941)

This two-piece fishhook in the shape of a V is designed to catch Pacific halibut of a specific size, dictated by the individual measurements of the hook's front opening, the distance of the bone point from the opposite arm, and the width of the arm on which the bone point is tied. Hooks like this one would catch only halibut of a certain age—neither young and small nor old and large enough to be difficult to handle (halibut have been caught as large as 400 pounds). Smaller, younger fish were thus spared to perpetuate the reproductive stock, preventing the depletion of the resource.

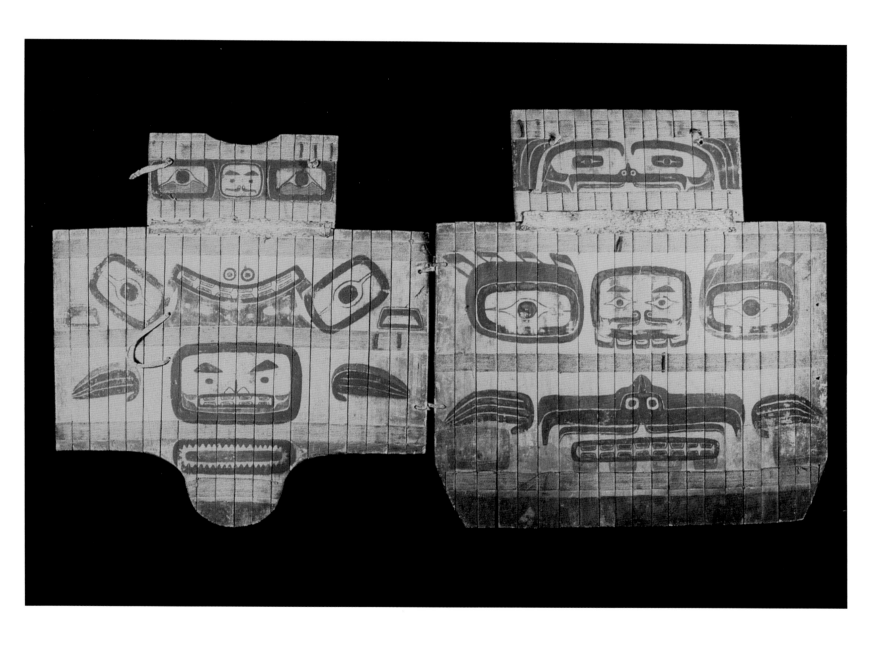

20
Armor
Tlingit or Chugach (Pacific Yup'ik)
Collected c. 1775–92, southeast Alaska

Painted wood with leather and
vegetable fiber
23¼ x 43⅜ in.
Museo de América, Madrid (no. 13914)

Although other examples of armor
from this area exist, this could well be
the breastplates and back plates of the
battle dress collected by Juan de la
Bodega y Quadra on his 1779 voyage.
As he wrote in his diary, "The Indians,
whose martial temperament no doubt
led them to invent defensive weapons,
go to war wearing breastplates and back
plates made of narrow slats woven
together with many threads, making
them flexible enough to be wrapped
around their bodies, leaving their arms
free." The painted designs represent the
clan affiliation of the owner, which is
determined by matrilineal descent. The

style of this painting, which is periph-
eral to most Tlingit painting styles,
suggests that the armor may be Chugach
or Eyak in origin, rather than Tlingit.

21
Flute
Tlingit
Collected c. 1775–92, southeast Alaska

Wood with abalone shell
15³⁄₈ in., length
Museo de América, Madrid (no. 13388)

A long cylinder of curved wood with a line of three holes, this flute narrates a story in bas-relief, featuring an iconography that alternates zoomorphic and anthropomorphic shapes. Although this instrument appears to be a flute, the absence of a mouthpiece and the fact that air cannot circulate in its interior, so it barely emits a hoarse croaking sound, would indicate that it is not actually a musical instrument but only an imitation.

22
Kayak Peg
Aleutian
Collected c. 1775–92, Aleutian Islands, Alaska

Ivory
2³/4 x ¹/2 in.
Museo de América, Madrid (no. 13040)

This peg depicts a zoomorphic figure. On one side, its ribs are clearly incised; on the opposite side is a curved tongue; and in the middle are two holes. Ropes were passed through these holes and used to transport the spoils of the hunt. The figure depicted is that of an otter, a very important symbol for the Aleutian people. The otter was considered the most powerful supernatural creature, as it helped shamans on their journeys of initiation. The sea otter was also a prime quarry for the hunters, who may have employed this zoomorphic form as a kind of talisman to propitiate a successful hunt.

23
Bowl
Chugach (Pacific Yup'ik)
Collected c. 1775–92, Prince William Sound, Alaska

Wood with shell inlay and animal fiber
4 x 9³/8 in.
Museo de América, Madrid (no. 13903)

In this oval bowl in zoomorphic form, the eyes and other highlights along the rim are perforated shell beads, and the mouth is incised. The animal's hollowed out body forms the bowl, in the center of which is another perforated shell inlay. The painstaking craftsmanship and the fact that when it was collected, traces of a sticky, greaselike substance were found suggest that the bowl was probably used in ceremonies of some type.

24
Whaler's Hat
Nuu-chah-nulth (Nootka)
Collected c. 1775–92, west coast of
Vancouver Island, British Columbia

Quills and vegetable fiber
11⅞ in., height; 11⅞ in., diameter
Museo de América, Madrid (no. 13570)

The designs woven in this hat depict a
whale hunt, which was a pursuit with
a strong ritual and spiritual foundation. This type of hat was reserved for
the chiefs of lineages with hereditary
rights to the whaling traditions. This
type of hat confirmed the status of the
wearer, referred to the rituals that preceded the hunt, and served as propitia-
tory objects. This particular hat was
probably collected at Nootka by José
Mariano Mociño, a naturalist who
traveled with Juan de la Bodega y
Quadra's 1792 expedition. It is like
those described by Mociño himself

and by the commanders of the
schooners *Sutil* and *Mexicana*. Similar
hats are worn by Chief Maquinna,
Chief Tetaku, and others in drawings
made by various illustrators who
formed part of the Alejandro Malaspina
expedition (see cat. nos. 26 and 29).

25
Hat
Chugach (Pacific Yup'ik)
Collected c. 1775–92, Prince William
Sound, Alaska

Painted cedar bark
4 in., height; 11⅝ in., diameter
Museo de América, Madrid (no. 13573)

This style of spruce-root weaving is the
same as that practiced by the Tlingit
and other Northwest Coast peoples,
though the painting is clearly only related in general appearance to the Tlingit
formline painting styles. Color distribution and other features of this painting resemble Tlingit work, but in detail
it reveals its Pacific Yup'ik origins. The
presence of this style of hat in Prince
William Sound is an example of the
interactions that took place between
the Tlingit and the Pacific Yup'ik, their
neighbors to the north, with whom
this hat appears to have originated.

26

N. Moncayo
Tais **of Nootka**
Juan de la Bodega y Quadra expedition,
1792

Pen and ink and watercolor on paper
11⅝ x 8⅞ in.
Library of the Ministry of Foreign
Affairs, Madrid (MS 146, no. 30)

In his *Noticias de Nutka* [*News from Nootka*], the naturalist José Mariano Mociño reports the following: "The dignity of the *Tais* [nobleman] is handed down from father to son, bequeathed to the sons when they are capable of governing and their fathers feel themselves to be getting old . . . The *Tais'* brothers are second-ranking nobles, but after two or three generations this status is lost as relatives more than twice removed are abruptly relegated to the *Mes-chi-mes*, or plebian, class, which is the lowest ranking. Women share the status of their fathers and husbands." As regards respect for the chieftain, Mociño writes, "The belief that the monarch . . . who governs them will in time become one of the blessed ones . . . obliges his subjects to venerate him."

27

Tomás Suría
Sardine Fishing
Juan de la Bodega y Quadra expedition,
1792

Pen and ink and watercolor on paper
11⅝ x 11⅞ in.
Library of the Ministry of Foreign
Affairs, Madrid (MS 146, no. 28)

In his diary, Juan de la Bodega y Quadra recounts how he ordered this drawing to be made and how this type of fishing was carried out. In his *Noticias de Nutka* [*News from Nootka*], naturalist José Mariano Mociño writes: "A nation of fishermen cannot link its properties to anything other than the beaches and the waters that bathe them. And so the people of Yucatl [Yuquot], like all the other inhabitants of these islands, take up arms to fight for the power to fish in their respective districts, and they believe that they are violating a public right when they travel to other waters for this purpose. As they obtain their main sustenance from the sea, they live constantly on its shores, changing their places of dwelling as fish become scarce in one place or abundant in another or if the seasons have discomfited them."

28
Vasques
**Interior View of Maquinna's House
Showing the Chief Dancing and His
Domestics Singing and Playing**
Juan de la Bodega y Quadra expedition,
1792

Pen and ink and watercolor on paper
11⅝ x 11⅜ in.
Library of the Ministry of Foreign
Affairs, Madrid (MS 146, no. 27)

In his diary, Juan de la Bodega y Quadra
recounts how Chief Maquinna "gave
me a dance, dancing alone to the
sound of the song sung by his relatives
and servants, beating the ground with
lance points and rifles to provide the
music's bass line, which was, however,
difficult to understand. At the end of
every brief dance, he had his brother
Qua-tla-zape present me with a rich
otter pelt, shouting out his expressions
of goodwill." The same scene is described by George Vancouver: "After
the meal, Maquinna gave us a demonstration of his nation's war maneuvers
. . . They performed a masked dance
that was so extravagant it made us
laugh: Maquinna, who played a leading
role, was a great success." Maquinna's
daughter is depicted in a seated position; the man in the top hat is the naturalist José Mariano Mociño. Bodega,
seated with his legs crossed, is explaining the ceremony to Vancouver, who is
seated to his right with his hat in his
hands. Later the two men agreed to
give the place both their names:
Quadra and Vancouver Island.

29
Tomás Suría
Maquinna, Leading Chief
Alejandro Malaspina expedition, 1791

Pencil and charcoal on paper
18¾ x 11⅞ in.
Museo Naval, Madrid (folder 1-27, cat. 2936)

This portrait of the Nootka chief, Maquinna, shows him wearing the typical chief's hat depicting whale-hunting scenes. The illustrators who accompanied the Spanish expeditions drew Maquinna on various occasions, and a number of different members of the expeditions described his character and behavior in glowing terms. His lineage has continued down to the present day, his name becoming the family surname. The naturalist José Mariano Mociño recounts in his *Noticias de Nutka* [*News from Nootka*], "We know three leading *Tais* in Nootka; the greatest of all in many respects is Maquinna, whose father died after [17]78 in a war against the Tla-umac."

30 *middle*
José Cardero
View of Majoa's Village
Alejandro Malaspina expedition, 1791

Watercolor on paper
10 x 17⅛ in.
Museo de América, Madrid (no. 2280)

The drawing shows the schooners *Sutil* and *Mexicana* anchored in the middle of La Atrevida Channel (now known as Broughton Strait, between Malcolm and Vancouver islands). In the background, the village known by the name of its apparent chief, Majoa, extends along the shoreline. The buildings were made of wooden planks, and their façades were decorated with large painted designs. In addition to the buildings shown in the drawing, numerous canoes of the early northern type ply the waters between the two Spanish ships. Though the artist rendered the canoe forms fairly accurately, it is puzzling that he portrayed them all being paddled stern first. The bow of such a canoe is the end with the short vertical cutwater extending up from the waterline. Perhaps it was the engraver who altered the drawing prior to the printing process.

31 *bottom*
José Cardero
Ceremony in Honor of Maquinna's Daughter
Alejandro Malaspina expedition, 1791

Watercolor and India ink on paper
9⅞ x 16½ in.
Museo de América, Madrid (no. 2268)

The drawing shows the celebration of the puberty rites of Nootkan Chief Maquinna's daughter. Important points in the life cycle were always inaugurated by a ceremony. For the Nuu-chah-nulth, leaving childhood behind and entering puberty involved a change of name. The scene depicted in the drawing is described in *Relación del viaje de las goletas* Sutil y Mexicana [*Chronicle of the Voyage of the Schooners* Sutil *and* Mexicana]: "Then the Chief turned to everyone and said: 'My daughter is no longer a child; she is a woman and hereinafter shall be known as Yzto-coti-clemot, the great *Taisa* [noblewoman] of Yucatl [Yuquot]' . . . The *Taises* and other nobles then began singing and dancing, and each one received an important jewel, which the princess threw from the *Quat-lat-zape* platform in the name of Maquinna."

32
José Cardero
Chief of Puerto del Descanso
[Neah Bay?]
Alejandro Malaspina expedition, 1791

Watercolor on paper
16½ x 9⅞ in.
Museo de América, Madrid (no. 2281)

This portrait was made of the chief of an anchoring ground located in Juan de Fuca Strait that was later described by the captains of the schooners *Sutil* and *Mexicana* in 1792. They had stopped in the same place a year earlier with the Alejandro Malaspina expedition. The members of the expedition noticed at the time a great number of one-eyed Makah people in the group, and the tendency of men to paint their faces red and wear either a single animal skin or blanket. The chief in the portrait is wearing a yellow cedar bark robe with a strip of sea otter fur on the edge. In later accounts from 1792, he is reported as wearing a necklace and a hat different from the one in the drawing, as well as five copper bracelets on his left wrist.

33
José Cardero
Roofless Winter House in Port Mulgrave (Yakutat, Gulf of Alaska coast)
Alejandro Malaspina expedition, 1791

Watercolor and India ink on paper
10³/₈ x 17¹/₈ in.
Museo de América, Madrid (no. 2250)

During Alejandro Malaspina's sojourn in Port Mulgrave (now known as Yakutat Bay), the members of his expedition had ample opportunity to observe the inhabitants. The following appears in Tomás Suría's diary: ". . . and then Tomás de Suría did a perspective drawing of the posts and beams that enclosed a long room, which was apparently to be used in winter. Then he spent a long time with the same objects at the ancient tomb (which he also drew)." (Although this work is signed by José Cardero, the painter Suría is the one who described it in his diary.) The uncovered house frame shows the manner of removing the roof and wallboards in order to construct temporary shelters at the summer and fall food-gathering sites. The boards would be returned to cover the frame of the winter house at the end of the food preservation cycle.

34
José Cardero
Grave of the Former *Ankau* of Port Mulgrave Who Died in a Raid
Alejandro Malaspina expedition, 1791

Watercolor and sepia ink on paper
11⁵/₈ x 16³/₈ in.
Museo Naval, Madrid
(MS 1726-67, cat. 2924)

"[There was] another grave, no further than two rifle shots from those already described; and although the purpose was the same, sheltering a small box and elevating another at a great distance from the ground, its ornamentation and paintings were much better finished; the hair that hung from the tops of the poles destined to hold the box and the tall pole behind it was probably erected in memory of the person whose ashes were deposited there . . . Some of the officers of the *Descubierta*, who visited the site accompanied by the *Ankau* himself, discovered that it was the grave of one of his wives" (from *Noticias sobre los habitantes de Mulgrave contenidas en una descripción física de las costas N.O. de la América* [*News about the inhabitants of Mulgrave contained in a physical description of the N.W. coast of America*] (Museo Naval, MS 425, fols. 150v, 151r, and 151v).

35
José Cardero
Pyre and Graves of the Family of the
Current *Ankau* in Port Mulgrave
Alejandro Malaspina expedition, 1791

Watercolor and sepia ink on paper
11 x 17⅛ in.
Museo Naval, Madrid
(MS 1723-5, cat. 2925)

"We could never understand whether
the colossal monster represented an
Idol . . . Close to him were several
pyres on which various bodies had
been cremated, and in the small box
beneath the claws or hands we could
glimpse an empty small basket, a
European top hat, a wolf pelt, and a
piece of wood. The monster was at
least ten and a half French feet, made
entirely of pine [Sitka spruce]; the
decorations on the box were small
[opercula] shells embedded in the
wood, and the figure on it was painted
blood red, except for the teeth, the
claws, and the upper part of the head,
which were painted black and white . . .
The figure was flanked by monuments
to two of the current *Ankau*'s sons"
(Museo Naval, MS 425, fols. 150v,
151r, and 151v).

English Expedition
1778

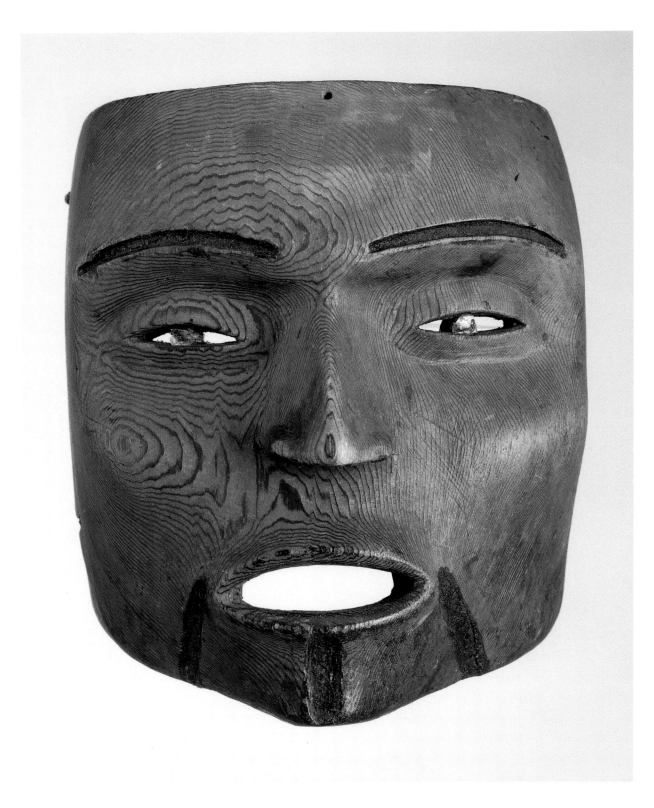

page 81
John Webber, *Nautilus of
Unalaska and Its Inhabitants* (detail),
John Cook expedition, 1778, water-
color on paper. Peabody Museum of
Archaeology and Ethnology, Harvard
University, Cambridge, Massachusetts

36
Mask
Nuu-chah-nulth (Nootka)
Collected 1778, west coast of
Vancouver Island, British Columbia

Balsam fir with bear hide, mica, and
traces of paint
8 1/8 x 4 7/8 x 6 7/8 in.
Museum für Völkerkunde, Vienna
(no. 223)

Collected at Nootka during James
Cook's third voyage, this beautiful
mask has the pronounced open mouth
commonly seen in eighteenth-century
Nuu-chah-nulth (Nootkan) art; it is
also seen in the masks collected at
Nootka in 1792 by Spanish explorers
(cat. nos. 13 and 14). There are two
types of Nootkan masks: those used
in the ritual dance of the wolves, the
tlukwana, and those with simple, clean-
cut, very expressive features created for

other ceremonials. Thin strips of bear
hide were set into the narrow grooves
at the eyebrows, mustache, and beard
lines. Used during the winter ceremonies, such masks portray ancestral
spirits or supernatural creatures that
are anthropomorphic in appearance.
Most of the rituals of the Northwest
Coast peoples took place in the winter
months, while the spring, summer, and
fall seasons were spent gathering in
food and other supplies.

37
Anthropomorphic Mask
Nuu-chah-nulth (Nootka)
Collected 1778, west coast of
Vancouver Island, British Columbia

Red cedar with traces of paint and
human hair
10 x 7¼ x 5¾ in.
The Menil Collection, Houston
(no. 73-07 DJ)

This is one of the few painted masks
collected by James Cook. Decorated
with abstract designs in green, which
are now scarcely visible, it is similar in
shape to other Nootkan masks collected
by Cook and by the Spanish expeditions. Thin hide strips were once glued
into the grooves cut in the brow, and
human hair was pegged into the top
edge of the mask. Early Nootkan mask
carvings often display soft sculptural
forms and more or less naturalistic

features, such as those seen here. The
deep relief of the eye socket beneath
the brow best reveals the Nootkan origins of this mask. The protruding lips
suggest a spirit that is either speaking
or singing. Although related to the lip
form common to Dzunukwa masks of
the Kwakwaka'wakw (Kwakiutl) peoples, those images also include very
hollow eye sockets, tiny nearsighted
eyes, and rich facial hair represented
by wide strips of bear fur.

38

Eagle-shaped Forehead Mask
Nuu-chah-nulth (Nootka)
Collected 1778, west coast of
Vancouver Island, British Columbia

Alder wood with abalone shell, nettle
fiber, and traces of paint
4³/₈ x 9 x 2¹/₂ in.
Museum für Völkerkunde, Vienna
(no. 222)

Particularly notable in this forehead
mask are the irises of the eyes, inlaid
with abalone shell. The shell is the
local Vancouver Island variety, while
most abalone shell inlay on the historic
Northwest Coast is of the California or
Mexican variety, *Haliotis fulgens.* Everyone on James Cook's third voyage who
saw this beautiful sculpture was interested in its style and purpose. Thomas
Davies produced a watercolor showing
various objects linked to the Yuquot
(Nootkan territory), among which this
forehead mask appears. The drawing
is now in the Hastings Museum and
Art Gallery in England. Forehead
masks were used in ceremonies performed during the winter festivals.
The old Native repairs in the cracks in
this mask, made with stitches of nettle
fiber cord, attest to its age and importance within Nuu-chah-nulth culture.

39
Female Figure
Koniag or Chugach (Pacific Yup'ik)
Collected 1778, Prince William Sound, Alaska

Bone, leather, and hair
8¼ x 3¾ x 2⅜ in.
University of Cambridge, Museum of Archaeology & Anthropology
(no. 1921.567.2)

Since prehistoric times, the Pacific Yup'ik have made small traditional figures of wood, bone, or ivory. Some of them have movable arms and legs in the style of figures made in Siberia; others are no more than heads or busts dressed in fur garments. Although they were generally considered magical or religious amulets or were used by shamans as ceremonial objects, others were children's dolls. This particular figure was acquired during James Cook's third voyage, but its exact purpose has never been discovered.

40
Kooh'minne (Rattle)
Nuu-chah-nulth (Nootka)
Collected 1778, west coast of
Vancouver Island, British Columbia

Wood with rawhide, abalone shell,
and traces of paint
4¹/₂ x 7⁷/₈ x 13⁵/₈ in.
University of Cambridge, Museum
of Archaeology & Anthropology
(no. 1922.948)

This rattle is made of two hollow
halves of wood joined together and
realistically carved in the form of two
birds, probably a species that lived in
the coastal areas. The wide body with
two heads is a very unusual depiction,
though the sculptural style of the rattle
is typically Nootkan. These rattles were
used for ritual purposes by shamans
and by chiefs and noblemen invested
with shamanic powers of transformation. They were also used in ritual
prayers preceding welcoming speeches
and as propitiating instruments to
accompany the various dances performed during potlatch ceremonies.
This particular rattle was collected
during James Cook's third voyage.

41

Bird-shaped Rattle
Nuu-chah-nulth (Nootka)
Collected 1778, west coast of
Vancouver Island, British Columbia

Wood with sinew
18^1/$_8$ x 3^1/$_2$ in.
Museum für Völkerkunde, Vienna
(no. 224)

The bird-shaped rattle consists of two
pieces joined by sinew cord. It was
collected by James Cook on Nootka
Island, a large island in Nootka
Sound, which opened into the waters
along the west coast of much larger
Vancouver Island. The rattle is similar
to one collected by the Spaniards
around 1792 (cat. no. 16) and to another collected by Cook on this same
voyage (cat. no. 40). It appears to be
some sort of fisher bird, perhaps a cor-
morant, which was very common in
this area. Rattles were important to
ceremonial activity for their ability to
invoke the spirit world and invite the
presence of the ancestors.

42
Club
Nuu-chah-nulth (Nootka)
Collected 1778, west coast of
Vancouver Island, British Columbia

Willow with stone blade, human hair,
fiber, and traces of paint
14⅞ x 3⅛ x 5⅛ in.
Museum für Völkerkunde, Vienna
(no. 211)

The handle of this club, sometimes
called a "slave killer," is in the shape
of a leg, which is topped by a head
crowned with locks of hair. The face
has a round mouth, from which the
stone blade protrudes like a tongue.
Written accounts suggest that such
clubs were used in rituals, possibly
sacrificial rites, although they might
also have been used in combats intended as demonstrations of strength.
Certain secret societies engaged in
these exhibitions of strength. Collected on James Cook's third expedition, the ceremonial weapon is similar
to the club acquired by Juan de la
Bodega y Quadra (cat. no. 17).

43
Club
Nuu-chah-nulth (Nootka)
Collected 1778, west coast of
Vancouver Island, British Columbia

Wood with stone blade, sea otter teeth,
and human hair
11 7/8 x 10 1/4 x 4 in.
University of Cambridge, Museum
of Archaeology & Anthropology
(no. 1922.949)

Carved in the shape of a human head
with an open mouth, from which the
blade protrudes like a long tooth, this
club is also embellished with human
hair and insets of sea otter teeth (some
of which are missing). Weapons of
this type were terrifying in appearance
and used by chiefs in the ritual killing
of slaves, usually captured or purchased for the occasion, in potlatch
ceremonies. Considered status symbols, they were part of the ritual paraphernalia used in major celebrations,
such as the secret societies' rites that
usually took place during the winter
season. This club was collected by
James Cook in 1778. The style of
carving and embellishment on this
club suggest that it is much older than
the related example (cat. no. 42).

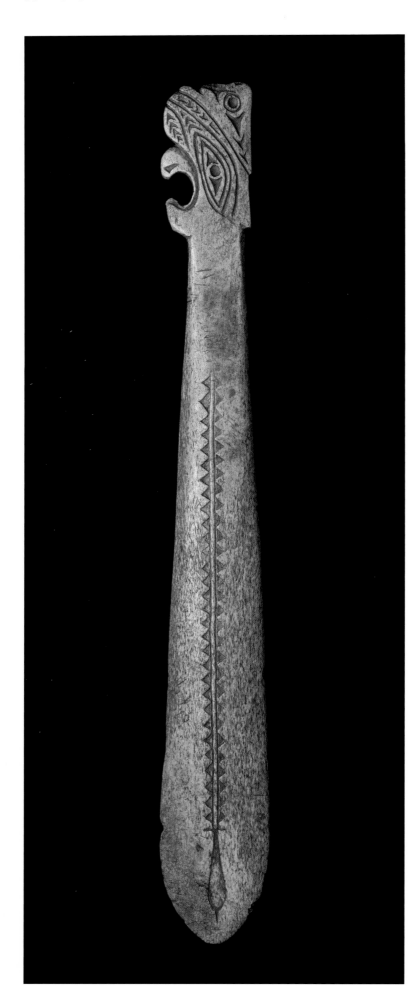

44
Club
Nuu-chah-nulth (Nootka)
Collected 1778, west coast of
Vancouver Island, British Columbia

Whale bone with unidentified
substance
22⅝ x 3 x ⅜ in.
University of Cambridge, Museum of
Archaeology & Anthropology
(no. 1922.954)

This whale-bone club, collected during
James Cook's third and final voyage, is
shaped in the typical Nuu-chah-nulth
style. The handle shows a stylized
thunderbird in profile with its beak
open, surmounted by an abbreviated
profile that is probably also a bird.
The imagery symbolizes the power of
the mythical world and is emblematic
of the highest-ranking chiefs. These
clubs were symbols of the status and
prestige of the chiefs, who gave the
clubs ceremonial names and referred
to them as such. The length of the
club is decorated with shallow two-
dimensional carvings filled with a red-
dish substance (probably spruce pitch
and red pigment).

45
Club
Nuu-chah-nulth (Nootka)
Collected 1778, west coast of
Vancouver Island, British Columbia

Whale bone with traces of paint
20½ x 3 in.
Museum für Völkerkunde, Vienna
(no. 212)

These clubs were more than weapons.
They were symbols of status and prestige linked to the whaling traditions
of the high-ranking families. Clubs
of this shape with the same types of
carved and incised designs were excavated from the Ozette archaeological
site on the coast of Washington at lev-
els that have been dated to 300–500
years ago. The continuity demon-
strated by such artifacts indicates that
Nuu-chah-nulth and Makah cultures
have been maintained over a very long
period of time: some objects date back
as many as 3,000 years.

46
Club
Nuu-chah-nulth (Nootka)
Collected 1778, west coast of
Vancouver Island, British Columbia

Whale bone
19½ x 3⅜ in.
Museum für Völkerkunde, Vienna
(no. 227)

This whale-bone club was collected by
James Cook in the area of Yuquot village (Nootkan territory). The grip of
this club is decorated with the profile
of a wolf, and the length of the blade
is carved with a row of shallow opposing triangles. Both this and the previous example (cat. no. 45) exhibit
sculpture and design styles that suggest
that these clubs were perhaps already
generations old at the time of their acquisition by Cook in the late eighteenth
century.

47
Monolithic Dagger
Nuu-chah-nulth (Nootka)
Collected 1778, west coast of
Vancouver Island, British Columbia

Stone
10¼ x 4⅛ in.
Museum für Völkerkunde, Vienna
(no. 209)

One end of this spindle-shaped monolithic dagger is deeply carved with concentric circles. Ethnographers believe
that it was used for smashing skulls—
as indicated by its name in the Yuquot
language, *see'aik*—in certain ceremonies
described in historic chronicles. Although there are various opinions as
to its true purpose, records exist of
similar objects being found among the
Kwakwa̲ka'wakw (Kwakiutl). This particular dagger was collected by James
Cook on his third and final voyage.

48
Monolithic Dagger
Nuu-chah-nulth (Nootka)
Collected 1778, west coast of
Vancouver Island, British Columbia

Stone with leather and traces of paint
11⅞ X 3¾ in.
Museum für Völkerkunde, Vienna
(no. 210)

This monolithic dagger was collected
by James Cook. The grip is carved in
the shape of an anthropomorphic
bird, although some may see it as a
stylized human head with cylindrical
eyes and an open mouth from which
strips of leather protrude like a tongue.
(The leather is what remains of a wrist
strap used to connect the weapon to
its owner.) From the time of the earliest European contacts with Northwest
Coast people, explorers were fascinated by these objects, which some described as "slave killers." Their form is
clearly related to the shape of stone
hand hammers used in pounding
splitting wedges or driving chisels,
though the hammers lack the daggers'
tapered point on the striking end.

49
Halibut Hook
Tlingit
Collected 1778, southeast Alaska

Wood with bone and spruce root
14¹/₂ in., length
Museum für Völkerkunde, Vienna
(no. 231)

Tlingit halibut hooks consisted of two parts joined together in a V. A bird poised over the mouth of a large fish is carved on one part of this hook. The large number of fishhooks included among the objects collected by explorers leads one to assume that the Native halibut hooks fascinated the Euro-American mariners. These hooks were very effective: they would catch only a certain, mid-size halibut, leaving enough fish in the habitat to perpetuate the species. The carved images were added for their spiritual power to draw the halibut to the bait. Similar to other fishhooks collected by members of the Spanish expeditions (see cat. no. 19), this particular hook was collected by James Cook in the last third of the eighteenth century.

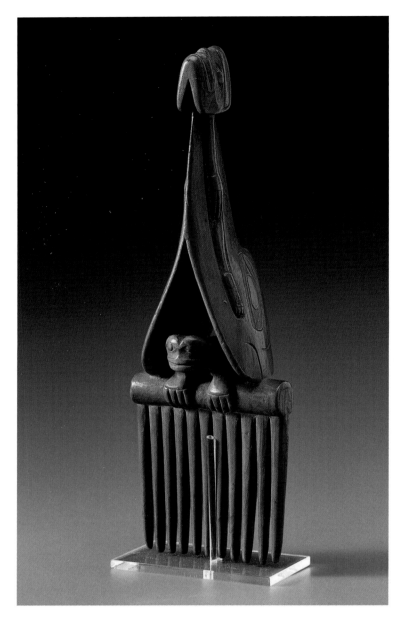

50
Comb
Probably Haida
Collected 1778, Queen Charlotte
Islands, British Columbia

Wood
8⁷/₈ x 3 x 2 in.
University of Cambridge, Museum
of Archaeology & Anthropology
(no. 1925.370)

Combs were used by both men and
women. This wooden comb depicts a
scene, possibly related to a shaman's
vision, in which a carved frog is seated
inside the head of a raven. In the
raven's mouth is a human figure whose
body extends down the length of the
beak, while its head protrudes from its
tip. The frog was considered an important aid to the shaman due to its
ability to pass through the spheres of
both water and land. This comb was
collected on James Cook's third and
final voyage. The delicacy and precision of the carving again underscore
the level of development attained by
pre-contact Northwest Coast peoples.

51
Comb
Nuu-chah-nulth (Nootka)
c. 1750, west coast of Vancouver
Island, British Columbia

Wood, possibly yew
6⁷/₈ x 4³/₄ x 1/4 in.
The Menil Collection, Houston
(no. 73-06 DJ)

Although the abbreviated imagery in
the incised designs on this comb may
have been intended to appear this way
by the original artist, it is possible that
the comb was at some time broken
and cut down to the current dimensions. Several eighteenth-century and
earlier Nuu-chah-nulth and Makah
combs are of the double-ended type,
with tine or teeth pointing in opposite
directions on both sides of a central,
decorated handle. The oval hole in
this comb may once have been in the
center of the whole object. If the teeth
on the other end broke, they may have
split off enough of the design area

with them to necessitate trimming the
handle back to these proportions. In
such a case, there would be space to
rectify the incomplete appearance of
the obverse and reverse designs. It is
not known with certainty whether
such a comb was for hair grooming
or for use as a weaving tool, though
many related, extant examples show a
type of wear consistent with the comb-
ing of human hair. This comb was
collected by James Cook in 1778 from
Yuquot village on Nootka Sound.

52
Box Lid
Nuu-chah-nulth (Nootka)
Collected 1778, west coast of
Vancouver Island, British Columbia

Wood with sea otter teeth and traces
of paint
$36^{5}/8$ x $6^{3}/8$ x $1^{3}/8$ in.
Museum für Völkerkunde, Vienna
(no. 215)

This is the lid of a box used to store
arrows, which was collected by James
Cook in 1778. During a hunt, arrows
were kept in leather quivers (as can be
seen in numerous illustrations), but
when they were at home, at least some
hunters stored their arrows in boxes
specially made for this purpose. The
carving on this particular example indicates that it probably belonged to a
prominent person in a high-ranking
family. The three human figures appear to illustrate a narrative story, the
text of which is unfortunately not
recorded. The style of incised line
carving and shallow sculptural relief in
these figures, typical of the southern
Northwest Coast in the eighteenth
century, formed the foundation of
later styles that developed in the hands
of inventive nineteenth-century artists.

53
Bowl
Nuu-chah-nulth (Nootka)
Collected 1778, west coast of
Vancouver Island, British Columbia

Wood
2¼ x 4 x 9¼ in.
University of Cambridge, Museum
of Archaeology & Anthropology
(no. 1922.947)

The Nootkan diet was based on different varieties of fish, just as the economy was based on fishing and the hunting of marine mammals. Among these fish were salmon, herring and their roe, various cod species, and halibut. The sea mammals they hunted for food included harbor and fur seals and whales, the hunting of which was restricted to chiefs and their crews, and involved numerous cultural regulations and ceremonies. The Nootkan diet was completed with mollusks, shellfish, and berries. This canoe-shaped bowl, collected during James Cook's third voyage, is carved with very basic sculptural forms at both ends. Bowls like this were used at potlatch ceremonies to serve seal or whale oil, some traces of which still remain.

54
Canoe-shaped Dish
Nuu-chah-nulth (Nootka)
Collected 1778, west coast of
Vancouver Island, British Columbia

Wood
7³/₈ x 9 x 28⁷/₈ in.
University of Cambridge, Museum
of Archaeology & Anthropology
(no. 1922.946)

This canoe-shaped dish was collected
by James Cook. The canoes of the
people who lived on the southern
Northwest Coast were light and fast,
and of a seaworthiness that was admired by the early explorers. Size varied
depending on whether the canoes
were to be used for warfare, fishing,
or trading, and whether they would be
traveling by sea or river. The bow of
this dish is embellished with a carved
thunderbird head, which indicates
that it was used by the families of
chiefs during major potlatch festivities.
The stern of the Nuu-chah-nulth
canoe is faithfully represented in the
form of this dish. The dishes used by
lower ranking families were similar in
size but lacked the embellishment of
decorative carving.

55

Rain Hat
Tlingit or Chugach (Pacific Yup'ik)
Collected 1778, west coast of
Vancouver Island, British Columbia

Painted spruce root
5¹/₂ x 10¹/₄ in.
Museum für Völkerkunde, Vienna
(no. 219)

In his *Noticias de Nutka* [*News from Nootka*], the naturalist José Mariano Mociño describes how these types of hats were made: "[they have] special forms for hats and cloaks. They begin by weaving both of them very thickly at the center, leaving the ends of the strands firmly fastened at the edges." The weaving technique is called twining and begins, as Mociño points out, at the center of the hat crown, proceeding outward and expanding in circumference toward the rim, where the ends are bound with specialized rows of weaving. This particular hat was collected by James Cook, and judging from its weave and painting styles, it originated in Prince William Sound, Alaska, where Cook made contact with the northern Native peoples. The painting appears to be a "modified Tlingit" style, which is commonly seen in Chugach or Eyak spruce root hats (see cat. no. 25).

56
Blanket
Nuu-chah-nulth (Nootka)
Collected 1778, west coast of
Vancouver Island, British Columbia

Cedar bark and wool
42⁷/₈ x 52 in.
Museum für Völkerkunde, Vienna
(no. 218)

Collected at Nootka Sound by James
Cook on his last voyage, this is one of
the oldest and most unusual blankets
still preserved today. It is an exceptional example, related in form and
style of weaving to the "raven's tail"
blankets of the early historic period on
the northern Northwest Coast and
also to the Chilkat-style woven robes,
with their formline designs and rectangular humanoid faces. The characteristics of this weaving also strongly
indicate that it most likely originated
among more northern peoples, such
as the Tlingit or Tsimshian, and was
carried to the Nuu-chah-nulth region
as a result of Native trade or warfare.
José Mariano Mociño's *Noticias de*

Nutka [*News from Nootka*] describes
how these robes or shawls were made
in the eighteenth century: "They have
no distaff other than their thighs and
fingers with which to spin the strands
of cypress, wool, and otter hair. They
first form a thick cord that is then
made finer and longer as they wrap it
around a rod nearly one foot long,
which they rotate atop a small board
with the same skill and agility as our
Indian women. The looms for their
fabrics are very simple. They hang the
warp from a horizontal stick four and
a half feet above the ground and their
swiftly moving fingers . . . replace all
tools."

57
John Webber
Man from Unalaska
James Cook's third voyage, 1778

Pen and ink on brown paper
17⅛ x 12 in.
Peabody Museum of Archaeology
and Ethnology, Harvard University,
Cambridge, Massachusetts (Belle J.
Bushnell Bequest, 1942, no. 41-72-
10/503)

The Aleutian is dressed in the typical
long cassock made from the skin of
small animals, wearing a parka, a bentwood visor or hunting hat, and nose
and lip ornaments. In the journal of his
third voyage, James Cook describes the
garments of the Unalaska as follows:
"on top of this garment, the men wear
another made of [prepared and dried
seal] intestines, which is water-resistant,
and a hood that covers the head ... All
of them [wear] a kind of oval cap made
of wood with an opening for the head:
they are painted in green and other
colors, and around the top part of the
crown are incrusted [inserted] long
whiskers of some marine animal [sea
lion] in which glass beads are inserted.
On the brim are one or two small figures made of bone [or ivory]."

58
John Webber
A Man in Prince William Sound
James Cook's third voyage, 1778

Pencil, gouache, and watercolor on
paper
17⅜ x 12⅜ in.
Peabody Museum of Archaeology
and Ethnology, Harvard University,
Cambridge, Massachusetts (Belle J.
Bushnell Bequest, 1942, no. 41-72-
10/501)

This delicate portrait is one of the first
illustrations of the inhabitants of the
area now known as Cook Inlet in
Alaska. It was intended to show their
facial features and physical characteristics as well as their garments. The
drawing shows the distinctive hair-
style, the male face paint, and the
characteristic garment of the region:
an *anorak* [parka] made of animal skin
decorated with fur strips. Personal
adornment consists of a necklace of
bone and beads, a long nose ornament, three labial pendants made of
beads strung together, and face paint.
A comparison of this and the following portrait (cat. no. 59) reveals the
differences in the way the two sexes
dressed.

59 *opposite*
John Webber
Woman of Unalaska
James Cook's third voyage, 1778

Pencil, pen and ink, and watercolor
on paper
17⅜ x 12¼ in.
Peabody Museum of Archaeology
and Ethnology, Harvard University,
Cambridge, Massachusetts (Belle J.
Bushnell Bequest, 1942, no. 41-72-
10/504)

John Webber, a Swedish-born artist,
accompanied James Cook on his third
voyage, one of whose objectives was
exploring the Northwest Coast and
the Alaskan coastline. Webber's paintings and watercolors illustrate incidents,
landscapes, scenes, and portraits of the
people of the various places described
in Cook's journal. This portrait of a
woman from Unalaska Island in the
Aleutians shows both her physical
characteristics and her dress. She
wears a sealskin *anorak* [parka]; her
hair is pulled back and gathered in a
knot at the neck. She wears a labret
and nose ornaments, and her cheeks
and chin are marked with the tattoos
characteristic of Unalaskan women.

page 103
View of an Otter Hunters' Settlement with Young Men Signaling Toward Puerto Nórdico Captain Pribiloff's voyage (detail), 1787–92. Armed Forces Geographic Service, Caroteca História, Madrid, (atlas no. 138, cabinet 3, no. 36) (see cat. no. 85)

60
Mask of a Human Face
Tlingit
c. 1800–50, southeast Alaska

Wood with traces of paint
8⅝ x 8 x 5 in.
Peter the Great Museum of Anthropology and Ethnology (Kunstkamera) of the Russian Academy of Sciences, Saint Petersburg (no. 5795-31)

In this realistically carved mask of a man's face, the small holes in the upper lip and chin must have originally held pegs that fastened strips of hide to the face, representing the mustache and beard. Tlingit shamans' masks were carved to depict their helping spirits, with whom they made contact by putting on the masks. These spirits guided the shaman in the spirit world and brought him information from the other side, such as events in the future, the knowledge to cure illness, or the patterns of the weather.

61
Mask
Tlingit, Chilkoot tribe
c. 1800–50, southeast Alaska

Painted wood
7³/₄ x 6¹/₂ in.
Peter the Great Museum of Anthropology and Ethnology (Kunstkamera) of the Russian Academy of Sciences, Saint Petersburg (no. 5795-32)

The shaman was one of the most significant figures in Tlingit society because he was believed to be the intermediary between the real world and the world of the spirits. One of the shaman's most important attributes was his mask. A shaman would have as many as eight masks, each representing a different *yeik*, or helping spirit. When the shaman put on a mask, the spirit it symbolized was believed to come into contact with him and help him in his tasks. The shamans who created these sacred objects made every effort to reproduce the features of either some powerful legendary figure or someone recently deceased, known to the clan for their curative powers.

62
Shaman's Mask
Tlingit
Collected 1890, Admiralty Islands, Alaska

Painted wood with leather
8¼ x 7 in.
Peter the Great Museum of Anthropology and Ethnology (Kunstkamera) of the Russian Academy of Sciences, Saint Petersburg (no. 211-6)

Many Tlingit shamans' masks represented female faces or, more precisely, female spirits, as indicated by the use of a flat, oval lip ornament known as a labret. The female spirit-presence in shamanic healing ceremonies is explained by the fact that certain older women enjoyed great prestige in Tlingit culture. With their knowledge of medicine and pharmacopoeia, they were considered shaman-women, not simply for their healing efficiency but also for their power to call forth spirits. This very expressive mask, collected by Russian missionary Georgi Chudnovsky in 1890, is probably an attempt to portray one of these women after her death. The naturalistic sculpture and asymmetrical painting are common features in Tlingit shamans' masks.

63
Shaman's Mask
Tlingit
Collected 1890, Admiralty Islands, Alaska

Painted wood with copper, animal hide, and human hair
11 x 7¼ x 4¾ in.
Peter the Great Museum of Anthropology and Ethnology (Kunstkamera) of the Russian Academy of Sciences, Saint Petersburg (no. 5795-31)

This shaman's mask is distinguished by the addition of copper sheet in the eyebrows, nostril flares, eyelids, and lips. Copper was a mineral of great value and prestige to the Northwest Coast people, and its use may indicate that this shaman's spirit came from among the Eyak or the Copper River area northwest of the Tlingit territories. The carving comes from the northern Tlingit, whose shamanic masks included portrayals of the spirits of the dead and animals related to both clan and family lineages. It was collected by missionary Georgi Chudnovsky near Angoon village in 1890.

64
Transformation Mask
Chugach (Pacific Yup'ik)
1780–1820, Prince William Sound, Alaska

Painted wood
29½ x 28⅜ in.
Peter the Great Museum of Anthropology and Ethnology (Kunstkamera) of the Russian Academy of Sciences, Saint Petersburg, Department of the Admiralty (1829, no. 633-31)

This mask represents the *inua*, or human spirit, of an otter, an emblematic animal with shamanic connotations. Among the Chugach and other peoples of Prince William Sound, the otter was associated with the kidnapping of men. This is a very interesting piece because masks of this type are not typical of the Chugach, which indicates that they borrowed it from the cultures of their neighbors to the west, the lower or central Yup'ik. With its two faces in one, it is characteristic of the masks called *baduchdljuk*, used in the Kuskokwim River region.

65

Forehead Mask and Headdress
Tlingit
Collected c. 1839–45, southeast Alaska

Painted wood with leather
9¹/2 x 10¹/4 x 14¹/8 in.
Peter the Great Museum of Anthropology and Ethnology (Kunstkamera) of the Russian Academy of Sciences, Saint Petersburg (no. 2448-3)

This forehead mask is carved with an image that could represent a sea monster, a porpoise, or a whale. The tapered snout may indicate a porpoise (not a common crest emblem but one that belonged to a particular Tlingit clan), with the wooden dorsal fin and painted leather pectoral fins filling out the image. The wooden "ears" atop the head of the mask may suggest that a composite, sea monster-type image is being illustrated. The comparatively

early collection dates of the Spanish, English, and Russian materials (in relation to the majority of American museum collections) helps to establish Northwest Coast styles in the early historic period. This mask was collected by the I. G. Voznesenskii expedition organized by the Russian Academy of Sciences.

66
Forehead Mask and Headdress
Tlingit
Collected c. 1839–45, southeast Alaska

Painted wood with copper, leather,
and sea lion whiskers
9 x 14⅛ x 21¼ in.
Peter the Great Museum of Anthropology and Ethnology (Kunstkamera)
of the Russian Academy of Sciences,
Saint Petersburg (no. 571-19)

This forehead mask most likely depicts
an eagle, the lower face representing
the body and the painted leather
appendages representing the wings.
It was worn on the forehead by the
leader of an eagle-moiety clan on
ceremonial occasions. The sea lion
whiskers were valued elements that lent
a dramatic aura to the headgear, and
the copper eyebrows brought the prestige of that element to the object. Clan
emblems of this type are symbolic

representations of animal species and
supernatural creatures that were adopted
as a result of mystical encounters. This
mask was collected by the I. G. Voznesenskii expedition, organized by the
Russian Academy of Sciences.

67 *opposite, top*
Battle Helmet with a Human Face
Tlingit
Collected c. 1839–45, southeast Alaska

Painted wood with human and animal
hair and abalone shell
7⅞ x 10¼ in.
Peter the Great Museum of Anthropology and Ethnology (Kunstkamera)
of the Russian Academy of Sciences,
Saint Petersburg (no. 571-17)

Battle helmets, an essential part of a
warrior's dress, were carved from a single piece of tough spruce to provide
maximum protection from club and
dagger attacks. Helmets were carved
with a variety of sculptural embellishments, from human images to animal
and bird forms. This one appears to
represent a human spirit, perhaps that
of an ancestor with an especially valor-
ous history. Abalone and human hair
inlays add color and life to the sculpture. With the advent of firearms,
these helmets were relegated to ceremonial purposes. This helmet was
collected by the I. G. Voznesenskii expedition organized by the Russian
Academy of Sciences.

68 *opposite, bottom*
Helmet with Eagle Mask
Tlingit
Collected c. 1839–45, southeast coast
of Alaska

Painted wood with shell and human
hair
9⅛ x 11 in.
Peter the Great Museum of Anthropology and Ethnology (Kunstkamera)
of the Russian Academy of Sciences,
Saint Petersburg (no. 2452-11)

Due to frequent battles between different
clans and tribes, the Tlingit developed
a whole range of military equipment
that not only protected the warrior but
also displayed the emblems of his clan.
Battle dress consisted of a tanned
leather undergarment, over which was
worn armor made of slats, arm and leg
protectors, and a helmet and visor. The
image of the clan emblem was carved
on the helmet, which might weigh as
much as 3 kilograms (7 pounds). This
sculpture appears to represent an an-
thropomorphized whale, with an abbreviated dorsal fin above the forehead
and leather pectoral fins on each side
of the face. It was collected by the I. G.
Voznesenskii expedition organized by
the Russian Academy of Sciences.

69
Mask
Tlingit
Collected c. 1839–45, southeast Alaska

Painted wood with abalone shell,
copper, sealskin, and human hair
8⅝ x 15 x 4 in.
Peter the Great Museum of Anthropology and Ethnology (Kunstkamera)
of the Russian Academy of Sciences,
Saint Petersburg (no. 2448-16)

The art of the Tlingit and other Northwest Coast peoples is based on a complex world of images with very special
meanings peculiar to a particular area.
This forehead mask most likely represents the sea monster *Gonakadeit*, a
composite creature with the features
of both a bear, indicated by the flared
nostrils and half-open mouth, and a
whale, with its pectoral fins represented
by the leather side panels. The inclu-
sion of valued trade materials like California abalone shell and copper sheet
added the prestige of these materials
to the headpiece, which in turn made
it a more valuable object. This mask
was collected by the I. G. Voznesenskii
expedition organized by the Russian
Academy of Sciences.

70
Helmet
Tlingit
c. 1780–1800, Admiralty Islands, British Columbia, and southeast Alaska

Painted wood with opercula and human hair
9 x 10¼ X 13⅜ in.
Peter the Great Museum of Anthropology and Ethnology (Kunstkamera) of the Russian Academy of Sciences, Saint Petersburg (no. 633-8)

This helmet may represent an image that comes from the Dakl'aweidí clan house known as the Killer Whale Dorsal Fin House. Tlingit artists often represented a whale's dorsal fin with a human face at its base—for example, on the song leader's staffs or crest hats. This unusually proportioned face may be one artist's way of depicting an abbreviated dorsal fin and human face, while maintaining the strength required of a battle helmet. The narrow, elongated face is not deeply carved and is similar in style of carving to other dorsal fin faces. The mustache and beard are formed by short human hair bundles pegged into drilled holes in the lip and chin. The opercula of the red turban marine snail are inlaid for the teeth. This helmet was in the Russian Admiralty Museum until 1836 when it was moved to its current home.

71
Battle Helmet with a Bear Image
Tlingit
c. 1800–40, southeast Alaska

Painted wood with opercula, copper,
and brown bear fur
7¹/₂ x 11⁷/₈ x 10⁵/₈ in.
Peter the Great Museum of Anthropology and Ethnology (Kunstkamera)
of the Russian Academy of Sciences,
Saint Petersburg (no. 5795-10)

This helmet was carved from a single
piece of wood and covered with the
fur of a brown bear to give it the appearance of this respected and ferocious animal. These depictions, which
usually refer to violent spirits, were
very appropriate for use in helmets:
psychological warfare was an important tactic. This helmet appears to
portray a bear, an animal much feared
as the most powerful carnivore of the
forest and the natural environment.
Its presence was always associated with

terrifying powers. The sculpture of the
face has been given a humanoid proportion, perhaps to illustrate the
human/bear heritage of the owner,
whose clan is believed to have descended from the bear. Copper disks
in the eyes and opercula as the teeth
add the richness of these imported
materials to the image.

72
Forehead Mask
Tlingit
c. 1790–1830, Sitka village (?)

Painted wood with opercula, abalone
shell, sea lion whiskers, brown bear or
sea lion hide, and leather
18 x 6 x 4 in.
Private collection

This very striking and fierce-looking
forehead mask is related in use
(though not in style) to other early
Tlingit forehead masks collected by
Russian mariners before 1845 (see cat.
nos. 101–3). The Russian American
Company Museum in the fur-trading
capital of Sitka, Alaska, had a large collection of Tlingit artifacts under its
roof when the territory was sold to the
United States in 1867. Edward G. Fast,
a member of the military contingent
sent to take over the administration of

the Alaska territory, "collected" these
objects and eventually turned them
over to the Peabody Museum of Harvard University. Some of these objects
were sold or traded over the years and
have since ended up in private collections. This magnificent example of
Tlingit crest art probably represents a
sea lion, based on the shape of its face,
and features a large spray of long sea
lion whiskers radiating out from the
edge of a fine rim that encircles the
creature's neck area. A bentwood

frame that supports sections of brown
bear or sea lion hide in the shape of
"ears" once provided a means to secure
the image to the wearer's head. The
Sitka Tlingit community includes a
clan structure known as the Sea Lion
House.

73
Forehead Mask
Tlingit
Collected c. 1839–45, southeast Alaska

Painted wood with abalone shell, fabric, baleen, sea lion bristles, and leather
16³/8 x 87/8 in.
Peter the Great Museum of Anthropology and Ethnology (Kunstkamera) of the Russian Academy of Sciences, Saint Petersburg (no. 2448-21)

The dancing headdress, known as *Sha'kee.at'* in Tlingit, is a type of headgear that was originally conceived by the Tsimshian. The inner frame of the headdress is formed of thin wood or baleen strips that are bent into an oval shape and tied to similar vertical pieces to form the foundation of the headgear. The frame is usually covered with downy bird skin, and sometimes red trade cloth or the tail feathers of

the red-shafted flicker (a small woodpecker) are sewn to the area bordering the wooden frontlet. Long sea lion whiskers once sprouted upward all along the upper circumference of the headdress frame. These were valuable objects possessed only by chiefs and members of the nobility. Because they featured the symbols of their owners, these masks were almost like coats of arms and were used only for ceremonial purposes, particularly for ritual dances. The carved imagery of this frontlet is difficult to interpret, and its exact iconography would only be known to the maker and the original owner's clan and family. The fine carving and inlay work, however, give us visual access to the artistry of its maker. This forehead mask was collected by the I. G. Voznesenskii expedition organized by the Russian Academy of Sciences.

74
Forehead Mask
Tlingit
Collected 1850, southeast Alaska

Painted wood with abalone shell, sea lion whiskers, cloth, flicker feathers, and leather
8³/8 x 8 x 77/8 in.
Peter the Great Museum of Anthropology and Ethnology (Kunstkamera) of the Russian Academy of Sciences, Saint Petersburg (no. 2448-19)

This frontlet depicts the raven, one of the creatures most important to the Tlingit as it is the emblem of one of the two moieties into which all the clans were divided. Clans owned properties—hunting and fishing grounds, sources of wood, and even potable water—as well as exclusive rights to trade routes. The carver of this frontlet was especially gifted, conceiving and refining the sculpture with unusual delicacy and fine finish. The iridescence of the abalone shell inlays beautifully accents the smooth and refined carving. Like most very early Tlingit frontlets, this one has no inlay on the thin rim that borders the central sculptural image. Several characteristics of this particular headdress combine to suggest that it was created in the eighteenth century. This forehead mask was collected by Doroshin in 1850.

75
Oil Bowl
Tlingit
Collected c. 1839–45, southeast
Alaska

Wood with opercula
5½ x 6¼ x 9 in.
Peter the Great Museum of Anthropology and Ethnology (Kunstkamera)
of the Russian Academy of Sciences,
Saint Petersburg (no. 2539-17)

This bowl made of a single piece of
wood is carved with the figure of a
beaver trying to bite the stick it holds
in its front paws. The top of the bowl
is decorated with inlaid opercula
shells. These bowls were used for serving the seal or *eulachon* oil that accompanied the smoked salmon at feasts
and potlatch ceremonies. Only the
high-ranking families could own a
sculptured bowl of this type, and the
carved image represents the emblem
of the matrilineal clan to which they
belonged. The bowl could thus be
said to be a status symbol of great
importance in this society. The bowl
was collected by the I. G. Voznesenskii
expedition organized by the Russian
Academy of Sciences.

76
Oil Bowl
Tlingit
Collected c. 1800–40, southeast
Alaska

Wood with opercula
3½ x 5⅜ x 11⅜ in.
Peter the Great Museum of Anthropology and Ethnology (Kunstkamera)
of the Russian Academy of Sciences,
Saint Petersburg (no. 2539-18)

Made of a single piece of wood carved
in the shape of a beaver, this bowl has
red turban snail opercula inlaid around
the opening. It would have been used
in potlatch ceremonies where the host
bestowed lavish gifts on his guests and
all his noble titles were read out. Potlatch ceremonies are still held today
on the occasions of funerals and wed-
dings and to mark other life cycles.
They can only be organized by wealthy
people who are also prominent members of the community, such as chiefs
and nobles. One of the valued gifts at
a potlatch was the rendered oil of the
candlefish, or *eulachon*, which was
served in bowls like this.

77
Shaman's Amulet
Tlingit
Collected 1890, Admiralty Islands,
southeast Alaska

Bone
2¹/₂ x 3³/₄ in.
Peter the Great Museum of Anthropology and Ethnology (Kunstkamera)
of the Russian Academy of Sciences,
Saint Petersburg (no. 211-25)

Although the shaman's most important attributes were his mask and rattle, amulets, such as this one in the
shape of an eagle's head, were also
essential to his work. The shaman
received his powers from encounters
with supernatural creatures, usually
in the form of certain animals, whose
appearance was only temporary: the
spirit could change form easily and
even become humanlike. As a reminder and proof of these encounters,
amulets were produced and worn by
shamans throughout their active lives.
It was believed that these amulets enabled them to connect with the spirit
and receive the powers they needed to
perform their rituals. This example's
crude and unorthodox style of design
and carving are typical of amulets
from the 1890s. Father Georgi
Chudnovsky, a Russian missionary,
collected this amulet in 1890.

78
Spoon
Tlingit
Collected c. 1839–45, southeast
Alaska

Mountain goat horn with copper
2³/₈ x 9¹/₂ in.
Peter the Great Museum of Anthropology and Ethnology (Kunstkamera)
of the Russian Academy of Sciences,
Saint Petersburg (no. 2539-34)

This spoon with a carved handle consists of two pieces fastened together
with copper rivets. The carving on the
handle depicts numerous superim-
posed zoomorphic figures: the lowest
one appears to be a wolf, and the
highest one an eagle crowned with a
cylindrical headdress similar to what
appears on some conical hats. Between
these two figures is a carving of an octopus, which appears to be swallowing
another figure. This delicately carved
piece was made from a pair of goat
horns—one was carved as the handle,
and the other was cut, boiled, opened
out, and riveted to the first to form
the bowl of the spoon. High-ranking
Tlingit families would own full sets of
such spoons, sometimes all made by
the same specialist carver. This spoon
was collected by the I. G. Voznesenskii
expedition organized by the Russian
Academy of Sciences.

79
Gambling Mat
Tlingit
Collected 1788, southeast Alaska

Painted rawhide
19¼ x 9⅞ in.
Peter the Great Museum of Anthropology and Ethnology (Kunstkamera) of the Russian Academy of Sciences, Saint Petersburg (no. 2448-29)

The Russians continued to send out reconnaissance missions from the Aleutian region until the second half of the eighteenth century. In line with the spirit of the times, explorers were instructed to collect objects for the Kunstkamera, or the Czar's art collection. This is one of the first objects to be acquired by the Russian navy in southeast Alaska. A mat for use with dice-like gambling pieces of bone or ivory, it features painted designs emblematic of one of the Tlingit clans on a thick sheet of stiff hide. The

skillfully conceived and finely painted design is typical of Tlingit style in the mid eighteenth century. It was collected during the 1788 expedition to southeast Alaska led by Dimitri Bocharav and Guerasim Izmáilov aboard the ship *Tres Santos.*

80
Shaman's Apron
Tlingit
Collected 1890, Admiralty Islands,
southeast Alaska

Painted deerskin with beads
18 1/8 x 41 3/8 in.
Peter the Great Museum of Anthropology and Ethnology (Kunstkamera)
of the Russian Academy of Sciences,
Saint Petersburg (no. 5795-14)

This apron was probably collected by
Father Georgi Chudnovsky, whose
name is linked to the last important
shipment of articles deposited in the
Saint Petersburg museum. In 1890,
Bishop Chudnovsky was sent by the
Russian synod to convert the peoples
of the Admiralty Islands to the east of
Baranof Island and the Russian settlement at Sitka. He spent six months
there and collected ninety-six objects,
including three shaman's aprons, one
of which is probably this example.
It is interesting to note that the items

collected by the missionary were essentially religious in nature—shamanic
headdresses, masks, rattles, a tambourine, and thirty-three amulets—
which indicates that he took his mission
to "extirpate idolatry" seriously.

81
Blanket
Tlingit
Collected 1778, southeast Alaska

Mountain goat wool and otter fur
41¾ x 57 in.
Peter the Great Museum of Anthropology and Ethnology (Kunstkamera)
of the Russian Academy of Sciences,
Saint Petersburg (no. 2520-7)

The weaving in this type of blanket is
known today as "raven's tail" because
of the motif of pendant black yarns
that resembles the tail of this bird.
Most of these blankets date from the
eighteenth century and the very beginning of the nineteenth century. They
are extremely rare: only eleven complete examples still exist, though fragmentary sections of about four others
have been discovered and identified.

They are much admired due to their
complex method of creation, no
longer used today, involving a variety
of weaving techniques. This style of
weaving evidently was overshadowed
by the development of Chilkat-style
weaving, which includes closely related as well as additional techniques
that allow the making of the circular
and curvilinear forms so characteristic
of the two-dimensional painting styles
of the northern Northwest Coast.
After the Tlingit weavers mastered the
Chilkat-style techniques, they stopped
producing robes in the "raven's tail"
style. In recent years, a large number
of weavers have taken up these dormant techniques and are once again
producing robes and other kinds of
woven regalia for ceremonial use.

82
Warrior's Shirt
Tlingit
Collected c. 1839–45, southeast Alaska

Painted deerskin
40⅛ x 27½ in.
Peter the Great Museum of Anthropology and Ethnology (Kunstkamera)
of the Russian Academy of Sciences,
Saint Petersburg (no. 2454-10)

In the 1840s, the Russian Academy of
Sciences sent I. G. Voznesenskii to
Russian America to collect objects for
the Czar's museums. He brought back
370 items, most of which were Tlingit.
His work was important, not so much
in terms of the number of objects he
collected as because of the records
that accompanied them. Thanks to
this information, we know that this is

a warrior's shirt, or tunic, made of
soft-tanned deerskin and decorated
with its owner's crests. The shirt was
worn beneath the slatted armor that
served as protection against enemy
blows. The painted image appears to
be a raven. The head, composed of
mirrored profiles, is turned beak-down
at the top of the design field, and the
wings (which also are composed of
profile heads) are joined at the lower
mandible. The tail is joined by formline designs that overlap to the wings
and is composed as a frontal-view
formline face with its feathers extending downward.

83
Man Considered to be a Young Noble
Captain Pribiloff's voyage, 1787–92

Engraving from *Russian Atlas of Reconnaissance Voyages in the Okhotsk Sea, Kamchatka, Bering Strait, Aleutian Islands and the Alaskan Coast*
22 x 18¹⁄₂ in.
Armed Forces Geographic Service, Cartoteca Histórica, Madrid
(atlas no. 138, cabinet 3, no. 38)

The young man is shown in typical Chugach dress, although the style of his cone-shaped hat was borrowed from the Chugach's Tlingit neighbors. He wears a garment made of numerous bird skins sewn together; his nose is pierced by a thin rod, probably made of bone; and he has two holes beneath his lower lip in which he wears traditional Chugach ornaments. The Chugach culture was a convenient bridge between the Native peoples in Russian America and the chiefdoms further south of present-day Alaska. Hunters from Prince William Sound and the Aleutian Islands traveled far along the Pacific coast in the employment of the Russian America Company, filling their orders for sea otter pelts. The men of Prince William Sound were a popular subject with the illustrators who accompanied the expeditions that began in the mid eighteenth century, and drawings very similar to this one were made by José Cardero, Tomás Suría, John Webber, and others.

84
Aleutians Seated in a Kayak (*Bidarka*)
Captain Pribiloff's voyage, 1787–92

Engraving from *Russian Atlas of Reconnaissance Voyages in the Okhotsk Sea, Kamchatka, Bering Strait, Aleutian Islands and the Alaskan Coast*
18¹⁄₂ x 22 in.
Armed Forces Geographic Service, Cartoteca Histórica, Madrid
(atlas no. 138, cabinet 3, no. 162)

In this scene depicting two kayaks, one carries a single occupant wearing the typical "clamshell" bentwood hunting hat and a waterproof jacket made from the intestines of seals or other sea mammals. He is poised with his *atlatl*, or throwing board, ready to throw a spear or dart. The hunter appears to have other arrowlike darts lashed to the kayak, which he paddles using a double-bladed paddle. Three people occupy the kayak shown in the lower part of the engraving. The first paddler has thrown a spear with the aid of his *atlatl*, while the other two paddlers continue to propel the *bidarka*. Many different varieties of skin-covered craft were used, from Barrow Point and St. Lawrence Island all the way to the lands of the Pacific Yup'ik on the Gulf of Alaska coastline.

85
View of an Otter Hunters' Settlement with Young Men Signaling Toward Puerto Nórdico
Captain Pribiloff's voyage, 1787–92

Engraving from *Russian Atlas of Reconnaissance Voyages in the Okhotsk Sea, Kamchatka, Bering Strait, Aleutian Islands and the Alaskan Coast*
18¹/2 x 22 in.
Armed Forces Geographic Service, Cartoteca Histórica, Madrid
(atlas no. 138, cabinet 3, no. 36)

This picture of a seaside settlement belonging to the Chugach band of the Pacific Yup'ik shows a Russian ship flanked by a number of two-man kayaks, whose paddlers are wearing the typical Tlingit-style Prince William Sound hat. A group of men and women observes them from the shore. The Chugach are part of the Pacific Yup'ik linguistic group that lives on the Alaskan coast around the shores and islands of Prince William Sound. They have close relations with the Tlingit, from whom they borrowed many cultural features and traditional designs, among them the conical hat and the celebration of potlatch ceremonies, at which the host demonstrates his wealth by bestowing gifts on his guests.

86
Yacutia Witch Doctor Invoking Spirits to Entrap Illnesses
Captain Pribiloff's voyage, 1787–92

Engraving from *Russian Atlas of Reconnaissance Voyages in the Okhotsk Sea, Kamchatka, Bering Strait, Aleutian Islands and the Alaskan Coast*
18¹/2 x 22 in.
Armed Forces Geographic Service, Cartoteca Histórica, Madrid
(atlas no. 138, cabinet 3, no. 30)

In this scene showing the interior of what is probably a subterranean Aleutian home, a shaman is performing a healing ritual. The ailing person is lying supported in bed, watching as the shaman beats a drum and dances. The shaman is easily recognizable, not only because of the instrument he is playing but also for the length of his hair, which was characteristic of shamans in this area. Two women seated with a child are looking on. The artist's rendering of the garments worn by the people in the engraving are considerably influenced by Russian dress.

North American Expeditions
1867–1910

87
Archaic Inuit Mask
Inupiak
c. 500, north Alaska

Wood
12 x 7⁵⁄₈ in.
Private collection, New York

Although its provenance is not known, the features of this mask seem to indicate that it was produced by one of the Native peoples of north Alaska. Similar naturalistic masks were collected in the mid nineteenth century on King Island and in the Port Hope region, although they were less finely and sensitively carved. The poor condition of the wood makes it likely that this mask was found in a cave or rock shelter. Masks that were protected in this way were able to survive the cold, dry Arctic climate for unusually long periods.

page 125
The Haida village of Xaina on the Queen Charlotte Islands (Haida Gwaii) in British Columbia (detail) (see fig. 27)

88

Mask of a Dying Warrior
Tsimshian, Kitkatla village
Collected 1885, north coast of British
Columbia

Painted wood with human and animal
hair and animal fur
12 x 8¾ x 6⅝ in.
Private collection

Used in dramatizations of the mythical past, this mask, with all its impres-
sive embellishments, conveys an
uncannily expressive presence. The
red paint across the eye socket may
indicate usage by a particular secret
society, while the formline designs in
red, blue, and black on the cheeks and
forehead are asymmetrically applied
like actual face paint designs worn by
Haida performers. The face is framed
by human hair while the mustache

and goatee are attached strips of animal fur. The tufts of ermine fur used
as ear pendants and the fine seal or
deer hair inserted for the eyelashes are
both uncommon touches that add to
the communicative power of the
image. The style of the painted designs suggests that the mask was made
in the period between about 1840 and
1860, though it was collected by
George T. Emmons in 1885.

89
Mask
Tlingit or Haida
Collected c. 1885, southeast Alaska
or Queen Charlotte Islands, British
Columbia

Painted wood with hair
11³/₈ x 9⁷/₈ x 4¹/₂ in.
Peabody Museum of Archaeology
and Ethnology, Harvard University,
Cambridge, Massachusetts (acquired
by the museum in 1869, no. 10/1699
1603)

A strong spiritual power imbued the
objects used by shamans, who were
powerful specialists in everything related to the supernatural world. Their
masks represented, and were manifestations of, different types of spirits that
helped the shamans in their rituals
and visions. When shamans died,
their objects, considered too powerful
to be seen by ordinary people, were
buried with them. This mask has lost
its mustache and eyebrows, which
were once made of wolf hide, judging
from a patch of the same material
pegged onto the chin to represent the
beard. The symmetrical and gently ac-
centuated forms of the face, and the
eyes with their upturned irises (which
indicate a trancelike state of being),
provide a dramatic and extraordinary
appearance to this image, further underscored by long locks of human hair.
The mask was acquired by George T.
Emmons during the second half of the
nineteenth century.

90
Portrait Mask
Coastal Tsimshian
c. 1830–60, north coast of British
Columbia

Painted alder wood with human hair
8¾ in., height
Private collection, New York

This delicately carved human face
mask has a captivating expression.
The forehead, cheekbones, and nose
are gently shaped, while the eyebrows,
mustache, and small facial ornamentations are painted on. The cross-shaped
painted field that divides the face into
squares is by no means common, and
its meaning is not known. The expres-
siveness of masks like this was surely

an aid to the people who wore them
for dramatic performances and dances,
helping to transport the audience to
timeless imaginary worlds. Few
Northwest Coast masks exhibit the
contained emotional and dramatic
power of this example.

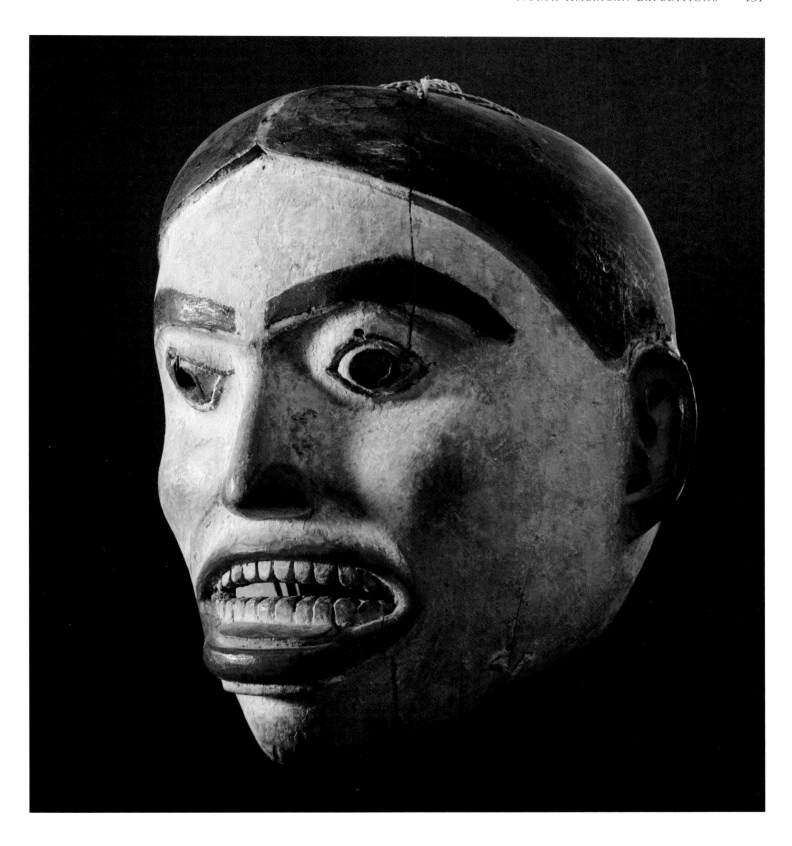

91
Mask of a Woman
Tsimshian
c. 1840–60, Nass and Skeena river
basins and coastal islands north of
British Columbia

Painted hardwood
9¾ x 8¼ in.
Private collection, New York

The downward tilt of the eyes, the
open lips showing carefully sculpted
teeth, the cheekbones that emphasize
the pronounced bone structure of the
face, and the white paint (which may
not have been part of its original appearance), all contribute to the drama
of this portrait of a woman wearing a
wooden lip plug, or labret. This realistic mask was used to depict a high-

ranking woman in dramatizations of
clan history or mythology. Its sculptural form is a Tsimshian artist's stylized
interpretation of the actual appearance
of the faces of his people.

92

Articulated Mask
Haida
c. 1790–1830, Queen Charlotte
Islands, north coast of British
Columbia

Painted wood with metal and fiber
8⅞ x 7¼ x 5¼ in.
Private collection

In this mask of a female, which features articulated eyes and mouth, the face is painted with designs made up of delicate parallel lines, and the nose is pierced with a metal ring. The hinged mouth includes an oval labial ornament, called a labret. Masks like this were used in theatrical performances that narrated historical, genealogical, or divinatory scenes, and in some

initiation rites. The articulated eyelids that appear in the masks of certain artists in this area lend an incredibly lifelike drama to the masks, especially when used in a firelit performance house. The small ears and rounded form of this mask are typical of Haida portrait masks of the very early nineteenth century.

93
Simeon Stihlda
Mask with Labret
Haida
c. 1860–80, Queen Charlotte Islands,
north coast of British Columbia

Painted wood with abalone shell
9 1/2 x 7 1/2 x 4 1/2 in.
Canadian Museum of Civilization,
Hull, Quebec (no. VII-B-7)

Haida masks with human faces were
sometimes modeled on the face of a
specific person and so are considered
portrait masks. One Haida carver of the
late nineteenth century, known today
as Simeon Stihlda, created a large
number of very detailed and sometimes
articulated portrait masks, of which
this is an example. His masks, like this
one, often have detailed hair (sometimes
sporting a carved texture), smallish

eyes, a narrow nose, and a tapered jaw
with a prominent, rounded chin. This
portrait, of an elderly Haida woman,
includes an abalone shell-inlaid labret
in the lower lip and sensitively carved
wrinkles about the face. The masks of
Stihlda appear never to have been put
to traditional Haida use, but rather
were sold to outsiders shortly after
being finished, as the generally clean
and unmarked interiors suggest.

94
Battle Helmet
Tlingit
c. 1700–90, southeast Alaska

Painted wood with opercula and human hair
8⁷/₈ x 10⁷/₈ x 10 in.
Private collection

This helmet was once part of a warrior's battle dress. It depicts a human face and was designed to have a particularly intimidating effect. Fine surface cracks reveal the tough, burly nature of this piece of wood, selected with strength and durability in mind rather than ease of carving. The comparatively shallow facial sculpture is indicative of very early eighteenth-century Tlingit carving styles. Conflicts were frequent among the Tlingit in the historic period and could be triggered by wrongs done to a person or to property. These required compensation, the amount of which was decided by the chiefs. In serious cases, should the accused or his close relations be unable to pay the compensation, the entire tribe was considered responsible for the wrong done. Most conflicts were settled by economic compensation, but homicide, even accidental killings, sometimes led to armed conflicts, which ended only when both sides had suffered equal losses.

95
Maskette
Tsimshian or Tlingit
c. 1790–1820, Nass and Skeena river basins and the north coastline of British Columbia, or southern southeast Alaska

Painted wood with copper and opercula
6 1/2 x 5 3/4 in.
Private collection, New York

This small mask is a true masterwork, apparently representing a mystical creature or metamorphic being. The refinement of its initial conception and the sculpture and the finish of its forms are outstanding. The protruding beaklike lips produce the effect of a bird's head in a human facial structure. The copper covering on the nostrils and eyebrows is a sign of wealth. Although the style of this mask is in many ways characteristic of Tsimshian art, small masks like this one are not commonly seen in that culture. The size of this finely carved maskette is more typical of Tlingit shamans' maskettes, which were fastened to a headdress frame covered with bird skin. The carving could, in fact, be from the hand of a southern Tlingit artist, some of whom were influenced by Tsimshian sculpture. Influences from other cultures, especially along the borders between First Nations, were common along the Northwest Coast.

96
"Trophy" Head
Nuu-chah-nulth (Nootka)
Eighteenth century, west coast of
Vancouver Island, British Columbia

Painted wood with abalone shell and
human hair
6¼ x 5⅜ x 4¾ in.
The Menil Collection, Houston
(no. X 820)

This wooden head has the stylistic
characteristics of the Yuquot in the
northern Nuu-chah-nulth region.
Particularly noteworthy are the red
and black facial painting, the shell
eyes, and the strands of hair drawn
through the holes on the upper part of
the head. Objects like this might represent an ancestor or a grim trophy
taken from an enemy in war. Carved

heads of this type were left on the
decks of James Cook's ships when they
anchored in Nootka Sound in 1778,
during the first English-speaking contact with Northwest Coast peoples.

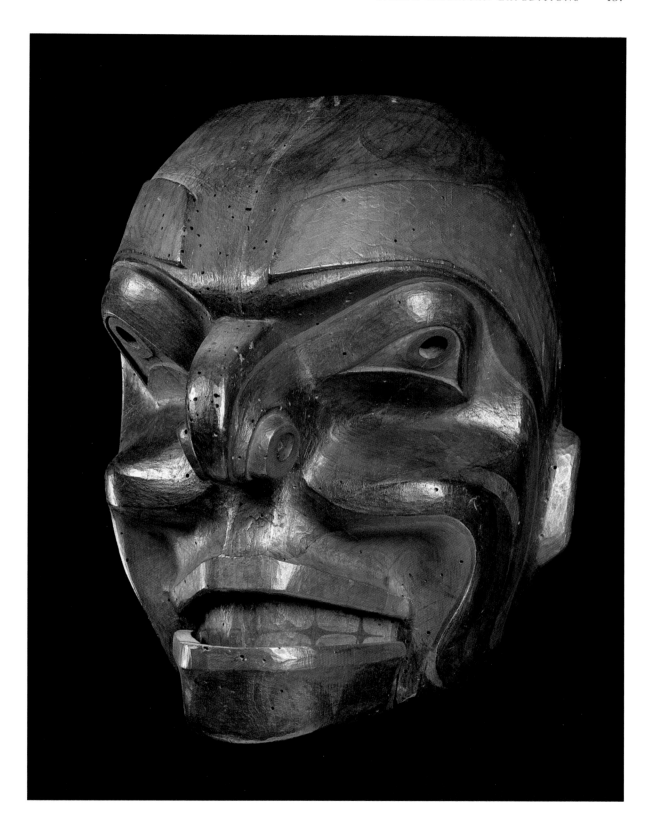

97
Orator's Mask
Haida or Heiltsuk
Nineteenth century, Queen Charlotte
Islands or north-central coast of
British Columbia

Painted wood
11½ x 9 x 8½ in.
Brooklyn Museum of Art (donated by
M. C. Eaton, no. 58.181.4)

This mask is identified as representing
an orator, the individual who would
recount the histories that were drama-
tized by the Winter Dance performers.
The lower jaw, articulated to produce a
more lifelike effect, would be moved
to imitate the actions of the performer
as he spoke. These types of masks were
once common in many of the cultures
of the Northwest Coast, and each tribe

or group had a rich mythology on
which to draw for dramatic subject
matter. The deeply carved and exaggerated features of this image are more
typical of Heiltsuk than Haida style,
though the mask could have originated
from either nation. The otherworldly
appearance of the image would have
been magnified by the shadows of a
firelit performance house.

98
Shaman's Mask
Tlingit
c. 1840–60, southeast Alaska

Painted wood with leather and opercula
11 x 7⅞ x 5⅛ in.
Peabody Museum of Archaeology
and Ethnology, Harvard University,
Cambridge, Massachusetts (no. 69-30-
10/1609)

This mask represents a bear with humanoid features—a mixture of human
forehead, nose, and cheeks with the
nostrils, snout, and ears of a bear.
From the forehead and both cheeks
emerge small images that represent
either bear cubs or the shaman's
guardian spirits, perhaps land otters.
The mysterious appearance of these
small figures from the face of the
larger image appears to represent the

overflowing of power from within the
central image. The bear, considered
lord of the forest, was an animal that
lived both in mythical realms as well
as in the present-day environment.
The shaman who used this mask in
rituals was transformed into a bear,
performing in continuous interaction
with the animal during the performance of his healing rituals.

99
Forehead Mask
Tsimshian
Mid nineteenth century, north coast of British Columbia

Painted wood with abalone shell and human hair
5½ x 9 x 8 in.
Canadian Museum of Civilization, Hull, Quebec (no. VII-B-17)

This finely carved forehead mask or headdress represents a beaver biting onto a stick that is held in its front paws. The beautiful blue-green California abalone shell pieces inlaid in the ears, eyes, nostrils, and incisor teeth, as well as along the stick, were included to catch the firelight and flash brightly in the ceremonial houses. The small snout, large eye sockets, numerous inlays, and the red-on-black dashing on the eyebrows are all typical traits of Tsimshian carving from the mid nineteenth century. This headpiece was once used in ceremonies dramatizing the origins of a clan, lineage, or family whose members were identified by the beaver. People who possessed specific symbols, titles, names, or social positions were entitled to certain hereditary privileges, among them the right to own land, songs, and dances, and to belong to a secret society.

100
Mask

Kwakwaka'wakw (Kwakiutl)
Collected 1901, northern part of Vancouver Island and adjacent mainland

Painted wood with copper and fabric
19 1/4 x 16 1/8 x 15 3/4 in.
American Museum of Natural History,
New York (no. 16/8534)

This mask with copper plaques was
purchased from George Hunt in 1901.
Representing a wasp or other insect,
it was used in the winter ceremonies
along with others representing a great
variety of creatures. The realistic art
of the Kwakwaka'wakw (previously
known as the Kwakiutl) is the most
spectacular and dramatic of the Northwest Coast in terms of style, form, and
cultural function. Much of this art was

associated with the important rituals
of the nation's secret societies, and
their social and cultural history.
Although there is very little information
about the characteristics of this art in
the eighteenth century, by the nineteenth century the influences of neighboring groups from both the north
and south can be noted among the
Kwakwaka'wakw.

101
Mask
Tlingit
Nineteenth century, southeast Alaska

Painted wood
9⅞ x 2¾ in.
Brooklyn Museum of Art (exchange
no. 05.589.7799)

This mask appears to represent a bear,
one of the animals identified with the
shaman, who acquired his powers by
wandering through the forest seeking
encounters with the spirits. The
shaman's spirits were represented by
his masks, of which there were usually
eight. Each spirit was identified by
some part of the animal—beak, jaw,
claws, etc.—which the shaman carried
in a bundle when he performed. The
spirits were also represented in the
shaman's masks and carvings. The
animals most frequently associated
with the shaman were the otter, the
mountain goat, the frog, the octopus,
the oyster catcher, and the bear. The
spirits of these animals appeared to
the shaman in human form, speaking
for the spirits of the dead.

102
Wolf or Bear Mask
Tlingit
Nineteenth century, southeast Alaska

Painted wood
7½ x 7⅞ x 13¾ in.
Laboratoire d'Ethnologie, Musée de
l'Homme, Paris (no. MH 82.30.3)

All the artistic production of the
Northwest Coast has a definite purpose and rich cultural symbolism.
Masks, like certain other objects, are
handed down in some instances from
generation to generation, which serves
to keep the nation's history alive. In
these cultures, history consists of stories
of alliances between people, animals,
spirits, and the natural world as a
whole. The handing over of objects is
so important to the Tlingit that when
a mask is inherited, steps must be
taken to ensure that it does not come
into the possession of any other clan.
After an artifact is "paid for" by being
brought out on behalf of the clan during appropriate ceremonies, the object
becomes an *at-óow*, or "an object possessed or treasured." These possessions
constitute the history and emblems of
the clans and are the basis of the entire
Tlingit tradition and culture.

103
Shaman's Mask
Tlingit
c. 1830–60, southeast Alaska

Painted wood
8 1/2 x 6 1/2 x 3 1/2 in.
Peabody Museum of Archaeology and Ethnology, Harvard University, Cambridge, Massachusetts (acquired by the museum in 1869, no. 69-30-10/1603)

Masks are among the most varied artistic creations of the Northwest Coast. The differences in the carving and details can indicate their tribal origins, although the masks of human faces are often the most difficult to identify. This mask, however, is classically Tlingit in the formation of its features; it is the type used by shamans in conducting their rituals. The aged and partially weathered appearance of the surface of this mask indicates that it was once stored in a gravehouse, along with the remains of its last owner. Despite the calm and innocuous expression on the face of this mask, a shaman's equipment was considered too powerful to remain in the village after the shaman's death. Their graves were usually distant from the main settlements, often on small, rocky islands that ordinary people would carefully avoid.

104
Mask
Tlingit
Late nineteenth century, southeast Alaska

Painted wood
12 1/2 x 9 7/8 x 4 3/8 in.
Peabody Museum of Archaeology and Ethnology, Harvard University, Cambridge, Massachusetts
(inv. no. 61-8-10/39085)

The sculptural arts of the Northwest Coast are characterized by portrayals of human or animal forms with exaggerated features such as ears, beaks, or jaws to identify the different creatures and mythic beings. This mask is a good example of those representing the spirit of an animal with an image that combines the attributes of animal and human. The composite figure may represent a bear or other land creature. The use of masks, names, and other symbols was part of the noble families' rights and inherited privileges.

105
Sun Dog Crest Helmet
Tlingit
c. 1780–1810, Klukwan village

Painted wood with opercula, bear
teeth, and brown bear hide
17⅛ x 12 x 14 in.
Private collection

Tlingit battle helmets (see cat. nos. 6, 8,
10, 67, 68, 70, 71, and 94) were made
as protective armor for warriors who
traditionally fought in largely hand-to-
hand combat, using stone and bone
clubs or daggers to incapacitate their
opponents. Because of the bravery and
sacrifice of the warriors on behalf of
their clan's survival, war helmets commonly attained the status of *at.óow,* or
clan emblem objects, upon their formal retirement. The Sun Dog helmet
was owned by Whale House of the
Gaanax.teidí clan of Klukwan village,
home of the spectacular house posts

carved by Kadjisdu.axch' II, a member
of the Kiks.ádi clan from Old Wrangell
(Kaasitl'aan village). The style of
workmanship in this venerable helmet
relates it to several other helmets in this
exhibition that were collected by Russian mariners in the early nineteenth
century. This helmet, collected by
Michael Johnson in 1976, appears in
a number of photographs taken in
and around the Whale House in 1895
by Lloyd Winter and Percy Pond,
pioneer photographers from Juneau,
Alaska (see frontispiece, page 2).

106
Articulated Mask
Coastal Tsimshian or Haisla
c. 1840–70, lower Skeena River and
its adjacent islands, or Douglas and
Gardner channels, central coast of
British Columbia

Painted alder wood and red cedar
with mica and quills
10 x 7⁷/₈ x 6⁵/₈ in.
Private collection, New York

This mask has eyes that move in their
sockets and an articulated jaw that can
be opened and closed by means of
cords fastened to its back. The forehead is embellished with two small
bird figures that are mounted on thin
quills, so they moved slightly with the
dancer's movements. The facial characteristics are typical of masks from
the north coast of British Columbia,
and the style of the painting, which
includes long fine lines in a combination of colors, is typical of masks dating
from the first half of the nineteenth
century. These masks were used in
dramatizations of tribal stories, in clan
reunions, and in *Naxnox* ("the power
beyond the human") ceremonies.
Naxnox masks enabled the dancer to
reveal spiritual powers as they appeared
in the physical world.

107
Articulated Mask
Coastal Tsimshian or Nishgá
c. 1780–1830

Painted alder wood or cottonwood
with human hair and leather
8¹/₂ x 8¹/₂ x 12 in.
Private collection, New York

Visually striking masks of unusual imagery like this one were used in a ceremonial known as *Naxnox*, the "power
beyond the human." The *Naxnox* is
staged by members of the community
who have inherited the rights to use
the names and mask-images that represent a wide range of spirit-beings
who exert their influence on the physical world. These ceremonies display
the powers of individuals associated
with these spirits and propitiate those
beings that govern the proper func-
tioning of the world. This mask,
whose full identify is not recorded,
features a long, thin beak with a delicately rounded tip. The representation
incorporates a movable lower mandible
that is joined to the face with a partial
covering of flexible leather, and an
upper beak that is carefully lapped or
half-mortised onto the rest of the mask.
The red pattern in the eye socket may
relate to human face-painting indicative of this spirit-image. The overall
form of the mask, especially the sym-
metrically oval ears and the forward-
cut rear edge, strongly suggests that it
was carved by the same Tsimshian
artist who created a very unusual
pair of masks carved in stone. These
much celebrated masks, one with
open eyes and one with eyes closed,
were collected from two separate
coastal Tsimshian villages near the
turn of the nineteenth century.

108 *left*
Articulated Mask
Haisla or Coastal Tsimshian
Collected 1882, Dean and Burke channels, central coast of British Columbia

Painted wood
14 1/8 in., height
Museum für Völkerkunde, Vienna
(no. 51.747)

Though apparently collected among the Nuxalk, this mask has characteristics that suggest it was made by a Haisla or Coastal Tsimshian artist from farther north along the British Columbia coast. The eyes and eye sockets, as well as the overall painting style, are not handled in the typical and distinctive Nuxalk manner of carving and painting. Like other neighboring nations, the Nuxalk celebrated winter ceremonies in which spirits were invoked to aid those who were about to enter secret societies. Like family or clan emblems and titles, the rights to names, songs, dances, and certain sacred rituals were inherited. However, their use required initiation into their secrets, a rite of passage similar to that experienced by shamans when they first went in search of the spirits. This mask was collected by P. Jacobsen, who was commissioned to carry out an expedition for the Berlin Museum.

109 *opposite, top*
Mask
Tlingit
Eighteenth century, southeast Alaska

Painted wood with abalone shell and leather
8 1/2 x 17 1/4 x 8 in.
Private collection

The long-nosed human face of this mask represents a mosquito, which were overly abundant in the area and have been depicted in many objects since ancient times. Mosquitos are connected with malevolent spirits that prey upon human beings. The skeletal structure of the face and the very unusual eye form help to lend this mask a somewhat heinous appearance. Information collected with the mask suggests that there were once several different noses that would be changed during the progress of a performance. The mask once had hide strips for the mustache and beard, and possibly painted moose hide panels that extended above the forehead. The teeth are made of abalone shell pieces inlaid between the lips. The painted formline U-shapes on the temples and lower cheeks are very unusual, composed with the negative parts of the designs (usually the unpainted spaces between the painted formlines) colored in red ochre. This "negative formline" technique may be unique to this mask, made during the historic period. Many contemporary artists have adopted this space-reversal technique in the last twenty-five years.

110
Forehead Mask
Tlingit
1800–40, southeast Alaska

Painted alder wood or birch
$14^7/8$ x $7^1/2$ in.
Private collection, New York

Gracefully carved from a single piece
of wood, this mask in the shape of a
long-billed bird might represent a
heron or a crane, both of which were
clan emblems. This type of forehead
mask with its slightly upturned bill
was probably used in dramatizations
of myths and clan histories rather than
in shamanic rituals. A number of features indicate that the mask is very old:
the compactness of the carving, which
achieves a maximum sculptural effect
while removing as little of the wood
as possible; the shape of the eye and
the surrounding hollowed eye socket;
and the patina and blue pigment
(of celadonite ore), which was traded
among the artists of the region. The
colors most used by the Tlingit were
greenish blue, red, and black.

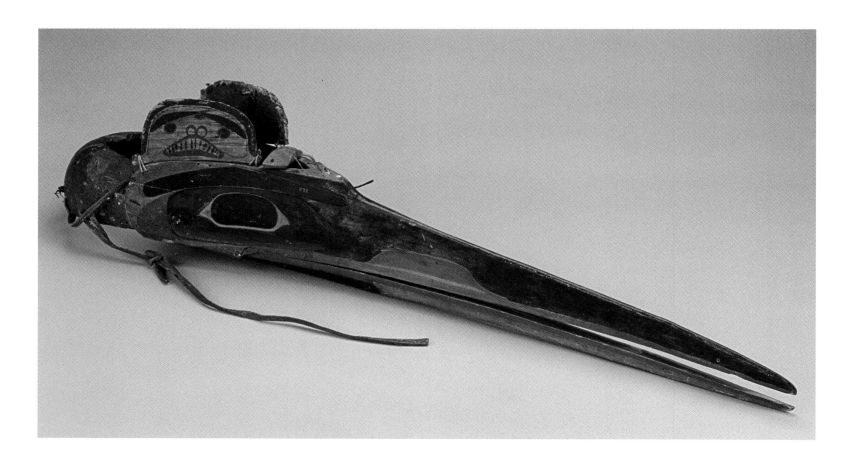

111 *opposite, top*
Bird Mask
Heiltsuk or Nuxalk
c. 1850–80, Milbanke Sound to
Burke Channel

Painted alder wood
11³⁄₈ x 28¹⁄₈ x 11³⁄₈ in.
Canadian Museum of Civilization,
Hull, Quebec (no. VII-X-214)

This mask, equipped with a device for
moving the jaw, was used in ritual
dramatizations that were part of ceremonies that made relations with supernatural and mythical creatures visible
and tangible. Heiltsuk and Nuxalk
styles often included use of the intense
blue pigment seen here, which contrasts
brightly with the vermilion red used
on the nostrils, lips, and ears. The
movable lower mandible is fitted within
the cheeks of the mask, and hinges on
a wooden pin fit into a hole drilled
through the cheek. Shrouded in cedar
bark or cloth to hide their human
form, skilled dancers wearing such
masks could realistically and dramatically imitate the movements and body
language of any bird species. Though
this mask may have been collected on
the Queen Charlotte Islands, it is
doubtless of Heiltsuk or Nuxalk manufacture and arrived in Haida country
via inter-nation trade or gifting.

112 *opposite, bottom*
Forehead Mask
Coastal Tsimshian
Collected 1879, north coast of British
Columbia

Painted wood with metal
43 x 8¹⁄₂ in.
Canadian Museum of Civilization,
Hull, Quebec (no. VII-B-126)

Masks and their accompanying cos-
tumes, songs, and dances were the
principal means of manifesting mythical characters in the dramas that re-
called the heroic feats of the nation's
founders. These performances reaf-
firmed the social and cosmic order,
thereby connecting the mythological
past with the present. They celebrated
the change of seasons, the rebirth of
an ancestor's spirit, or the acquisition
of guardian spirits: all powerful stim-
uli for the development of Northwest
Coast art. This mask was collected by
I. W. Powell in 1879, though its true
identity and meaning were not
recorded.

113
Raven Mask
Kwakwa̱ka'wakw (Kwakiutl)
Late nineteenth century, Knight Inlet,
British Columbia

Painted red cedar with cedar bark
39 x 12¹⁄₂ in.
Brooklyn Museum of Art (donated by
Herman Stutzer, no. 15.513.3)

In certain Northwest Coast cultures,
masks represented the form in which
the first ancestor appeared to his descendants and founded their lineage.
Others made visible the characters of
myth and history. This raven mask was
made to participate in the exorcism of
the cannibal spirit from dancers known
as the *Hamat'sa*. The *Hamat'sa's* initiat-
ing spirit, known as *Baxbakwalanuksiwe*,
had three monster bird associates, the
Raven, the Huxwhukw, and the Galok-
wudzuwis, or Crooked Beak. These
bird masks (as they were called in the
original story) accompany *Baxbakwalanuksiwe* as the cannibal spirit preys on
the bodies of human beings. This raven
mask is of an older nineteenth-century
type, made perhaps as early as 1860–80.
Graphite mixed with the black pigment
gives the surface a grayish sheen, and
the design detailing is absolutely minimal. Shrouds of shredded cedar bark
(which tops the head) once curtained
the head and face of the dancer.

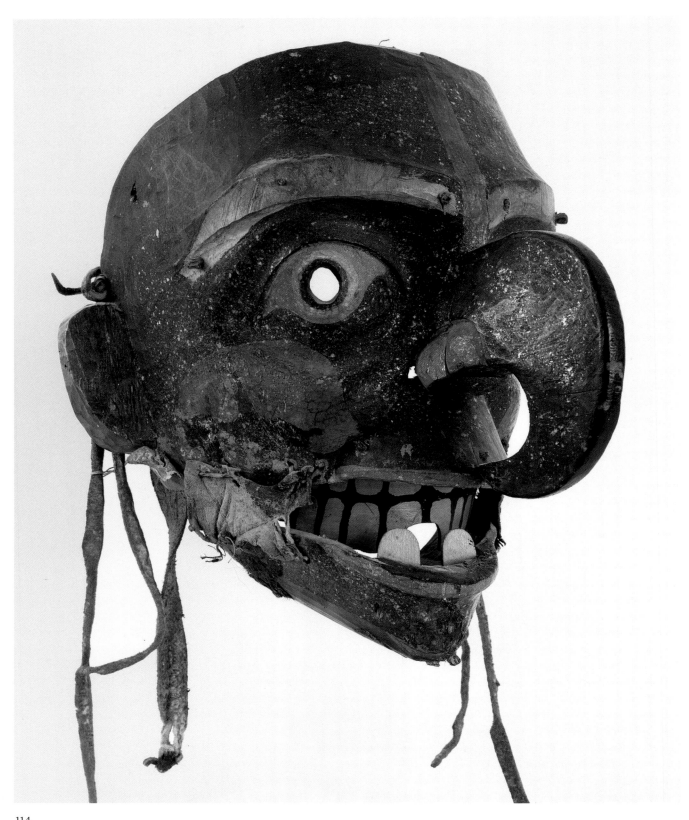

114
Articulated Mask
Probably Heiltsuk
c. 1800–50, southeast Alaska

Painted wood with leather
9⅝ in., height
André Nasser Collection, New York

This mask of a fantastic creature that is half-human, half-bird testifies to the links between humans and the mythological animals that founded the family lineages. The theatricality of the shaman's role (all participants were referred to as "doctors") in the winter ceremonies is underscored in this transformational mask with its exaggerated features and an articulated jaw that heightens the dramatic effect. This mask once had hide and fur strips attached on the eyebrows and upper lip, which would have magnified its monstrous appearance. Flakes of graphite and/or mica create sparkles in the paint texture. The Heiltsuk (also called Bella Bella) celebrated a creature known in English as the Wild Man of the Woods, and this mask may represent one such forest being.

115
Articulated Mask
Tsimshian
Collected 1909, Gitikshan, Skeena
River Basin, north coast of British
Columbia

Painted wood with leather
8¼ x 7¼ x 8¼ in.
American Museum of Natural History,
New York (no. 16.1/621)

This mask represents a raptor, possibly
an eagle or an owl, with a large curved
beak that is movable and large circular
eyes that also pivot up and down.
When closed, the eyes are white; when
open, they are red. The round, hollow
eye sockets and black beak suggest the
owl image, the changing eyes perhaps
its ability to see in daylight and dark-
ness. This signifies both transformation

and opposition. The mask was held
to the head by means of cords drawn
through the holes on the sides of the
face. The movable eyes must have
made the mask quite startlingly dramatic. George T. Emmons acquired
it from among the Gitikshan, a village
on the Skeena River.

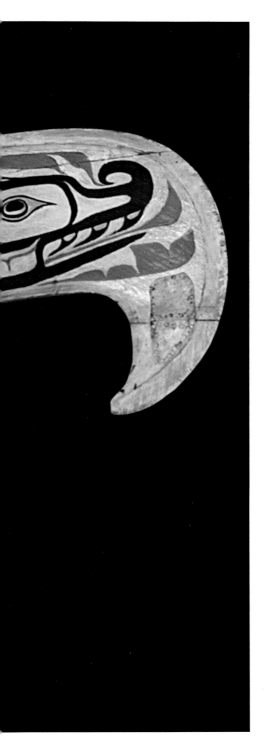

116 a *(open)* & b *(closed)*
Transformation Mask
Kwakwaka'wakw (Kwakiutl)
Collected 1908, Alert Bay,
British Columbia

Painted red cedar with leather, nails,
and metal
17 x 29½ x 12½ in. (closed)
17 x 29½ x 71 in. (open)
Brooklyn Museum of Art (museum
expedition 1908, no. 08.491.8902)

Transformation and ancestry were central to the masks used in certain winter ceremonies, and the most dramatic of these were the mechanical masks of this type. At the high point of the performance, the dancer would open the mask from within, displaying a totally different appearance, sometimes featuring a human face or that of an animal ancestor. The beak of this mask opens outward to reveal a painting of the *Sisiutl*, a mythical two-headed serpent, which in this case has a humanoid face in the center. The top of the head opens upward, with the painting of a human being on the inside. The inside of the lower mandible displays the painting of a split-profile bear. Though many Northwest Coast cultures made mechanical masks dramatizing transformation, the Kwakwaka'wakw created more of such masks and in a greater variety than any other First Nation of the north Pacific coast.

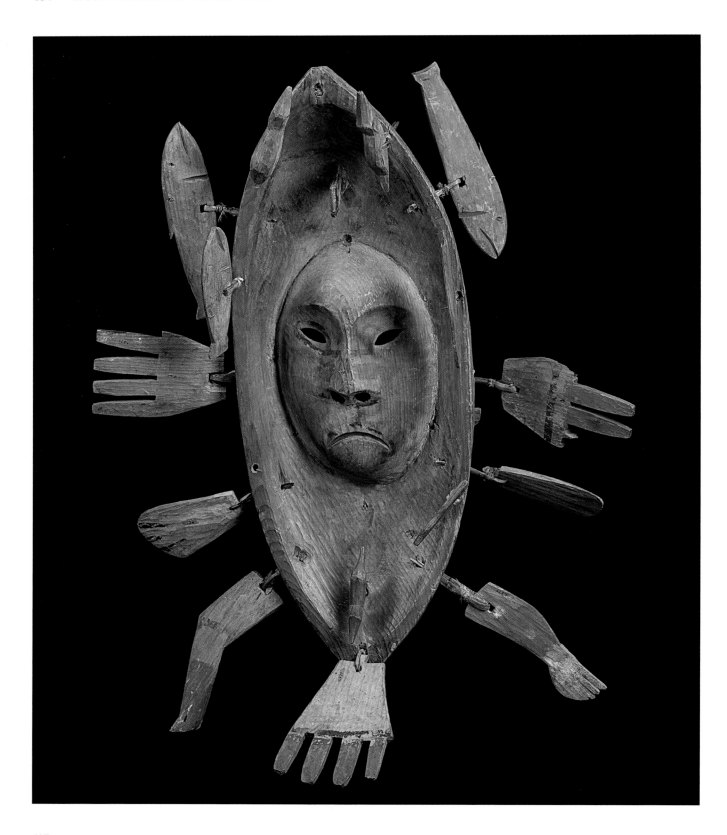

117
Dance Mask
Yup'ik
Collected 1898, Yukon River delta, west Alaska

Wood with traces of paint and fiber
22 x 16 in.
Private collection

The central form of this mask appears to represent a boat, probably the large, skin-covered *umiaq* of the Bering Sea hunters. In the center of the *umiaq* is a face with the downturned mouth sometimes indicative of a sea-dwelling spirit. This face may be the *inua* of the *umiaq*, since all things animate or inanimate are seen by the Yup'ik as possessing a spirit, or it may (more likely perhaps) represent the *tuunraq*,

or helping spirit, of the hunter and owner of the mask. Images of fish, birds, seal flippers, legs, and thumbless human hands surround the *umiaq*, all symbolic of the activities pursued by the hunter. The collector of this mask, Joseph Chilberg, acquired a large and significant group of Yup'ik objects in west Alaska in the late nineteenth and early twentieth century. In 1909, Chilberg sold a large collection of

Yup'ik material to George Heye, founder of the Museum of the American Indian, and he also supplied material to other museums and private collectors. Chilberg maintained a museum of Yup'ik material culture in Long Beach, California, until 1935.

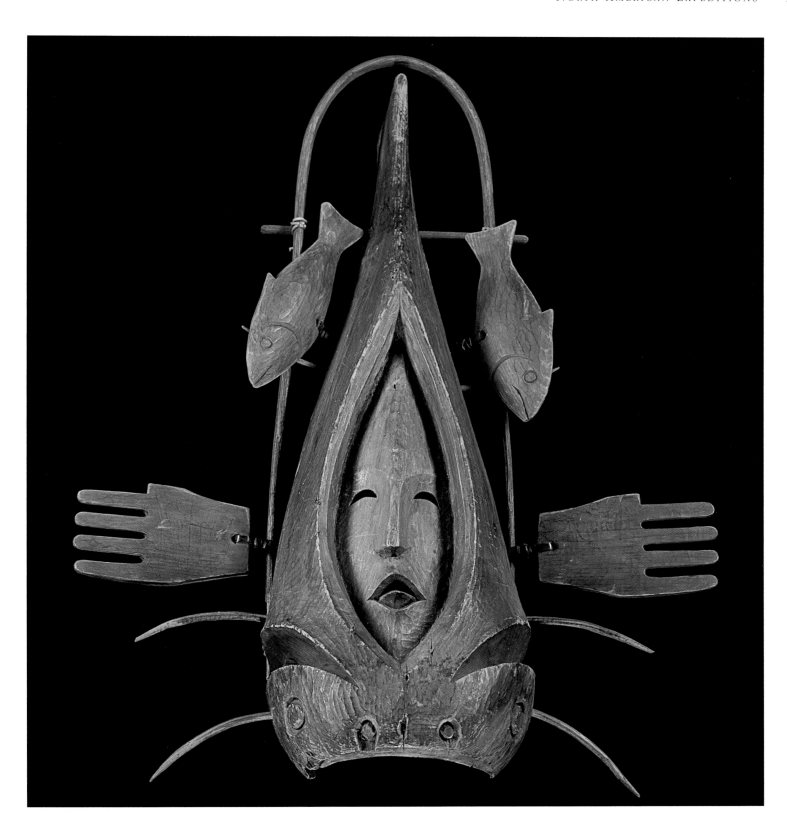

118
Dance Mask
Yup'ik
Collected 1898, Yukon River delta,
west Alaska

Painted wood with fiber
22 x 16¹/₂ in.
Private collection

Yup'ik dance masks have been widely
recognized for most of the twentieth
century for their ethereal, surrealistic,
and spiritual qualities. They were
sought out by Euro-American painters
and collectors of the Surrealist school,
who admired and celebrated these
qualities in their work. This mask,
which appears to represent a large fish,
also displays the creature's *inua*, the
inner spirit that in this case is portrayed
by a fishlike humanoid face. Thumbless, four-fingered human hands extend
out on both sides of the mask and its
inua face, and two small fish shapes
are fastened to the bentwood arch that
encircles the mask's tail. Four short,
thin, bentwood appendages protrude
from the lower corners of the mask; they
may have once had additional small
figures or perhaps downy feather tufts
attached to them. The entire image
beautifully encapsulates the skill and
natural ease with which Yup'ik carvers
manifested the spiritual dimensions
of their interrelationship with the
subarctic, Bering Sea coastal environment. Wearing such a mask in dance
constitutes a means of prayer to the
spirits of the creatures that supplied food
for the villages, asking that they allow
themselves to be taken by the hunters
and fisherman. The mask was collected by Joseph Chilberg in 1898.

119
Otter Mask
Central Yup'ik
Collected 1898–99, Yukon River delta, west Alaska

Wood
15½ in., height
Private collection

This mask, which apparently represents the *inua*, or inner spirit, of the otter, has a face that is half-seal, half-human, transmitting the idea of balanced forces and transformation. It also includes representations of two of the small finger masks worn by the women who accompanied the large masked figures in the dances performed during the important winter festivals. This type of mask was often one of a pair that was complementary rather than identical, reflecting the Yup'iks' dual concept of nature. This mask has the typical upturned male mouth. It was collected by Joseph Chilberg in 1898–99.

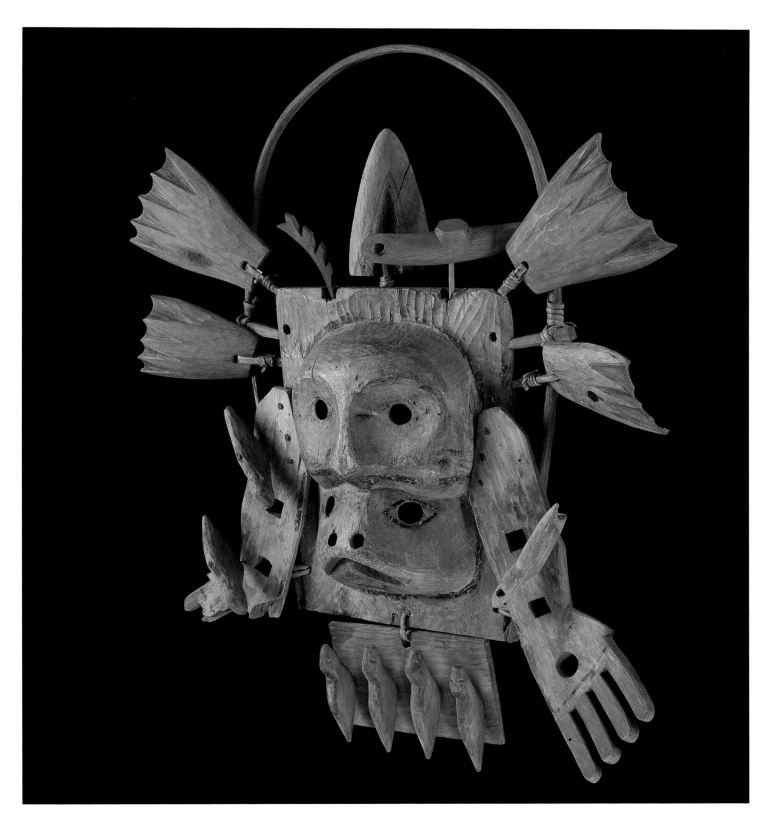

120
Dance Mask
Yup'ik
Collected 1898, Yukon River delta,
west Alaska

Painted wood with fiber
25 x 20 x 3½ in.
Private collection

Yup'ik masks for the most part represent the spirits or events encountered by the shamans (*angalkuq*) in their dealings with the non-physical world, or they depict the *inua* (inner spirit) of the animals the hunters pursued for sustenance. Yup'ik masks were traditionally made for a single season's use, and then either burned or left out in a remote tundra location to decompose over time. Private or museum collectors often paid the owners for masks they may have otherwise destroyed. This double-image mask exhibits human and seal features. The two "opposite" faces allude to the interdependence of sea and land beings. Four seal flippers (one of which, interestingly, appears to be of different manufacture, perhaps older), both rear and pectoral, along with what may be the seal's tail, extend outward from the center rectangle of the mask. Human arms and hands (one of which is broken) reach out toward the viewer. These thumbless hands are pierced by a large hole, both indications of the hunter's desire to allow some animals to escape his grasp, in order to maintain the resource. The dance mask was collected by Joseph Chilberg perhaps in 1898.

121
Long-faced Mask
Chugach or Koniag (Pacific Yup'ik)
Nineteenth century, Prince William Sound, Alaska

Wood
17¹/₂ x 7¹/₄ in.
Private collection, New York

The masks from the Prince William Sound region are simple in form and design, with little or no painting and carvings that are usually flat and quite rudimentary, perhaps representing some spirit. This mask has a high forehead with high, slanted eyebrows carved in relief and forming an angle to the nose. The eyes are oval, and the mouth is quite prominent and twisted downward. Masks like this were used by shamans when enacting spiritual dramas. The mask's features would be highlighted by the dim lamp or firelight that was used in the dwellings that housed these events.

122
Nepcetaq Mask
Yup'ik
c. 1830–60, south Norton Sound and
Lower Yukon

Wood with animal teeth, quills, and
sinew
20 x 23 in.
Private collection

Nepcetaq means "the ones that stick (or cling) to the face" and describes how the shaman would use his power to draw a mask to his face and dance with it without using his hands, any strings, or other means to hold the mask in place. Yup'ik traditions involved powerful, semi-human spirits who controlled the passage of animal spirits from the sky world to the earth. The four holes in the large backboard represent the passages that the animal spirits would take on their journey to the world. The shaman, or *angalkuq*, used such a mask to demonstrate his power and to draw animals near to the

hunters. Masks that were newer when collected retain their brightly painted surface and the self-tied, radiating feather ornaments, of which only fragments remain in this older and more subtly carved example. Many feathers were once looped by their quill tips through the small holes in the outer edge of this mask and tied in place with a length of sinew, strung from one quill to the next around the perimeter. Three small animal teeth remain of those once set into the lips of the central face, all of which would have added a bristling countenance to the mask.

123
Shaman's Mask
Tlingit
c. 1780–1850, southeast Alaska

Painted wood with human hair and
leather
9¾ x 9⅛ in.
Private collection, New York

This expressively sculptured mask is
surrounded by a wide corona, painted
a brilliant vermilion red, a pigment
obtained in trade. The image represents a small animal with humanized
features that might be a bear, a marmot,
or a small rodent. The deep, precise
sculpture enhances the strong emotional content of this carved face. The
exact meaning of the corona is not
known, though its importance to the

representation of the shaman's spirit
helper, or *yeik*, explains its presence.
The Burke Museum collection (Seattle)
includes a mask with similar small
mammal features that appears in photographs of the funeral of the chief of
the Shakes lineage. Its presence among
other clan-owned objects indicates
that it was a piece of clan regalia, not a
shaman's mask. In 1909, J. R. Swanton
stated that the masks displayed by a

Shakes clan, the Nanya.ayí, included a
marmot, which may pinpoint the
identity of the Burke Museum mask.

124
Mask
Nuxalk (Bella Coola) or Kwak-
waka'wakw (Kwakiutl)
Collected 1889, central coast of British
Columbia and north Vancouver Island
and adjacent mainland areas

Painted wood with human hair
11½ in., height
André Nasser Collection, New York

The masks of the nations that lived
in the center of the Northwest Coast
are noteworthy for their spectacular
appearance and their often intense,
bright colors. They represent fantastic
birds, sea monsters, land animals, and
transforming supernatural creatures.
Masks like this were used by the Nuxalk
and Kwakwaka'wakw in their winter
ceremonies, during the initiation
of young men as members of secret

societies. This mask is sculpted in classic Nuxalk three-dimensional style,
though the characteristics of the painting are more typically Kwakwaka'wakw.
Nuxalk masks often are painted blue
on the face, while green eye sockets
and painted details are more common
among Kwakwaka'wakw masks. Many
Nuxalk objects made their way to
Kwakwaka'wakw ownership in the
nineteenth century, and this mask

appears to have been repainted by its
new Kwakwaka'wakw owner. Charles
Warren collected this mask in 1889.

125
Headdress Frontlet
Tlingit
Late eighteenth or early nineteenth century, southeast Alaska

Painted wood with abalone shell
7½ x 6 x 3 in.
Canadian Museum of Civilization, Hull, Quebec (no. VII-B-689)

Possibly collected from the Haida (and identified by its museum as such), this headdress frontlet is clearly carved in an early historic period Tlingit style. The rich shell-inlaid imagery includes an anthropomorphic thunderbird as the main figure, with a dragonfly between its knees. The large, round eyes and paired wings of this insect (the emblem of a clan from Angoon village) are clearly represented. Frontlets are known to have been traded or gifted from one First Nation to another, which spread this headdress tradition

from its origins among the Tsimshian as far south as the Kwakwaka'wakw and Nuu-chah-nulth of Vancouver Island. This frontlet is missing the characteristic framework that enabled it to be worn as a headdress (see cat. nos. 73 and 74). These headdresses, most often identified with the Tlingit and Haida cultures in the northern part of the Northwest Coast, are part of the regalia worn by high-ranking people at ceremonies all over the Northwest Coast today.

126
Naakusht'aa (attribution)
Flying Raven Clan Hat
Tlingit
c. 1810–40, Klukwan village

Painted wood with abalone shell,
leather, and human hair
11³/4 x 17¹/2 x 15³/8 in.
Private collection

Tlingit clan hats are some of the most
treasured objects owned by house-
groups in different lineages. Over
time, the clan members in a particular
village would proliferate and require
separate quarters, prompting the
construction of a new house in which
several extended families would reside.
This hat, with the Flying Raven crest
emblem manifested in its form, was
owned by the Frog House of the
Gaanax.teidí clan of Klukwan village,
twenty-two miles up the Chilkat River
from the town of Haines, Alaska. The
raven image has the very unusual feature of movable wings, which can be
raised up and down to reveal early
nineteenth-century style red formline

designs on the underside. Relief-
carved black formline designs appear
on the flanks of the hat. The firm-
edged style in which the raven is
carved and the prolific inlay of large
abalone-shell pieces throughout the
object point to the work of an artist
named Naakusht'aa, a carver of the
Dakl'aweidí, an eagle side-clan with
the killer whale emblem. This artist,
according to notes by Tlingit ethnogra-
pher Louis Shotridge, also created the
house posts of the Frog House, the
Frog *Shaadakooẋ* [hat], and the Frog
grave marker photographed by Lloyd
Winter and Percy Pond in 1895. The
clan hat was collected by Howard
Roloff in 1978.

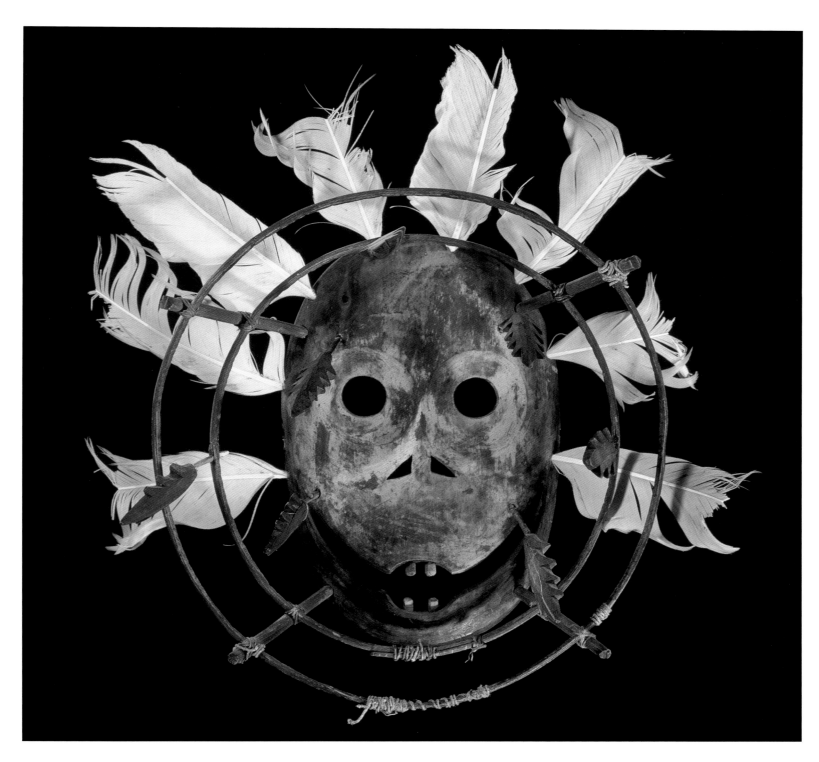

127
Pair of Masks
Yup'ik
Collected 1893, Cape Vancouver, Nelson Island, Alaska

Wood with feathers, caribou hair, and quills
15³/₈ x 20¹/₂ in., each
Sheldon Jackson Museum, Sitka, Alaska (nos. IIH1, IIH2)

The stark, expressive simplicity of this magical pair of Yup'ik dance masks epitomizes the infinite ability of wood, basic tools, and natural materials to convey the power and mystery of Native experience. It has been suggested

(by Ann Fienup-Riordan) that the crescent-shaped eyes and the light spots on the masks' black background may represent the moon and stars, and that these masks may illustrate a widely recognized story or event. The masks were collected by the Reverend Sheldon Jackson in 1893, and related masks were collected from other sites along the Yup'ik coastline in the 1880s and 1890s. Edward W. Nelson has remarked that a similar mask, also from Cape Vancouver, presents a *tuunraq* (also *tunghak*), the Yup'ik name for the helping or "familiar" spirits that assisted the shamans in their spiritual work.

128
Mask Representing *Uksoak*
Central Yup'ik
Collected c. 1875, Alaska

Wood with feathers
11³/₄ in., diameter
Private collection

Most of the masks used in the year's five major festivals, which were both religious ceremonies and social events, were nonidentical pairs. Ignorance of this fact led to their being separately acquired, so that many are now in different collections. Such is the case with this mask, which represents *Uksoak*, or the Spirit of Autumn. A. H. Twitchell acquired it in the second half of the nineteenth century. Its mate is now in the Rhode Island School of Design's Museum of Art.

129
Mask
Central Yup'ik
Collected 1898–99, Yukon River delta,
west Alaska

Wood with feathers
15½ in., diameter
Private collection

The Yup'ik believed that all of nature's creations—human beings, animals, places, and inanimate objects in general—were possessed of a spirit that could act in such a way as to either benefit people or cause evil to befall them, and that these spirits were controlled by the shaman. The edges of this mask are decorated with concentric circles, evoking the ripples that appear on the surface of the water when a stone is cast. This was a phenomenon believed to possess life and a spirit. Perhaps the bird-shaped face in the center of the mask represents an *inua*, or inner spirit, and the appendages in the form of hands and legs symbolize its power. The mask was collected by Joseph Chilberg in 1898–99.

130
Shaman's Mask
Central Yup'ik
c. 1860–80, Kuskokwim River Basin,
Alaska

Painted wood
30 x 27 in.
Private collection

Shamans could use their power to influence the forces of nature and animals, even to control them and restore
the natural order when it was disturbed
by circumstances such as illness. However, in order to be able to do this,
they had to observe a strict fast and
survive trances during which their
souls embarked on long and dangerous
voyages through the world's different

spheres. The shamans' visionary powers worked like X-rays to penetrate the
bodies of others and reveal their visions.
This power is depicted in this extraordinary mask portraying a *tunghak,* or
supernatural spirit. The hole in the
center represents the path that permits
passage from one sphere to another.
The upturned corners of the mouth
denote that the figure is male.

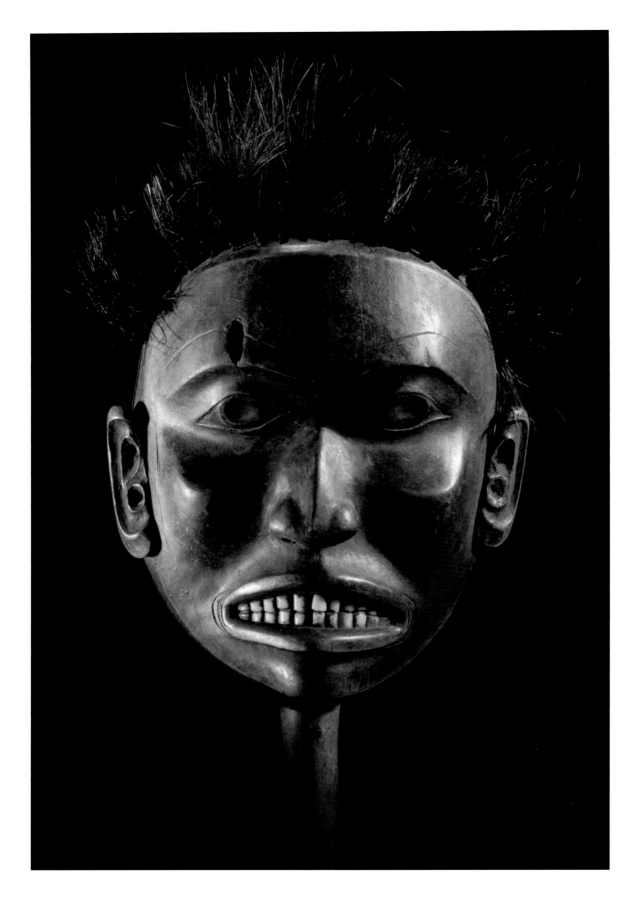

131
Globe-shaped Rattle
Tsimshian, Nishgá, or Gitksan
c. 1780–1820, Nass and Skeena
river basins, north coast of British
Columbia

Painted birch with bone or ivory and
human hair
11 1/2 x 6 in.
Private collection, New York

The globe shape commonly employed
for a shaman's rattle naturally suggests
a human skull, and the face carved here
has taken further advantage of the form.
The rear hemisphere of this rattle is
covered with a design composition
made up of broad formlines with
small negative areas carved in relief, an
indication both of its age and of the
wide distribution of that early historic
period style. The face of the rattle is
unusually masklike, with fine naturalistic sculptural detail. The painstaking
workmanship is typical of Tsimshian
production, and the total appearance
of the sculpture denotes an object of
exceptional quality. The subtle treat-
ment of the features, particularly the
slightly hollowed irises of the eyes and
the sharply formed mouth and cheeks,
gives the facial expression a mysterious
and piercing appearance.

132
Oyster Catcher Rattle
Tlingit
c. 1780–1830, southeast Alaska

Painted wood with ermine skin and leather
8¼ x 3⅞ x 5½ in.
Peabody Museum of Archaeology and Ethnology, Harvard University, Cambridge, Massachusetts (acquired by the museum in 1869, no. 69-30-10/1790)

This shaman's rattle is carved in the form of a black oyster catcher, a small shorebird that was apparently a powerful ally of Tlingit shamans. All extant examples of this type of rattle appear to be Tlingit in origin. While they all share the same oyster catcher form, with its sensually curved neck, they vary completely in the arrangement of figures on the back of the bird. (Oyster catchers do not ordinarily carry their heads in this manner, except during a brief "dance" they occasionally perform among a group of birds, which may be a mating ritual.) The group of figures on this rattle, in addition to being uncommonly dense in composition, is reversed from the more usual arrangement. In most such rattles, the large-mouthed figure next to the bird's neck is adjacent to and facing the handle of the rattle, while the various human and animal-spirit figures follow suit. The central image here is a shaman torturing a witch to extract a confession by twisting the suspect's hair behind its head. The witch's *yeik* (apparently a bear) protrudes from its chest (see cat. no. 136), while three other bear-spirits crowd around, and unidentified spirit-images lie close to the bird's back.

133
Shaman's Rattle
Tsimshian
c. 1800–50, Nass and Skeena river basins, Queen Charlotte Islands, north coast of British Columbia

Painted wood
10¼ in., length
André Nasser Collection, New York

Spherical rattles made of two hollow halves fastened together appear to emulate a skull form. Rattles were ceremonial objects that led to the supernatural world by means of their sound, and they were used by shamans who functioned as intermediaries between the humans and the spirits or supernatural creatures that gave them their power. Shamans' objects were commonly decorated with carvings of the spirits who aided them. The delicate human face portrayed on this rattle most likely represents one of those helping spirits. The thin eyebrows and lips, prominent cheekbones, and broad, flattish nose are all conventions of Tsimshian sculptural styles. The radial fluting around the rim of the rattle is reminiscent of the form of cockleshells, an intertidal bivalve commonly harvested for food.

134
Dance Staff Ornament
Tlingit
1800–60, Klukwan village, southeast Alaska

Painted spruce with leather, human hair, abalone shell, and opercula
17 in., length
Private collection, New York

This small orca or killer whale carving was made to fasten to a round staff for use as a clan-emblem dance wand. This whale is visually related to a one-piece killer whale staff once owned by the Nanya.aayí clan leader known as Chief Shakes of the Stikine Tlingit, who lived in the area of Wrangell,

Alaska. The style of the two-dimensional design is characteristic of the art produced in the early decades of the nineteenth century. Staffs were part of the ceremonial paraphernalia used by the chiefs, one of their purposes being to mark the rhythm of songs and dances as they were struck against the ground. They were usually decorated with the owner's clan symbols or with motifs that referred to the myth of his family origin. In this case, it is the killer whale, which can be recognized by its blunt snout, wide mouth with abundant teeth, blowhole (inlaid with abalone shell), and large dorsal fin embellished with locks of human hair.

135 *opposite, left*
Chief's Staff
Heiltsuk or Haida
Collected 1864, Queen Charlotte Islands or the north central coast of British Columbia

Wood
55½ in., length
André Nasser Collection, New York

This beautifully sculptured staff, carved with forms characteristic of the heraldic and emblematic totem poles, features three semihuman mythological figures. The uppermost figure wears a spruce-root hat that extends far upward like a giant stack of nobility rings. Most unusual is the center figure, which

stands behind and peeks through the legs of the upper figure. The bottom image is seated on a platform that is supported by four thin columns. The sculptural form of the faces on the three figures and the very uncommon composition are more indicative of Heiltsuk, rather than Haida, work. Staffs were tapped against the ground by chiefs (or often their speakers) to emphasize their words or to mark or accentuate the rhythm of songs and dances. The master of *H.M.S. Grappler* collected this staff in 1864.

136

Raven Rattle

Tsimshian

c. 1820–50, Nass and Skeena river basins and adjacent islands, north coast of British Columbia

Painted maple or birch
13¼ in., length
Private collection, New York

Raven rattles, at least in the historic period, were the property of chiefs. The spiritual nature of the composite figure on the back of the raven, however, is a clear reference to the shamanic character of this rattle's origins. Though raven rattles vary little in their overall composition, they are one of the most fascinating and enigmatic objects from the Northwest Coast. In this rattle, a humanlike figure with a bear's head and claws and a long tongue is reclining above the raven— the emblem of certain matrilineal clans and hero of a variety of myths. The joining of tongues is a common indication of the exchange of power and spiritual intimacy. Unique to this rattle's human-bear image is the tiny shaman's *yeik*, or helper-spirit, emerging from its stomach. Although unusual in a rattle figure, this is a common image in shaman's grave guardians and other small figures. The gently rounded forms, very finely carved details, and overall dynamic lines clearly illustrate the mastery of its sculptor.

137
Comb
Tlingit
c. 1800–30, southeast Alaska

Wood with candlefish oil
5³/4 x 2¹/2 x 1¹/4 in.
The Menil Collection, Houston
(no. 74-049 DJ)

This comb depicts a mythical scene in which a large animal, most likely a bear, is devouring a human being, starting with its feet. Many Northwest Coast stories speak of various interactions between humans and bears. One is the story of Kaats, a man who married a bear and had human-bear offspring. The wear on the teeth of this comb illustrates its long use, underscored by the polish on the surface of the carving. The obvious genitalia on the human are not a common feature of Northwest Coast work, though the delicacy, refinement, and finish of this small object certainly are.

138
Shaman's Amulet
Tlingit
c. 1730–1830, southeast Alaska

Sperm whale tooth
5³/₄ in., length
Private collection, New York

This small carving is in the shape of an archaic style canoe, atop which sits a bear with octopus tentacles on its body. On the back of the bear, a newly initiated shaman, known as *ixt'* in the Tlingit language, is reclining. The two-dimensional designs engraved on the surface of the canoe are done in a very archaic style, indicating that this

amulet was passed from generation to generation of shamanic practitioners. The amulet refers to the shaman's spiritual voyages and was worn around the neck as a talisman. It was used during shamanic practices, ceremonies, and healing rites, which included handling and sucking ill spirits from the diseased parts of the body. The shaman's amulets and other equipment were viewed with suspicion because of their connection to the shaman, whom people saw as having supernatural powers and the ability to cross the boundaries between life and death.

139
Shaman's Amulet
Tlingit
c. 1700–1820, southeast Alaska

Sperm whale tooth
3³/₄ in., length
Private collection, New York

Shamans' amulets are said to have been the most powerful objects used in healing rituals. Made in secret and protected from profane influences, the amulets were generally carved by the shamans themselves or commissioned from professional artists. The images testified to the shaman's direct contact with supernatural powers as he moved

back and forth between the human and spirit worlds to reactivate his healing and clairvoyant skills. The amulets were also thought to have the powers inherent in the creatures that provided the materials used to make them: walrus tusks, whale teeth or bone, and the horns of mountain sheep. The very early style of carving on this amulet illustrates several composite images, metaphors for the transformation that is central to the work of the shaman.

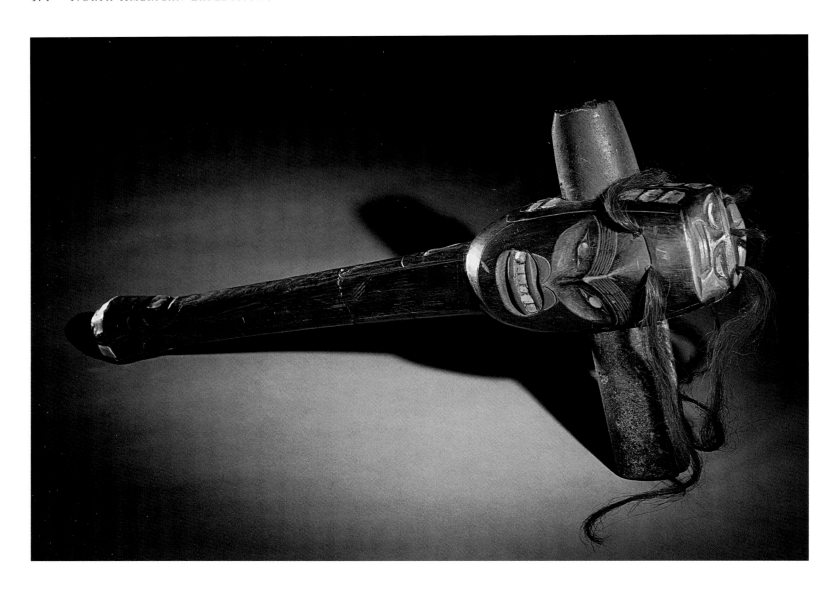

140
"Slave Killer" or "Copper Breaker"
Club
Kwakwaka'wakw (Kwakiutl)
Collected 1905, Vancouver Island and
adjacent mainland

Painted wood with resin, stone, hair,
and abalone shell
20 x 11 x 4³/8 in.
Brooklyn Museum of Art (museum
expedition 1905, no. 05.588.7289)

Clubs known as "slave killers" are pre-
sumed to have been used to kill slaves
during certain potlatch ceremonies.
Slaves were sacrificed only on rare occasions, after which their owners were
compensated with new titles and new
songs with value equal to that of the
slaves. Slavery had existed since ancient
times in this part of the world. Individuals became slaves if they were taken
as prisoners of war and no ransom was
paid for their release. Slaves became
part of their master's property and were
trained in the rules of the household
and resource gathering. Similar looking clubs were also used, at least cere-
monially, for the "breaking" of coppers,
the large shieldlike objects made of
sheet copper that represented great
amounts of wealth (see cat. no. 151).
Among the Kwakwaka'wakw, cutting
or breaking pieces from a copper and
giving them to a rival chief was a form
of insult, which had to be assuaged by
returning copper pieces of equal value.
If unable to respond appropriately, the
rival was considered not to be of true
high standing in his community.

141 *opposite, top*
Club
Haida
c. 1850–80, Queen Charlotte Islands,
British Columbia

Wood with traces of paint
2 x 23⁵/8 x 3¹/8 in.
Canadian Museum of Civilization,
Hull, Quebec (no. VII-B-81)

The Haida obtained their major sustenance from the ocean, although the
roots and berries they gathered were
also an important part of their diet.
Halibut, salmon, shellfish, and marine
animals were extremely important to
their economy. They used a variety of
harpoons, hooks, and nets for fishing.
Once sea lions and seals had been har-
pooned, they were hauled up to the
canoe, where they were dispatched
with a club and either hauled aboard
or towed behind to shore. This long
club appears to represent a sea lion
with small human faces carved on its
body. The blending of the human figure in the mouth and on the snout of
the sea lion is particularly masterful.

142 *opposite, bottom*
Antler Club
Tsimshian
Probably eighteenth century, Nass
and Skeena river basins, north coast
of British Columbia

Caribou or elk antler
4³/4 x 16³/4 in.
The Menil Collection, Houston
(no. X 140)

Numerous objects of this type exist
and are believed to be weapons based
on Athapaskan club types made of
caribou antler. Historic accounts indicate that they were war clubs, though
they were evidently also used for
killing slaves when high-ranking chiefs
chose to demonstrate their disdain for
wealth by destroying or giving away
their property. Some such clubs appear to have had metal points attached
to the end of the protruding arm
below the carved head. Judging from
the degree of wear and polish on this
example, it was probably handed
down from generation to generation,
identifying all its owners as members
of the same clan or secret society.

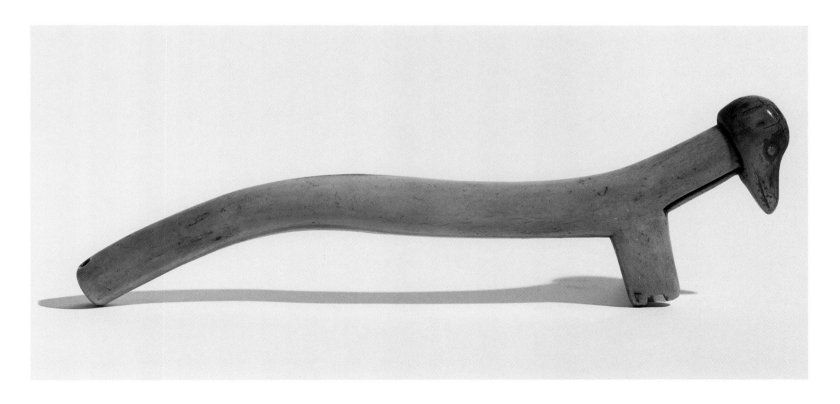

143
Toothed Club
Tlingit or Haida
c. 1880–1910, southeast Alaska or
Queen Charlotte Islands, British
Columbia

Wood with bear teeth
24⅝ x 2½ x 6¼ in.
Peabody Museum of Archaeology
and Ethnology, Harvard University,
Cambridge, Massachusetts (acquired
by the museum, H. F. Wollcott & Au-
gustus Hemenway Funds, 1914,
no. 14-27-10/85889)

Carved in the style of the late nineteenth century, this unusual club may
have originally been a common
wooden fish or seal club that was
"dressed up" with the addition of a
row of bear teeth inlaid on the edge.
This may have been done to make the
object more appealing to a curio
buyer, since by this time, for all practical purposes, traditional warfare had
ceased. The two-dimensional compositions on this club lack many traditional characteristics, which indicates
that this club was carved in the period
when artistic conventions, particularly
the two-dimensional variety, were no
longer being conveyed in the master-
apprentice tradition. This breakdown
in tradition was largely the result of
the devastating epidemics of the nineteenth century, as well as the strong
pressures from the dominant cultures
to marginalize and assimilate Native
peoples. Such policies nearly brought
an end to Northwest Coast cultures as
they were known, though most cultural
institutions (with the major exception
of traditional languages) have seen
enough of a revival in the last quarter
century to now be assured of survival.

144 *opposite, top*
Hunting Hat
Yup'ik
Collected c. 1868–85, Lower Yukon,
Alaska

Wood with ivory, sinew, and root
7⅞ x 13⅜ x 14⅛ in.
Canadian Museum of Civilization,
Hull, Quebec (no. IV-E-91)

These hats, which date back more than
2,000 years, were used by Inupiaq
hunters of the Bering Sea as status
symbols, indicating their rank, and to
protect their faces. Made from a single
piece of driftwood by thinning, steam-
ing, and bending the plank into this
conical form, they were decorated
with pieces of ivory carved into a traditional variety of shapes. Some were
marked with spiral carvings, the significance of which is largely unknown,
and others were carved in the shape of
animal heads or bodies, which were
intended to magically assist in the
hunt. The Aleutian-style hats, which
differed in proportion and decoration
from these, were sometimes called
"clamshells" due to their shape. The
hats used by the Yup'ik of the Lower
Yukon and Norton Sound area were
more conical in shape and painted
only with overall color or simple forms.

145 *opposite, bottom*
Hunting Visor
Inupiaq
Collected c. 1868–85, Norton Sound,
Alaska

Painted wood with ivory, cordage, and
feathers
6⅛ x 19⅞ x 10¼ in.
Canadian Museum of Civilization,
Hull, Quebec (no. IV-E-90)

Like the hunting hats, bentwood visors
were used by the hunters of sea mammals in the Bering Sea and Aleutian
Islands to protect their eyes from the
glare of the sun, while also providing
a symbol of status and rank. Although
they all served the same purpose, their
form varied according to region. Visors
from the Norton Sound area are generally flat with rounded edges and
often display a handful of feathers at
the back. Those from the Aleutians
are somewhat longer, painted with different colored designs, and decorated
with abundant sea lion whiskers.
Both visor styles are often decorated
with ivory inserts in the form of side
plaques or carved animals mounted
on the front surface.

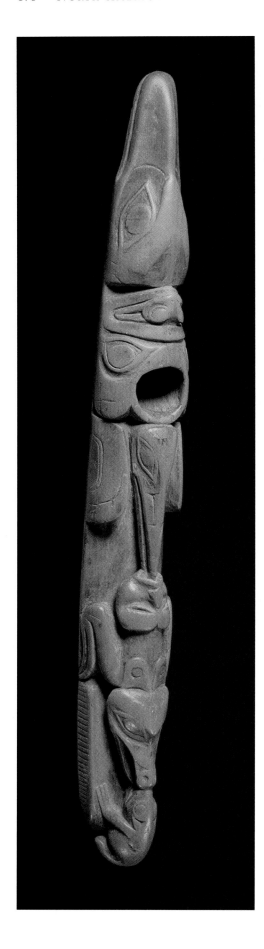

146
Throwing Board (*Atlatl*)
Tlingit
c. 1750–1810, southeast Alaska

Yew
14 in., length
Private collection, New York

Tlingit throwing boards are most likely shamanic objects rather than true throwing boards, like those used by the Pacific Yup'ik (see cat. no. 84). Because they were used symbolically to battle the evil spirits that caused misfortune, illness, and chaos, the images of the spirits represented were more important than the functionality of the weapons themselves. The transformational nature of the imagery in this example, which includes several kinds of shamanic conventions, readily demonstrates its spiritual connections. The frog in the mouth of the bearlike image, the bird's beak joined with the mouth of the humanoid face, the blending of that face with the wolflike image, and the land otter image whose mouth is joined with that of the wolf are all examples of shamanic representations. Very few Tlingit throwing boards have survived to the present day, and those that have appear to have been created in the eighteenth or very early nineteenth centuries. The carvings on this particular throwing board indicate that its origin was in the very early historic period or perhaps even before Euro-American arrival on the Northwest Coast.

147
Throwing Board (*Atlatl*)
Tlingit
Pre-eighteenth century, southeast Alaska

Wood with abalone shell
13½ in., length
André Nasser Collection, New York

Although throwing boards date back more than 5,000 years and were used from Australia to Mexico, in areas where they were called *atlatl*, they remain one of the least well-known weapons. Throwing boards extended the leverage action of the hunter's forearm, increasing the arrow's speed and range. They were commonly used by the Alaskan Yup'ik and the Alutiiq, who preferred them to bows and arrows. Because only one hand was needed to operate them, they had an important advantage when hunting from kayaks. The throwing boards produced by the Tlingit were delicately carved with their traditional two-dimensional and sculptural motifs; however, their "functional" aspects were minimal. They were not used as true weapons but were employed symbolically by shamans as weapons against malevolent spirits. The sculpture and design of this unusual *atlatl* suggest that it is a very early example, perhaps made generations prior to the arrival of Euro-Americans in the beginning of the historic period.

148
Ceremonial Club
Kwakwaka'wakw (Kwakiutl)
c. 1850–70, north end of Vancouver
Island and adjacent mainland

Wood with abalone shell and human
hair
14⅛ x 9¼ x 2⅜ in.
Canadian Museum of Civilization,
Hull, Quebec (no. VII-E-56)

The Kwakwaka'wakw winter ceremonies included numerous rituals
and demonstrations of the power of
supernatural beings and the ancestors'
contacts with them. These ritual performances were among the most elaborate on the entire Northwest Coast.
Masked figures, known as *Nuhlamahla*
(literally, Fool-Dancers), were in charge
of maintaining the strict rules of these

rituals, insulting and reprimanding
anyone who violated protocols. In ancient times, violators were even killed,
evidently with clubs like the one
shown here: the terrifying appearance
reflects its function. By the late nineteenth century, weapons such as this
and the threat of their use had become
symbolic rather than actual.

149 *opposite, left*
Wood in the Shape of a "Copper"
Kwakwa̱ka̱'wakw (Kwakiutl)
Collected 1905, Vancouver Island,
British Columbia

Painted wood
50 x 20 in.
Brooklyn Museum of Art (museum
expedition, 1905, no. 08.491.8895)

Coppers are highly valued objects that
represent a concentrated amount of
wealth. Among the Kwakwa̱ka̱'wakw,
coppers would be cut (they used the
term "broken") and the pieces given to
rivals in order to intimidate "lower"
chiefs with the power of wealth.
Coppers were bought and sold by the
chiefs of family lines when they were
raising monies to distribute at potlatch
occasions. This object is a copper
made of wood, featuring the image of
a bird, possibly the *Kolus*, one of the
names given to the thunderbirds of
the Kwakwa̱ka̱'wakw. The head and
downturned beak are at the top of the
design field, the feet and talons are
below the head, and the wings are
on each side below the characteristic
T-shaped ridge that is referred to as
the "backbone" of the copper. Each
important copper had a name that was
known and respected by the community. This wooden version may have
been made to place on the grave of a
deceased chief to represent one of the
coppers he had owned in his lifetime.

150 *opposite, right*
Saayeina.aat
Double-Whale Dagger
Tlingit
c. 1750–90, southeast Alaska

Steel with cloth and leather
19¹/₂ x 3⁷/₈ in.
Private collection, New York

This metal dagger has a swiftly taper-
ing, double-edged, ribbed blade end-
ing in a blunt point. The hammered
and engraved pommel is in the shape
of an emblematic whale. Drilled holes
simulate the spaces between the teeth.
This very old piece of metalwork is
one of at least two daggers made by
the same Tlingit metalsmith, a woman
named Saayeina.aat, who is said to
have used iron from a meteorite. Prior
to Euro-American arrival in the area,
the Northwest Coast peoples obtained
metal from Asian shipwrecks, Native
trade routes from California, or the
Bering Strait. In the post-contact period, they obtained iron and steel (as
well as copper) through trading for
metal objects and tools, which they
usually transformed into their familiar
styles by forging and cold-working.

151
"Copper"
Haida
End of nineteenth century, Skidegate,
Queen Charlotte Islands, British
Columbia

Painted sheet copper
29³/₄ x 22¹/₄ x 1³/₄ in.
Brooklyn Museum of Art
(no. 16.749.1)

Objects like this were used exclusively
on the Northwest Coast. Made of
sheets of copper that have been cut
and decorated in a special way, each

work had its own name and was one
of the most valuable objects that could
be given away at a potlatch. In 1882,
Johan Adrian Jacobsen described the
price of $4,000 for a copper similar to
the one shown here, which indicates
just how valuable these objects were.
The figure depicted here is a bear, its
form defined by softly rounded and
delicately composed formlines in
black. Such an image invested the
copper's owner not only with the animal's power but also with the prestige
belonging to it as a clan emblem.

152
Feast Ladle
Northern Northwest Coast People
c. 1850–80, southeast Alaska or north
British Columbia coast

Wood
25½ in., length
Museum für Völkerkunde, Vienna
(no. 51.664)

This large spoon or ladle is made of
a single piece of wood, with a sculptured frog on the handle. The frog
was a clan emblem in several northern
Northwest Coast First Nations, and
the carving here indicates that this
ladle was owned by a member of one
of those clans for use at potlatch ceremonies. Among the Tlingit, the frog is
an emblem of raven-moiety clans,
while among the Haida, it is the emblem of eagle-side clans. The frog was
also among the animals that appeared
to the shaman and gave him esoteric
information about the supernatural,
though such functions did not preclude
the status and importance of the frog
as a clan crest emblem. Large ladles
like this were used to serve fish or seal
oil and other foods to guests, whose
well-being was the responsibility of
the hosting clan. The oil residue left
in the bowl of this ladle attests to its
traditional use.

153
Ladle with Skull
Heiltsuk (Bella Bella)
Collected 1905, central coast of British
Columbia

Painted wood with bear hide
28 x 9 x 7⅞ in.
Brooklyn Museum of Art (museum
expedition, 1905, no. 05.588.7297)

The Heiltsuk are known for their over-
the-top artistic styles and for the wide
range of mythological creatures that
were represented in their masks, house
posts, and dance paraphernalia. A
large wooden ladle like this, boldly
embellished with carved skulls, was
most likely used in the Cannibal (*Tanis*)
Society initiation ceremonies. According to Charles Newcombe, who collected the ladle shown here, it was
probably used for the symbolic feeding
of human beings to the cannibal initiate.

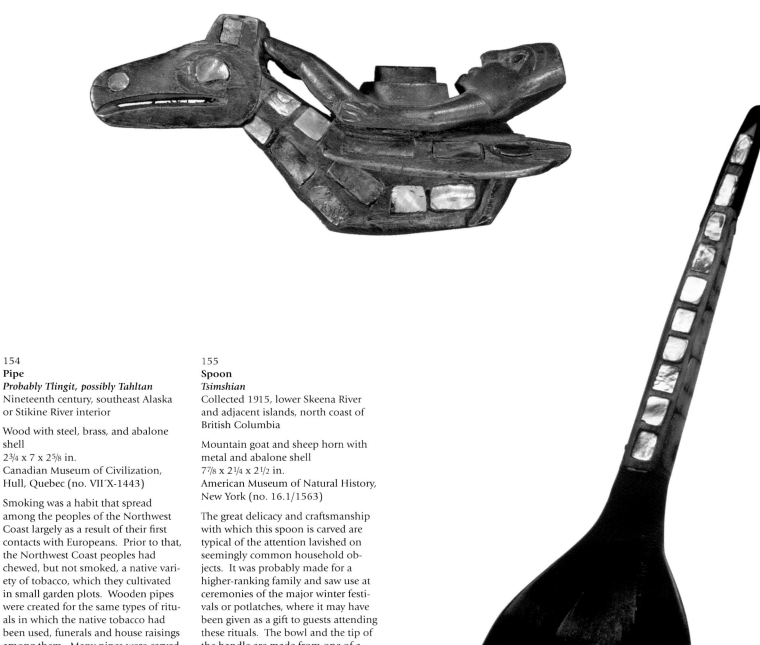

154
Pipe
Probably Tlingit, possibly Tahltan
Nineteenth century, southeast Alaska
or Stikine River interior

Wood with steel, brass, and abalone
shell
2³/4 x 7 x 2⁵/8 in.
Canadian Museum of Civilization,
Hull, Quebec (no. VII´X-1443)

Smoking was a habit that spread
among the peoples of the Northwest
Coast largely as a result of their first
contacts with Europeans. Prior to that,
the Northwest Coast peoples had
chewed, but not smoked, a native variety of tobacco, which they cultivated
in small garden plots. Wooden pipes
were created for the same types of rituals in which the native tobacco had
been used, funerals and house raisings
among them. Many pipes were carved
from sections of musket stocks obtained in trade, and some incorporated a short piece of the gun barrel as
the bowl. In this way, the powers associated with the weapons were transferred to the pipes. The human figure
lying on its back in this pipe, which
features a metal-lined pipe bowl, is
reminiscent of raven rattle forms
(see cat. no. 136).

155
Spoon
Tsimshian
Collected 1915, lower Skeena River
and adjacent islands, north coast of
British Columbia

Mountain goat and sheep horn with
metal and abalone shell
7⁷/8 x 2¹/4 x 2¹/2 in.
American Museum of Natural History,
New York (no. 16.1/1563)

The great delicacy and craftsmanship
with which this spoon is carved are
typical of the attention lavished on
seemingly common household objects. It was probably made for a
higher-ranking family and saw use at
ceremonies of the major winter festivals or potlatches, where it may have
been given as a gift to guests attending
these rituals. The bowl and the tip of
the handle are made from one of a
pair of mountain goat horns, with a
narrow piece of mountain sheep horn
used to add length to the handle. The
ten pieces of abalone shell add their
jewellike quality to this fine spoon,
which was acquired in 1915 by George
T. Emmons. Emmons assembled several collections of Northwest Coast art,
consisting of more than 5,000 objects,
which he made available to major
museums across North America.

156
Bowl in the Form of a Bird
Heiltsuk or Haisla
Nineteenth century, north British Columbia and adjacent islands

Wood with abalone shell
5 1/8 x 13 x 6 5/8 in.
Laboratoire d'Ethnologie, Musée de l'Homme, Paris (no. MH 47.47.1)

A single piece of wood is carved in the shape of a raven, with the central part of the body hollowed out for use as a bowl. The large ovoid-shaped eyes are inlaid with pieces of abalone shell. Bowls like this sometimes contained the food served to guests, or they were used to hold fish or seal oil, which was much appreciated as a condiment and preserving agent. *Eulachon* (or candle-fish) oil was also used to stoke the fire and make the flames roar; by showing disregard for its value as a sign of wealth, this was thought to increase the host's prestige. The thin formlines and abundantly detailed designs on this bowl are indicative of mid nineteenth-century Heiltsuk or Haisla work.

157
Bowl
Haida
Nineteenth century, southeast Alaska and Queen Charlotte Islands, British Columbia

Wood
4 1/2 x 6 1/8 x 7 in.
Laboratoire d'Ethnologie, Musée de l'Homme, Paris (no. MH 85.78.27)

Bowls like this were used to hold the various foods and fish or seal oils consumed at potlatch ceremonies. One of the most appreciated foods was salmon, which was either dried or smoked in various styles for preserva-tion. The salmon's flavor was enhanced with widely traded candlefish oil, which was served in bowls like this elegantly shaped example. The high, upswept ends and low sides are, of course, re-lated to the forms of Northwest Coast canoes, and the raised ridges on the inside are thought to be related to the structural folds of birch-bark containers from the Native peoples of the interior of Alaska and British Columbia.

158
Bowl in the Shape of a Frog
Tlingit
c. 1860–1900, southeast Alaska

Wood with copper and abalone shell
5³⁄4 x 8¹⁄4 x 10 in.
Peabody Museum of Archaeology
and Ethnology, Harvard University,
Cambridge, Massachusetts (donated
by Lewis H. Farlow, 1980, no. 73135)

Bowls and ladles used in Northwest
Coast feasts and ceremonies were decorated with the clan's symbols and
emblems, as is the case of this bowl
in the shape of a frog. Additional
embellishments, such as copper, were
intended to display the wealth of their
owners. The abundant use of copper
sheet obtained in trade, valued since
ancient times, testifies to the gradual
changes that took place in Northwest
Coast art following European contact.
In this unusual bowl, collected by
Nicholson, copper sheet has been used
to cover the rim and most of the limbs
and eyebrows of the frog, while bright
abalone shell, also acquired in trade,
highlights the eyes, nostrils, and mouth.

159
Ceremonial Bowl
Kwakw̱aka'wakw (Kwakiutl)
c. 1860–90, Fort Rupert, north
Vancouver Island and adjacent
mainland

Wood with opercula and shell
22³/₈ x 14¹/₂ x 16¹/₂ in.
American Museum of Natural History,
New York (no. 16/8573)

This elaborately designed bowl used in
the major winter ceremonies was acquired from George Hunt in 1901. He
described the principal carved motif as
a representation of a wolf whose tail,
in accordance with the conventions of
Northwest Coast art, has been transformed into an eagle, creating a double image. Franz Boas interpreted this
common image as a grizzly bear-eagle,
but its full meaning and significance
has not yet been definitely identified.
The eyes and the edge of the bowl are
inlaid with opercula, a valuable object
of trade obtained from the red turban
marine snail that was frequently
used to decorate ceremonial objects
produced by the Kwakw̱aka'wakw
(formerly known as Kwakiutl).

160
Bowl
Tlingit or Haida
c. 1700, southeast Alaska or Queen
Charlotte Islands, British Columbia

Spruce
6 x 8¼ x 13 in.
Private collection, New York

The carving on this oval bowl combines the forms of a frog and a bird.
The archaic design, the simplicity of
the sculpture, and the dark patina of
grease all indicate that this bowl is
very old and was probably produced
before Euro-Americans arrived on the
Northwest Coast. The seven subtle
grooves surrounding the rim of the
bowl are a particularly elegant finishing touch. The sheer delicacy with

which the frog and bird heads, and the
subtly relief-carved limbs of each creature are defined is one of the most remarkable aspects of this outstanding
container. Sitka spruce is a common
tree on the northern Northwest Coast
and one that carves quite beautifully,
though it is seldom recognized and
identified in ethnographic or art historical literature. Like certain hard-
woods, such as alder wood or maple,
spruce does not impart a strong flavor
to food, as does red or yellow cedar.

161
Serving Spool
Nuu-chah-nulth/Makah
Eighteenth or early nineteenth
century, west coast of Vancouver Island
and northwest Washington

Wood
17 in., length
André Nasser Collection, New York

This is a very unusual object. The
faces at each end are carved in an archaic style that indicates the spool is
probably very old. Similar wooden
spools in certain museum collections
have been identified as serving spools.
These were used to tightly wind a
small diameter cord around the leader
of a whale harpoon line, usually a
stout (⅝ inch diameter) twisted sinew

rope, to protect the sinew surface from
wear. Several such wooden spools
were excavated from the Ozette archaeological site on the north coast of
Washington state. Entombed at this
site are parts of five houses that were
inundated by a catastrophic mudslide
between 300 and 500 years ago. The
Makah artifacts discovered there have
illuminated the historical record on
pre-contact Northwest Coast life.

162
Mortar
Haida
Nineteenth century, Queen Charlotte
Islands, north coast of British Columbia

Whale vertebra
6⅞ x 13¾ x 13 in.
Laboratoire d'Ethnologie, Musée de
l'Homme, Paris (no. MH 38.175.1)

This mortar, made from the vertebra
of a whale, is decorated with the head
of a bird. The fins of the vertebra were
used to make a symmetrical axial design. The mortar was probably used
to prepare the tobacco mixture consumed by the Haida as snuff. Even
before the Europeans arrived, *nicotiana
quadrivalvis* was cultivated in small
plots, to be mixed with lime and then
chewed. It was only after seeing Euro-
American sailors smoking tobacco in
pipes at the end of the eighteenth century that the Northwest Coast people
began making pipes for smoking the
herb.

163
Bowl
Tlingit
Nineteenth century, southeast Alaska

Painted wood
6 x 11⅜ in.
Laboratoire d'Ethnologie, Musée de
l'Homme, Paris (no. MH 82 30 23)

This semispherical wooden bowl has
an unusually executed formline design
wrapped about its circumference. The
use of red color in the ovoid-shaped
forms is not common, though it occasionally appears to better balance the
distribution of color overall. Designs
of this type are often ambiguous as to
the representation of specific clan emblems. Clans are groups, identified by
emblematic animals, that constitute
one's political, social, and ceremonial
life, inherited along the maternal line.
The relationship with emblematic animals originated when an ancestor had
a supernatural encounter with a particular animal. The symbol of this animal was then used by the family in the
most important objects it produced,
such as bowls like this.

164
Box
Haida
Nineteenth century, Queen Charlotte Islands, north coast of British Columbia

Painted cedar
22¼ x 18⅛ x 17⅜ in.
Canadian Museum of Civilization, Hull, Quebec (no.VII-B-1276)

Made of cedar and decorated with typical northern Northwest Coast paintings, this box uses primary formlines that are dark, curving, and of varying width, while the secondary formlines are red. Ovoid-shaped elements predominate and are the conceptual "centers" of design areas from which U-shapes and other design movements emanate and intermingle. The artist that painted this box was a design master who used inventive junctures and unusual compositions to fill out the sides of this container with paintings that flow smoothly and elegantly about the surface. This artist followed certain design conventions and yet improvised with innovative ideas of his own. The four sides of this kind of box are made of a single plank of wood—three corners are specially kerfed, or notched, and then the board is steamed and bent to form the box. The bottom is shaped and fitted, then pegged or sewn to the lower edge. The lid of this box is missing, but one would have been made of a thick plank that was hollowed out (to make it lighter and less susceptible to cracking) and fitted to the upper edge.

165
Box
Tlingit or Haida
Collected 1896, Queen Charlotte
Islands, British Columbia and south-
east Alaska

Painted wood with fiber
12¼ x 11⅜ x 14⅛ in.
American Museum of Natural History,
New York (no. 16/1122, Bishop,
1869-90-94)

This wooden box featuring four
painted bas-relief panels illustrates an
early style of the conventionalized,
zoomorphic figures of the Northwest
Coast. The comparatively thick formlines and very simple red design areas
are indicative of northern Northwest
Coast styles of the early historic period.
The design arrangement is like the previous one (cat. no. 164) with profile
designs on each panel of the box.
When the box is viewed from the corner, the profiles come together in the
frontal view of a formline-style face.
The arrangement of motifs is repeated
on the other two panels. This box was
collected by S. Kirschberg in 1896.

166 a & b *opposite, top and bottom*
Box Panels
Coastal Tsimshian or Haisla
c. 1850–70, north coast of British
Columbia

Painted red cedar
16 x 28 in.
Private collection, New York

The artists of the Northwest Coast decorated objects with designs that are
symbolic representations of animals,
birds, heavenly bodies, or other emblems of the owner's clan. They also
depict his lineage, wealth, and status.
Wide chests of this type were used to
store the ceremonial objects used in
potlatch ceremonies. This particular

design is painted in one of the most
inventive and unique styles known to
any northern Northwest Coast artist.
In this composition, unusually wide,
black primary formlines are combined
with untypically narrow red, or secondary, formlines, with additional
unusual touches like the red-on-black
hands painted in the lower corners of
one panel. Certain individuals of the
mid nineteenth century struck out in
inventive new directions that were
quite different from the conventional
paths blazed by their predecessors.

167 a & b *opposite, top and bottom*
Box Panels
Tlingit
c. 1750–1820, southeast Alaska

Painted red cedar or spruce
12¾ x 25¾ x 15¾ in.
Private collection, New York

These carved and painted panels are fine examples of bas-relief carving in the archaic Tlingit style. The work of an inspired artist who used the layout of more traditional designs while introducing some original personal touches, the panels alternate fine incised lines with other wider and deeper carved out areas that form the outline of the painted images. A human face is depicted on each of the long panels, and beneath it is what

may be the front view of a bird, whose beak appears in the center of the panel between the two eyes. Rectangular U-shapes are used to represent its feathers on one side, while on the other the legs and talons of the bird are shown. This box may have been made to hold a shaman's paraphernalia, which would be protected from uninitiated eyes by the fierce looking faces carved in each panel.

168
Box Drum
Kwakwaka'wakw (Kwakiutl)
Collected 1898, southeast Alaska

Painted wood
29 x 17 x 33⅜ in.
Canadian Museum of Civilization, Hull, Quebec (no. VII-E-50)

This large percussion instrument made of wood has four painted surfaces, one panel of which is decorated with a black, red, and green thunderbird design. Box drums were made in the same bent-corner techniques as were boxes, chests, and certain bulging dishes. Their low, bass drumlike sound was used to accompany the wooden plank drums and deerskin-covered tambourine-style drums that

punctuated the rhythms of traditional songs. This one is unusual, being painted with the opening oriented upward—most northern Northwest Coast box drums have the opening on one side rather than on the top. This Kwakwaka'wakw painting has visible influences from both the historic northern Northwest Coast formline tradition and the southern proto-Northwest Coast style, which predates the development of the formline design conventions. If the drum was in fact collected in southeast Alaska, it must have arrived there as a result of trade, as several hundred miles lie between Alaska and the Kwakwaka'wakw homelands of Vancouver Island.

169
Hat
Tlingit
c. 1830–60, southeast Alaska

Painted spruce roots
12¼ in., diameter
Private collection, New York

Unlike older, eighteenth-century painted compositions for Tlingit hats, where the decoration was concentrated in the upper half of the hat surface, this beautifully composed and executed painting extends over the entire hat from crown to brim. On the front of the hat is a face with two large ovoid eyes and a wide mouth, inside

of which is a human face with outstretched hands. Two human profiles are painted in the ovoids that appear on each side of the hat near the edge, positioned like pectoral fins. Behind them, painted in red formlines, are the bodies, arms, and legs. The overall design probably depicts a sea monster myth that is part of a clan history. The clan caretakers so highly valued and respected such hats that they were sometimes kept in specially woven covers, shaped like the hats themselves in a simpler weave, and passed down from generation to generation.

170
Shaman's Cape
Tlingit
c. 1750–1820, southeast Alaska

Painted moose or deer hide
38 x 26¼ in.
Private collection, New York

This rare, well-preserved shaman's garment is painted with clearly defined, archaic-style designs that contrast sharply with the color of the hide. The partly symmetrical design is outlined in wide black lines with a few secondary touches of red. On the longest part of the cape is the face of a spirit being within whose jaws appear

human arms and legs rendered in red. A red, headless human figure also appears between two profiles of creatures with spiral-shaped nostrils and long mouths filled with teeth. The paintings may represent emissaries from the spirit world, who reveal to the shaman the causes of illness and enable him to predict the future, or they could be portrayals of the shaman himself in his flight toward the supernatural world.

171
Hat
Tlingit or Haida
c. 1750–80, southeast Alaska or Queen Charlotte Islands, north coast of British Columbia

Painted spruce roots
12¼ in., diameter
Private collection, New York

Fiber arts, such as basket, hat, and fabric weaving, were the purview of women artists on the Northwest Coast. Spruce roots are harvested, peeled, and finely split into materials from which beautifully woven baskets and hats like this one are created over a period of weeks. Traditional gender roles left carving and painting to the men of the village who were trained in those arts. This painted design, done by a male artist, portrays a whale defined with black formlines. There are no secondary formlines *per se*, though there are "tertiary" areas that are painted with a greenish blue, which comes from celadonite, an iron ore. The crown is enhanced with a four-pointed star design. The similarity of this form to hats illustrated by European artists at the end of the eighteenth century indicate that this beautifully woven hat is very old.

172
Hat
Haida
Collected c. 1867–68, southeast Alaska
or Queen Charlotte Islands, north
coast of British Columbia

Painted spruce roots
7³/₈ x 14¹/₂ x 14¹/₂ in.
Peabody Museum of Archaeology
and Ethnology, Harvard University,
Cambridge, Massachusetts (no.
69.30.10/2159)

The truncated cone-shaped hats made
from spruce roots and painted with
emblematic designs usually belonged
to the nobility, the high-ranking families of a Northwest Coast community.
These hats illustrate the division of
labor by gender: they were woven by
women and painted by men, sometimes as a husband and wife team.
This very fine and smoothly woven hat
is of the tall, mid nineteenth-century
style in shape, and it is decorated with
a very open design that leaves a lot of

background showing around the
painted forms. This style of composition is common on Haida hats of the
second half of the nineteenth century.
The photograph is of the rear center of
the hat design, the part that is in red
formlines; the head of the design is
done in black primary formlines.

173 & 174
Set of House Posts
Nuxalk (Bella Coola), Talibo village
Late nineteenth century, near Dean and Burke channels, central coast of British Columbia

Red cedar
78³/4 x 23⁵/8 x 23⁵/8 in.
83 x 27¹/2 x 23⁵/8 in.
Canadian Museum of Civilization, Hull, Quebec (nos. VII-D-401 and VII-D-402)

This set of posts supported the main roof beams of a Nuxalk house. They were carved from two sections of a cedar tree and depict grizzly bears. The tops of the posts are slightly concave to hold the horizontal beams in place. The bears are seated on their hind legs with their front legs drawn up and the paws facing outward. The houses of the Nuxalk (also called Bella Coola), the Kwakwaka'wakw, and the northern Nuu-chah-nulth (also called Nootka) were rectangular with low-peaked gable roofs, which were topped with large, split and adzed cedar roof planks. Because the grizzly bear was a symbol of great power and authority, these posts probably belonged to a chief's house, referring to the origin story of the owner of the house and his family lineage.

175
Fragment of a Totem Pole
Tsimshian
Collected 1926, Prince Rupert area,
north coast of British Columbia

Red cedar
14¹/₈ x 66¹/₂ x 24 in.
Canadian Museum of Civilization,
Hull, Quebec (no. VII-X-331)

The first Europeans to reach the Northwest Coast in the eighteenth century
reported the existence of totem poles
inside Native houses (see cat. no. 28).
They were rarely seen outside of the
houses except on the northern Northwest Coast, especially among the
Haida, whose houses were sometimes
entered through the mouth or stomach
of the animals depicted on the poles.
This sculpture was once part of a larger

monument, though exactly which
monument and what its purpose was
have not been recorded. The unusual
face appears to represent an anthropomorphic fish, or perhaps a whale, if
the two square mortises on the back
were for supporting a dorsal fin. On
the sides, sculptured pectoral fins are
embellished with relief-carved two-
dimensional designs composed like a
profile face.

176
Totem or Figure of an Orator
Kwakwa̱ka'wakw (Kwakiutl)
Collected 1905, Smith Inlet, British Columbia

Painted wood
116 in., height
Brooklyn Museum of Art (museum expedition, 1905, no. 05.588.7418)

This large sculpture portrays an orator during a potlatch ceremony. Traditional oration was a highly developed art, equal to that of a traditional singer or dancer. It took a lifetime of training and practice to speak in the special dialects of the Native languages that were reserved for ceremonial events. A sculpture of this type is rare, only a few having survived from the late nineteenth century. The image represents the ancestry of the family lineage, and when an orator made his speech from behind the image, speaking through its mouth, it was the accumulated power of the hereditary family line that was believed to be speaking. Some of these figures are carved with the speaker's hands held up on either side of the speaking mouth.

177
Dance Curtain
Nuu-chah-nulth (Nootka)
c. 1880–95, Nitinat Lake

Painted cotton fabric
81 x 247 in.
The Menil Collection, Houston
(no. 71-44 DJ)

Painted (and sometimes carved in relief) interior house screens are an ancient tradition among Nuu-chah-nulth and Makah communities, as well as elsewhere on the Northwest Coast. House screens incised with thunderbird, whale, and serpent images that are several centuries old were recovered from the Ozette archaeological site on the coast of Washington. Toward the end of the nineteenth century, Nuu-chah-nulth ritualists began to use house screens painted on cloth instead of the adzed wooden boards employed

in the past. Cloth "curtains" were easier to transport and keep hidden from Indian agents who were charged by the government with eliminating Native ceremonial and religious activity. The artist who painted the smoothly flowing, interconnected red, black, and blue formlines of this image drew from both older Nuu-chah-nulth design styles and certain northern formline traditions, combining the two in powerful movements representative of the potent forces of the natural world. The lively and energetic creatures represented

in this painting include a baleen whale, in whose body two wolf images can be seen, and a thunderbird, above the broadly spanning wings of which are two serpents. The serpents' bodies are composed to fill the more or less triangular shapes in the "sky field" of the design. The remaining space is completed by free-form designs in red, one section of which contains a right-angle corner with an inward "crease" very reminiscent of a bent-corner box kerf. This curtain was collected by Howard Roloff in 1975.

GLOSSARY OF TERMS

ALEUT
One of the two branches of the Inuit-Aleut language family that covers the entire Arctic cultural area. Spoken in the extreme west of the Alaskan Peninsula and throughout the entire Aleutian Islands chain, it is divided into two main dialects: Eastern Aleut, spoken from the western Alaskan Peninsula to Amukta Island, and Western Aleut, spoken from Seguam Island to the Commander Islands in the Russian Federation. Aleut speakers and inhabitants of the Aleutian Islands and the western part of the Alaskan Peninsula, all of whom share the same cultural model and history, are called Aleuts or Aleutians.

ALUTIIQ/SUTPIAQ
The name used since 1982 to designate both the Pacific Yup'ik language and the Pacific Yup'ik peoples (Koniag and Chugach).

BELLA BELLA
See Heiltsuk. Bella Bella is the name formerly applied to the Heiltsuk nation and the settlement now known by the Heiltsuk name of Waglisla.

BELLA COOLA
See Nuxalk. Bella Coola is the name derived from the Kwakwala language that was formerly applied to the Nuxalk nation. Bella Coola continues to be the name of a river and a town.

CHILKAT
A band of the northern Tlingit that lives around the Chilkat River at the head of Lynn Canal. Their name has been applied to the style of weaving seen in beautiful ceremonial blankets and aprons, the original techniques for which were invented by Tsimshian women in the eighteenth century. The blankets were produced from thigh-spun yellow cedar bark fiber and mountain goat wool. Male artists painted symbolic designs on a "pattern board" that served as the guide for the women's design work. In the middle of the nineteenth century, privileges obtained through marriage transactions enabled the Kwakwaka'wakw to start making and using these blankets, which have long been prized possessions displayed by chiefs on ceremonial occasions.

CHINOOK
Native people and language family derived from the Penutian trunk. Chinook speakers lived on the Pacific coast between Willapa Bay in Washington state and Tillamook Point in Oregon, and on both banks of the Columbia River from its mouth to past the point where it joins with the Willamette River. Lower Chinook was the basis of Chinook jargon, a lingua franca widely spoken on the entire Northwest Coast during the nineteenth and early twentieth centuries.

CHUGACH
A band or tribe of the Pacific Yup'ik. The two main Pacific Yup'ik bands are the Chugach and Koniag. The Chugach live in the territory surrounding Prince William Sound in southern Alaska.

CHUKCHI
Ethnic band located in a broad area in the extreme northeast of Siberia on both sides of the Arctic Circle, between the Bering and Chukchi seas and eastern Siberia. Their language belongs to the large paleosiberian group, and their culture is closely related to the Koriak culture. Although the word *Chukchi* is used to refer to the entire nation, it means "rich in reindeer" and actually applies only to the band that inhabits the interior. The coastal band refers to itself as "the sea people," and both bands refer to themselves collectively as *luoravetlan*, or "the true people." The inland Chukchi not only are hunters but also tend reindeer.

COAST SALISH
Native nation made up of a greatly varied number of Salish-speaking groups. The Salishan language family consists of twenty-three languages, sixteen of which are spoken in the Northwest Coast area; the others are located in the interior of the states of Washington, Idaho, and Montana, and the province of British Columbia. In the coastal region, the Coast Salish nation is traditionally divided into three groups. The northern Coast Salish are settled on the southeastern coast of Vancouver Island and the adjacent mainland near Georgia Strait in British Columbia. Among their linguistic and cultural divisions are Comox, Pentlatch, and Sechelt. The central Coast Salish are located around the southern tip of Vancouver Island, the islands of Georgia and Juan de Fuca straits, the lower Fraser River valley, and adjacent areas in Washington state. Among their linguistic-cultural divisions are Squamish, Halkomelem, Nooksack, Northern Straits, and S'Klallam. The southern Coast Salish are settled around Puget Sound in Washington state. Among their linguistic-cultural divisions are Lushootsed and Twana. The southwestern Coast Salish are settled on the Pacific coast of Washington state between the Hoh River and Willapa Bay. Among their linguistic-cultural divisions are Queets, Quinault, and Chehalis.

ESKIMO
Eskimo means "eater of raw meat" and was used by neighboring tribes to designate the Native peoples of the entire Arctic region.

EYAK
Native people and language of the Eyak-Athapascan family, whose speakers lived on the southern coast of Alaska between Prince William Sound and Yakutat Bay. At the end of the eighteenth century, they were at least partially absorbed by the Tlingit, in the area of Controller Bay and south toward Yakutat Bay. Their culture is more akin to the Chugach than the Tlingit of the Northwest Coast culture region.

GITKSAN
Native people of the Northwest Coast. One of the principal divisions of the Tsimshian language family, they are found dwelling on the middle and upper parts of the Skeena River in northern British Columbia. In many publications, they are generically called Tsimshian, of which their language is a subtype.

HAIDA
Native people and language of the Northwest Coast. They live on the Queen Charlotte Islands in British Columbia and on the southern coast of Prince of Wales Island, Alaska, where they are known as Kaigani Haida. The Haida language is not related to any other known language.

HAIHAIS

Native people of the Northwest Coast who inhabit the northern coast of British Columbia in Milbank Sound and further inland around Finlayson and Marthieson channels. Their language is Heiltsuk, which belongs to the northern branch of the Wakashan family. In most traditional literature, the Haihais, Haisla, Heiltsuk, and Owekeeno are grouped together under the general name of northern Kwakiutl. They all belong to the same linguistic family, but they have different sociocultural characteristics.

HAISLA

Native people of the Northwest Coast, located in northern British Columbia near the upper part of Douglas Channel and around Gardner Channel. Their language is part of the northern branch of the Wakashan family.

HEILTSUK

Native people of the Northwest Coast who inhabit the northern coast of British Columbia between Spiller and Burke channels and around Dean and Fisher channels. In traditional literature, they are called Bella Bella, the original name of a European fort and the neighboring Native settlement. Now they are once again known as Heiltsuk, after their language, which belongs to the northern branch of the Wakashan family.

INUIT

Plural form of the word *inuk*, meaning "the true men," and the name now used to designate the people formerly known as Eskimoes (the word *Eskimo* is today considered politically incorrect). The Inuit inhabit the Arctic area from south of Alaska along the coasts of the Bering Sea, the Arctic Ocean, and Greenland. The inhabitants of the coasts of the Chukchi Peninsula in Siberia also belong to the Inuit culture. The Inuit language, one of the two branches of the Inuit-Aleut family, consists of two clearly differentiated subgroups. Yup'ik, which includes five languages, is spoken on the Chukchi Peninsula and from Norton Sound to Prince William Sound in Alaska. Inupiaq-Inuit includes a series of related dialects spoken from Norton Sound to the region of Barrow, Alaska, on the north slope and in the rest of the Arctic region as far as Greenland. To underscore certain differences in culture and artistic traditions, the word *Inuit* is usually used to designate Canadian Inuit, while northern Alaskan Inuit are known as Inupiaq, south-

western Alaskan Inuit are known as Yup'ik, and Inuit of Siberia and St. Lawrence Island are known as Yuit.

INUPIAQ (Inupiaq-Inuit)

One of the two divisions of the Inuit branch of the Inuit-Aleut language family spoken throughout the Arctic region. The Inupiaq language consists of a series of dialects spoken all the way from Seward Peninsula in Alaska to north of Norton Sound and throughout northern Alaska and the Arctic coasts of Canada, reaching as far as the coasts of Greenland.

KAIGANI

The only Haida band that lives in the extreme south of what is now southeastern Alaska. In the early eighteenth century, shortly before the first Spanish expedition of the period, Haida bands from the extreme northwest of the Queen Charlotte Islands won the southern half of Prince of Wales Island and Sukkwan, Long, Dall, and Forrester islands from the Tlingit. This group is called the Kaigani Haida. The Kaigani are named after the first village that was established on the southern tip of Dall Island. Their culture is essentially the same as the rest of the Haida, but because the Kaigani remained on the United States side when the U.S.-Canadian border was drawn, they developed certain cultural and linguistic differences in relative isolation.

KISKAGASS

Deformation of Gisgagas, a Gitksan village whose name is sometimes also written as Kiskagass or Kishgagass. In ancient sources, these names are all used as synonyms for Gitksan. Gisgagas was the Gitksans' northernmost winter settlement, while Kuldo was the settlement located farthest to the east.

KITKITSH

Deformation of Gitsees, a Tsimshian coastal village whose name means "village of the salmon traps." The name is sometimes also transcribed as Kitzeesh. It was the riverside settlement closest to the coast, very near the mouth of the Skeena River.

KONIAG

Yup'ik-speaking band or group. The Koniag and Chugach are the two main bands of what are generically known as Pacific Yup'ik.

The Koniag live on Kodiak Island and the Alaskan Peninsula as far as Cape Kupreanof in southwestern Alaska.

KORIAK

Native Siberian people located on the Kamchatka Peninsula. The Koriak are divided into two clearly differentiated groups. The most numerous group lives in the inland and tends reindeer. The coastal Koriak make a living from fishing and hunting sea mammals. The Koriak and Chukchi cultures are closely related.

KWAKIUTL

See Kwakwa̲ka'wakw. The Kwakiutl belong to the Kwakwa̲ka'wakw nation located between Hardy Bay and Malcolm Island, north of Vancouver Island. Franz Boas, assisted by George Hunt, produced most of the work that serves as the basis for academic studies of Kwakiutl anthropology. The name Kwakiutl was mistakenly used in traditional anthropology to generically designate all the peoples of the same linguistic division.

KWAKWAKA'WAKW

Group of Northwest Coast peoples who speak the Kwakala language, which is classified as Wakashan. It is the name by which these bands refer to themselves, although in traditional anthropology they are incorrectly called Southern Kwakiutl. The name Kwakwa̲ka'wakw translates literally as "Kwakwala-speaking peoples." These bands speak different dialects and inhabit the northern part of Vancouver Island and the adjacent islands and mainland, as well as the area around the Queen Charlotte and Johnstone straits off the central coast of British Columbia. They are among the peoples of the Northwest Coast whose traditional culture and language are best preserved.

MAKAH

Native people of the Northwest Coast located at the northwestern tip of the Olympic Peninsula in Washington state. Their language belongs to the Wakashan family— they are its southernmost representatives. The name Makah (meaning well-fed, or generous hosts) was given them by their S'Klallam neighbors, but it continues to be officially used for legal reasons. They call themselves by their Native name of Kwideech-cha-aht, which refers to the fact that they live adjacent to Cape Flattery, on the opposite side of the Juan de Fuca Strait from their Nuu-chah-nulth linguistic counterparts. Spain's late eighteenth-century settlement of Núñez Gaona was in Neah Bay, the principal Makah settlement of today.

NISGA'A

Native nation of the Northwest Coast and one of the linguistic-cultural divisions of the Tsimshian family. The Nisga'a are settled the length of the Nass River basin in northern British Columbia. Traditional sources usually list them generically as Tsimshian. Because they are so isolated from Western culture, the Nisga'a have preserved their traditional language and culture to a greater extent than most First Nations and are one of the groups that is most active in pursuing land claims in British Columbia.

NOOTKA

See Nuu-chah-nulth. Nootka is a name mistakenly given by history and traditional anthropology to the Mowachaht people and by extension to the Nuu-chah-nulth nation to which they belong. The name also appears in historical Spanish records (where it is written as Nutka) to designate the Mowachaht settlement of Yuquot, located in Nootka Sound. Now the name is used only for the bay, the island on which Yuquot is located, and a small settlement or fishing camp located a few miles north of Yuquot where fish canneries were previously located. The name Nootka originated with a misunderstanding between James Cook and the Mowachaht, who tried to tell him that he could go around to get from where he was to the village of Yuquot because Yuquot was located on an island.

NUNIVAK

Inuit band that speaks a dialect of the central Yup'ik language. The Nunivak live on Nunivak Island in the Bering Sea, opposite the southwestern coast of Alaska. Along with the inhabitants of this mainland area, they are generically called "southwestern Alaskan Inuit."

NUU-CHAH-NULTH

A self-identification (meaning "all along the mountains") used for the people of the western coast of the Vancouver Island cultural area. They all speak dialects of the same language, which belongs to the Wakashan linguistic family. Traditionally they were incorrectly called Nootka (or Nutka in Spanish-language records). Later called "West Coast People," they decided in 1978 they wanted to be known as Nuu-chah-nulth, and they are now legally and officially recognized as such. The Nuu-chah-nulth Tribal Council, which administers legal matters for all of the fourteen related bands, has its headquarters in Port Alberni, British Columbia.

NUXALK

Native nation located on the central coast of British Columbia near Dean and Burke channels. The Nuxalk were formerly called Bella Coola, the anglicization of *bilcoola*, the name by which they were known to the Kwakwaka'wakw. The Nuxalk language is an isolated branch of the Coast Salish linguistic family. Nowadays the Nuxalk nation is more commonly called by its proper name.

OWEEKEENO

Native people of the Northwest Coast, settled on the south-central coast of British Columbia in Fitzhugh Sound and around the Rivers and Moses inlets and Owikeno Lake. Their language, Oowekyala, belongs to the northern branch of the Wakashan family.

QUILEUTE

Native people of the Northwest Coast, settled on the coast of the Olympic Peninsula in Washington state. Historically they extended from the south of Cape Alava to Destruction Island. Their language belongs to the Chimakuyan family. On July 14, 1775, they killed six sailors from Juan de la Bodega y Quadra's ship.

TANAINA

Of all the Native peoples on the Pacific Coast, the only ones whose language belongs to the large Athapascan family. Precisely because of this linguistic filiation, anthropologists include the Tanaina in the sub-Arctic cultural area. They live on the land surrounding Cook Inlet in south-central Alaska, where they are settled to the north of the Pacific Yup'ik-speaking Koniag and Chugach.

TLINGIT

Native nation of the Northwest Coast located on the islands and channels of the southeastern Alaskan panhandle. At the end of the eighteenth century, the southern Tlingit territory was infringed upon by the Kaigani Haida. The Tlingit language is believed to be distantly related to the Eyak-Athapascan family.

TSIMSHIAN

Language family with no known relation to any other North American language. Tsimshian speakers are settled in northern British Columbia. Among speakers of different subdivisions of the Tsimshian language are the Nisga'a, the Gitksan, the coastal Tsimshian who live on the lower part of the Skeena River and the adjacent coast, and the southern Tsimshian on the islands and coast south of the Skeena River. The coastal and southern Tsimshian are the two bands whose cultures are properly known as Tsimshian.

WAKASHAN

Large language family that, together with the Nuxalk, almost completely covers the Northwest Coast area known as the Central Region. The Wakashan linguistic family includes the Haisla, Haihais, Heiltsuk, Owekeeno, Kwakwaka'wakw, Nuu-chah-nulth, and Makah. The name comes from an observation made by James Cook's expedition and others of the early European travelers who described how people from these groups customarily shouted *wa-kash* as a greeting and an expression of joy. The term *wa-kash* simultaneously means "hello," "welcome," and "hurray!"

YUP'IK

One of the two clearly differentiated linguistic divisions of the Inuit branch of the Inuit-Aleut trunk language, which covers the entire Arctic region. There are five Yup'ik languages, which are spoken exclusively from Sirenikski in Siberia to St. Lawrence Island and on the American continent from Norton Sound to Prince William Sound. For purposes of cultural simplification, the term Yup'ik generally refers to the Native peoples of southwestern Alaska.

PROJECT TEAM

Exhibition

Curators
Paz Cabello
Alberto Costa Romero de Tejada

Head, Fine Arts Division
Imma Casas

Coordination
Mercedes Basso
Ariadna Bello
Sílvia Sauquet

Installation Design
Lluís Pera

Installation Coordinator
Carles Comas

Graphic Design
Lali Almonacid

Conservation
Cecília Illa
Teresa Berrios

Transport
TTI, Barcelona

Insurance
Aon Artscope
Cabinet Morel & Cie SA
GDS, Correduría de Seguros

Publication

Spanish Edition

Coordination
Mercedes Basso
Ariadna Bello
Sílvia Sauquet

Catalogue Entries
Paz Cabello
Araceli Sánchez
Ana Verde

Translation
Ignasi Sardà

English Edition

Editor and Additional Catalogue Entries
Steven C. Brown

Copy Editor
Polly Koch

Assistant Editor
Geraldine Aramanda

Collections Curator
Susan Davidson

Translation
Patricia Mathews

Design
Don Quaintance, Public Address Design
Elizabeth Frizzell, Production Assistant

Typography
Composed in Giovanni

Color Separations
Grafitex, Barcelona, and
C+S Repro, Filderstadt, Germany

Printing
Dr. Cantz'sche Druckerei, Ostfildern-Ruit,
Germany

Photography Credits

Specific sources and photographer credits are noted below; otherwise photographic material has been supplied by the owner

Archivo Oronoz, Madrid: fig. 6

Sylvia Ball, New York: cat. nos. 114, 124, 133, 135, 147, 161

L.B. Bogdanov, Saint Petersberg: cat. nos. 60, 61, 62, 63, 64, 65, 66, 67, 68, 69, 70, 71, 73, 74, 75, 76, 77, 78, 79, 80, 81, 82

Hillel Burger, Cambridge, Massachusetts: fig. 3; cat. nos. 57, 58, 59, 89, 98, 103, 104, 132, 143, 158, 172

Craig Chesek, New York: cat. nos. 115, 165

Davidson: fig. 31

D. Destable, Paris: cat. nos. 102, 157

Hughes Dubois, Brussels and Paris: fig. 20

Werner Forman Archive Limited, London: cat. no. 130

Lynton Gardiner, New York: cat. nos. 100, 159

Edward de Groff: fig. 26

B. Hatala, Paris: cat. nos. 156, 163

Paul Hester, Houston: cat. no. 96

Hickey & Robertson, Houston: cat. nos. 37, 72, 88, 92, 94, 105, 109, 126, 137, 142, 177

Bill Holm, Seattle: figs. 28, 30

Justin Kerr, New York: cat. nos. 116, 140

Richard Maynard: figs. 27, 29

Barry McWayng: cat. no. 127

Stephen S. Myers, New York: cat. no. 155

Jordi Nieva, Barcelona: fig. 22

Luis Olivas, Madrid: cat. nos. 83, 84, 85, 86

Stan Schnier, New York: cat. nos. 117, 118, 119, 120, 122, 128, 129

Smithsonian Institution Press, Washington, D.C.: fig. 5